DON'T FORGET M

Don't Forget Me

The Eddie Cochran Story

Julie Mundy
and Darrel Higham

MAINSTREAM
PUBLISHING

EDINBURGH AND LONDON

First published in Great Britain in 2000 by
MAINSTREAM PUBLISHING COMPANY
(EDINBURGH) LTD
7 Albany Street
Edinburgh EH1 3UG

This edition 2001

ISBN 1 84018 449 3

Picture credits: The Cochran Family; Rockstar Records;
Harry Hammond; *Oldham Evening Chronicle*; Michele
Morley; Neil Foster; Sharon Sheeley; O'Neill Photo Co;
Freeman Hover. Every effort has been made to
acknowledge correctly and contact the source and all
copyright-holders of each photograph. We apologise for
any errors or omissions, which will be corrected in
future editions

A catalogue record for this book is available from
the British Library

Typeset in 10.5 on 14pt Janson
Printed and bound in Great Britain by
Creative Print and Design Wales

Contents

Introduction

Whether the subject is politics, sport, cars, motorcycles, architecture, fashion, films or music, the 1950s have always been, and will continue to be, a marvellous area of study for the budding historian. It was a decade when cars were as curvaceous as the blonde-bombshell movie actresses dominating the silver screen, when science fiction started to grip the imagination, when good boys and girls never went on a date without a chaperone, and when Mum and Dad always knew best. At the turn of the 1950s, five years after the Second World War had ended, the mood was surely one of optimism as the world's war-weary population looked forward to a brighter, peaceful future.

But the new decade proved to be just as turbulent as anything that had preceded it. The Cold War between America and Russia nearly developed into full-scale nuclear conflict, American troops stormed into Korea, and Britain was showing force in the Middle East over the Suez Canal. But some would argue that all these events pale into insignificance when compared to the real trouble that began brewing when the decade was still young: teenagers, teenage rebellion and more importantly, rock'n'roll.

The first rock'n'roll star to shape the future of popular music and fuel this teenage controversy was Elvis Presley. He began his career recording for the small independent Sun Records label in Memphis in 1954, and the music that he created was pure rockabilly – a raw hill-billy version of rock'n'roll. Everything about Elvis was different, almost dangerous, compared to what had gone before. His elaborate clothing and his long hair painstakingly styled into a greasy pompadour added to an overtly sexual stage act, which outraged parents, church officials and school authorities throughout the southern states of the USA.

But it didn't all start with Elvis. The origins of rock'n'roll can be traced back to black blues artists of the 1930s who used the phrase as a term to describe sexual intercourse. White country artists were just as important in the early development of this explosive musical form, blending the blues with their own music to produce a brand of country boogie, an early formation of rock'n'roll, which was carefully developed and popularised by artists such as Carl Perkins, Little Richard, Jerry Lee Lewis, Chuck Berry, Buddy Holly and Gene Vincent among others.

Every major artist from this groundbreaking era has had his or her career documented in print or on celluloid, with the exception of one.

Probably the most talented and yet underrated of all the early rockers was Eddie Cochran. He has been ill-served by rock historians since his untimely death in 1960 at the age of twenty-one. He crammed a great deal into his short life and musical career, one which lasted only five years, and was certainly the most diverse of all the rockers. In fact, to dismiss him as 'just another rock'n'roll artist' would be a great mistake. It seems inconceivable that this artist, who heavily influenced everyone from The Beatles to Marc Bolan and from Jimi Hendrix to The Stray Cats, as well as countless rockabilly bands still performing around the world today, has been overlooked for so long.

Writing and researching the information in this book has taken nearly three years, as the story reaches far beyond the handful of rock'n'roll classics Cochran is known for today. Over the years, the dedication of writers and researchers such as Rob Finnis, Spencer Leigh, Michael Kelly, Trevor Cajiao and Tony Barrett have provided the foundation upon which this book is built, and it would have been impossible to undertake this project without their support, along with the encouragement of Eddie's family, friends, associates and fans from around the world.

'There Are Three Steps To Heaven'

Step One . . .

I bought my guitar because it was like Eddie Cochran's. It was in the local paper and I'd been looking for one and they are hard to find. The advert just said 'Orange Gretsch guitar 100 bucks'.

I called up the guy and said, 'Hey, is it like Eddie Cochran's?'

He replied, 'I dunno, it's orange and it's all in pieces, so you'd better get up here.'

I went up to look at it and there it was – just like Eddie's. The guy had it all taken apart and he was going to refinish it. Luckily the pickups and all the screws were still together in a box and the guitar was just sitting there without any strings on it.

It's funny, as you make a couple of bucks you think, well, now, I'll try the other guitars, the Les Pauls, the Strats, but none of them could ever take the place of that one guitar I bought when I was seventeen.

Brian Setzer

For real country-style tone, for exceptional playing convenience, comfort and for regular he-man looks, the Gretsch 6120 Chet Atkins Hollow Body Guitar included a wealth of design features for the country musician.

As new, the advertised price for this impressive instrument was $385, although in 1955 the teenaged Eddie Cochran purchased his Gretsch second-hand from a small local music store near his home in Bell Gardens, Los Angeles. The instrument was originally on loan to musician Gary Lambert, who, after ordering a new Country Club Gretsch, was given the 6120 to use until his own guitar arrived.

At the time of his purchase the young Eddie Cochran was already playing with a variety of local bands and was regarded as something of a local celebrity through his partnership with Hank Cochran in their country duo, the Cochran Brothers.

After reaching the teenager's hands, the Gretsch remained Eddie's main instrument throughout his entire career, becoming as closely associated with his image as it was with his music. Today, the 1955

Gretsch 6120 is referred to by vintage guitar dealers and musicians as simply 'the Eddie Cochran model'.

Eddie's first guitar was a Kay. Although far less glamorous than the Gretsch, it was a simple, inexpensive yet effective instrument for any beginner. The Kay was originally owned by Bill Cochran, who managed to teach Eddie a couple of chords before entering the services and leaving the instrument in his younger brother's hands.

Bill was the eldest son of Frank and Alice Cochran. Born in 1905, Frank was raised in Oklahoma City, while Alice, two years younger, was from Ada, Oklahoma. The couple met as a result of a double date, where they were both matched with different partners, and they got married in 1923. Their first child, Gloria, was born the following February. Two more children arrived while the couple were living in Oklahoma where Frank worked as a machinist – Bill was born in June 1925 and Robert two years later in November 1927.

At the close of the decade, the Black Monday stockmarket collapse in Wall Street on 29 October 1929 heralded the beginning of the Great Depression. Following the First World War, a drop in foreign trade and an increase in domestic production contributed to the economic slump that gripped not only the United States but also the rest of the world during the 1930s.

It wasn't until the Second World War that the United States began to show a recovery, but for many families it was too late. Businesses, banks and agriculture prices had collapsed, resulting in a massive increase in unemployment, peaking in 1933 when a staggering sixteen million people lost their jobs throughout the country.

Although Oklahoma's economy had grown during the First World War, it suffered greatly during the 1930s; the economic crisis, added to soil exhaustion and drought, plunged the agriculture-dependent state into depression. After joining the ranks of the unemployed, Frank Cochran moved his family six hundred miles north to Albert Lea, Minnesota, where their fourth child, Patricia, was born in 1932. Taking a job downtown as a houseman for a packing company called Wilson & Co., Frank moved his family into their new home at 108 Shell Rock.

In 1938 the Cochran family moved again, this time just three blocks away to 909 Marshall, and it was here (and not in Oklahoma as most music encyclopedias or similar works mistakenly inform readers) that Edward Raymond Cochran was born on 3 October 1938. His delighted older siblings all played an active role in looking after the new addition to the family.

We were a blessing for Mother; we kids took care of Eddie. I used to put him to sleep and he loved music while he was sleeping. He used to lie beside me and hold my thumb and suck his other thumb while I played *Beer Barrel Polka*. He went to sleep with music everywhere.

Bill Cochran

In 1944 Eddie was enrolled in the Northside School in Albert Lea. The family's address was now 230 Charles, where they had moved three years earlier. Frank had left Wilson and Co. for a new job as a machine operator in the Olsen manufacturing company.

Nineteen-year-old Bill Cochran was away in the forces, serving in the Marines and the Navy, but before leaving he had purchased a Kay guitar. After teaching his youngest brother a couple of chords, he left the instrument in Eddie's hands. Eddie was more interested in the drums, though, but in his quest to learn that instrument he was told that he would have to learn the rudiments of the piano first. He then decided on the trombone, but the school orchestra's musical director suggested he should play the clarinet instead, informing his family that Eddie 'didn't have the lip' for the instrument. Apparently, on sight of the clarinet, Eddie refused to join the orchestra and finally asked his brother Bob to show him a few chords on Bill's guitar.

This time Eddie took to the guitar immediately. Aided by Nick Manaloff's *Complete Chord And Harmony Manual*, he quickly advanced his technique and, in Bill's absence, cleaned and polished the guitar as if it were his own.

Around this time Eddie also developed a passion for hunting, one which continued throughout the rest of his life. He owned a gun from an early age. His schoolfriends Terry Cole and David Lindahl recall Eddie's interests as fishing, shooting and simple childhood pleasures such as playing cowboys and indians.

Hank Hickey, who later married Eddie's sister Patty, has fond memories of seeing Eddie grow up in Albert Lea: 'His best friend David was the Sheriff's son and they had fun following Patty and me around while we were courting. They were typical younger brother types – they followed us to the movies and then sat up in the balcony and bugged us no end. He and David Lindahl used to play cowboys and indians in the jail. They were very lucky – not many boys got to play in an actual jail, but they had the run of it!'

'There were so many kids on the block,' Terry Cole remembers. 'The three of us sort of hung around together for our mutual benefit, to sort of protect each other. Eddie was older than me. I was a year behind him and David. We used to run amongst the houses between Charles and First Street and terrorise the neighbourhood playing cowboys and indians. Eddie loved Hopalong Cassidy and Tom Mix.

'I remember Eddie sitting on the front steps playing his guitar. It sounded neat. It sounded good to us.'

By the end of the 1940s the Cochran children were growing up fast. Gloria, Bill and Bob were all married and their father had another new job, working as a car mechanic at the South Broadway garage. It was during this period that Frank decided to move back down south to Oklahoma with Alice and Eddie. They went to Midwest City, where he took a job at Tinker Airforce Base. A machinist by trade, Frank worked at the base – the primary reason for Midwest City's existence – as a civilian. The family had barely settled in, however, when Eddie became seriously ill; it was enough to persuade Frank and Alice to move back to Albert Lea and rejoin the remainder of their family.

Although no one in the family can recall the cause of Eddie's illness, his sister Patty remembers their return to Minnesota. 'They moved down to Oklahoma for just a short while, but then they moved back up to Albert Lea. Dad had a job at Tinker Airforce Base, Bill was in the service and so Daddy, Mom and Eddie went, and I stayed in Albert Lea with Gloria. As a matter of fact, Mom was very unhappy down there because Eddie had gotten so sick and she just wanted to be back where her girls were.'

Patty's husband Hank agrees: 'Eddie got sick – really, really sick –

while they were in Midwest City, and the family were very concerned. So the two girls went down there and we followed a couple of weeks later. But they didn't last long when they returned to Albert Lea either. Frank worked at the same factory I was working in. I was in the engineering department and he was a machinist. He only worked there for two or three months before Bill talked them into going to California.'

By the time the Cochran family returned to Albert Lea, the eldest son Bill had already left the service and had settled in California with his wife Betty. 'I was in the Navy and I was attached to the Marines, so I wore both uniforms. Bob went into the Navy as well, as Dad had done before us – he was in the Seabees for a while. I met Betty while I was stationed in California and I married her just before I got out of the service in '46. We went back and lived a year in Albert Lea and then we came back out here in '47. I went back in '51 and started to talk to my family about coming out here. Bob and Gloria were both married by then.'

Alice also had a sister in California and Bill urged the rest of his family to join him on the West Coast. So, packing all their possessions in two cars, the Cochran family embarked on the long journey to California, finally reaching their new home in Bell Gardens, a suburb south-east of Los Angeles.

Possession, Mom? This guitar's my friend, my best friend

Eddie Cochran

Leaving behind all his childhood friends, Eddie clutched his guitar for the entire journey to California. The small town of Albert Lea and the prairies of Minnesota, bordering Canada and reaching across the Midwest to Lake Superior, couldn't be further removed from the Golden State of California and the vast metropolis of Los Angeles.

The world capital of the motion-picture industry, LA was looked upon as a city where you could find your fortune. The famous Holly-wood sign was erected in 1923 as an advertisement to draw people to the new homes rapidly being developed throughout the area as the booming modern city flourished into one of the world's largest urban areas.

The Californian population grew extensively during the 1930s as many Oklahomans migrated to the West Coast after the drought had turned their state into a dust bowl. Joining the 'Okies' in their search for a new life were the Cochran family who initially moved in with Bill while they found a place of their own to live. As Bill remembers, some of their first homes were far from permanent: 'They were living in Bell Gardens,' he explains. 'My aunt had lived out here for years, so they moved into a trailer on the back of her property. They had a little apartment first, before moving out to a house. Many people in Bell Gardens were into western music, so that's how Eddie really started playing as well.'

The family eventually settled into their new home at 5539 Priory Street in Bell Gardens. Frank began work as a machinist in a missile factory and in September 1951 his twelve-year-old son Eddie was enrolled in Bell Gardens Junior High.

It was here that he met Fred Conrad Smith, and the friendship between the two would last throughout Eddie's musical career. Born in Los Angeles in 1939, Connie 'Guybo' Smith, as he was known, started playing bass in the seventh grade for the school band, as well as the steel guitar and mandolin. The two boys were soon inseparable, constantly jamming together along with fellow student Al Garcia, and rehearsing frequently at the Cochran family home in Bell Gardens.

One early public performance from the pair is recorded in the Bell Gardens Junior High school newsletter. 'On Friday, 19 March 1954,' it states, 'the school orchestra directed by Mr Riles played for an assembly at Bell Gardens Elementary school.' Part of this perfor-mance featured a guitar duet where the fifteen-year-old Eddie, accompanied by Guybo on steel guitar, performed *Just Married* and *Walking The Dog*.

Eddie played other roles in extra-curricular activities, most notably as editor-in-chief of the student newsletter, *The Live Wire*, and as chief justice in the Student Court, an organisation set up to help students gain respect for school rules. A student would be sent to this court for any violation, no matter how minor, of the school rules.

According to *The Live Wire*, officials for the court were chosen because of their outstanding citizenship, high grades and mature thinking.

In early 1953 Eddie, along with Guybo and Al Garcia, formed a musical group called The Melody Boys. Their first gig was at the Towngate Hall in San Francisco. It was also around this time that Eddie met local musician Chuck Foreman. Five years his senior, Chuck was the first person to record the young Eddie Cochran.

'I was born in Long Beach in 1933 and grew up around the Anaheim and Buena Park area of Los Angeles and Eddie lived over in Bell Gardens. I started in music from day one, really; my sister had been trained in opera and another sister played in popular dance bands. They formed all-girl bands and they started me out on piano and keyboards at a very early age. Then I played in school bands and things of that sort. I was one of the few musicians who had actually learned to read a chart, and I was working in what was big at that time in Los Angeles: country and western, or "country swing" as it was known then.

'Eddie was fourteen when we met. He knew five chords, two of which were wrong, and he had a little Gibson with a DeArmond pickup on it. What he wanted to be was a singer, but at the time he was just beating rhythm.

'What drove him into lead work was playing around with a lot of other young people who got together over weekends and evenings to jam a little bit. I think he got so frustrated with people who were trying to be lead players, or "take-off guitarists" as we called them in those days. He would get so frustrated, knowing that he could do it better, as well as it being easier and less frustrating than what he was doing on rhythm.

'We would go anywhere to get the chance to practise with other people and get some ideas. I can't remember exactly who introduced me to Eddie – it could have been Warren Flock or one of the Carlton Brothers. Most of us were about eighteen or nineteen years old and Eddie was a little kid, but he sang and he played rhythm guitar and he was lightning fast at learning things. So if you wanted to play one of the instrumentals that was big at the time, Eddie could pick it up real quick. If someone showed him something, he wouldn't forget it – he would sit around and practise it and find the formation of the chords. Everybody was so amazed at how quick he went from almost zero to eclipsing everybody else. It was just outstanding.'

Throughout the summer of 1953 Chuck and Eddie began experimenting on Chuck's two-track recorder. 'Eddie was fascinated by his own sound being played back,' Chuck remembers. 'That's why we recorded many vocal tunes like *Candy Kisses* and *Heart Of Stone* – he was basically a rhythm-guitar player singing. Within a year we were playing the other stuff like *Poor People Of Paris* and *Jamming With Jimmy*. In a period of one year he learned so fast because he really was intense, he was unbelievably intense, with his guitar and his music. It just got worse, too. You'd go to a party and everybody would be having a few beers and necking – and what was Eddie doing? He was playing the guitar.'

Chuck also explains how he and Eddie would work together on a song using overdubs. In 1953 this technique was still in its infancy, and enabled a single musician to record one or more parts onto the same track.

'Generally, the original bottom-end track was actually an overdub in itself,' says Chuck. 'When we had the advantage of having the two tape-recorders, that was a kick. We would do the basic thing – I'd sit there and pat my foot and sing, or we'd hum it together and Eddie would beat a nice rhythm track to it. Then we'd play that back and on some tunes Eddie would tune down the bottom string of his guitar to simulate a bass line. So we had an overdub to start with and we'd play that back and either both play lead together or Eddie would sing and I'd play, and that was the final track. All of this was recorded at the slowest speed available because we didn't have any tape. We were constantly recording, but we were using the same tape over and over again because we didn't have any money to buy new ones. We were all dirt poor, counting pennies out to put gas in the car to go and jam.

'We would also experiment with a piano to get a reverb sound with mics – that was a common practice in those days. We would put a small speaker in the bottom of the piano and take the damper off the strings so they would resonate. Then we would open the top of the piano and hang a little microphone in the top, then bleed in part of that sound with another mic.'

The recording techniques mentioned, including their basic attempts at overdubbing, may seem primitive by today's digital standards, but in the summer of 1953, Chuck and Eddie's recordings were remarkably advanced – especially when you take into consideration that these were only intended as home recordings. In fact, these early attempts at basic overdubbing made a huge impression on the young Eddie. Throughout his recording career he continued to expand his knowledge and technique to the point where he felt confident enough to create a record playing all the instruments himself.

Although it was of immense value to Chuck and Eddie, many musicians remained sceptical about overdubbing and were unable to grasp the opportunities this breakthrough in technology presented to them. Many felt the skill of performing live in the studio was under threat. Chuck agrees: 'The only person doing multiple recordings for release at that time was Les Paul. Everyone else had to walk out on the stage, plug the guitar into the amplifier and just do it – something that's almost unheard of now.

'In the old days so much had to be done live. No one expected lip-synching, no one expected pre-recorded backgrounds or tracks – you had to really be able to do it. We didn't have the equipment, either: the most advanced thing on the market at that time was a Fender Bassman amp. In those days, the idea of a singer going in and doing a vocal when the band completed their tracks three weeks ago was unheard of. Those things didn't happen in the 1950s. You could either do it or you couldn't. I remember the horror that was felt when you realised you could record on different tracks, and if the sax man was playing flat they could turn him off. That was unheard of in the early days. It was a different world, musically, compared to today.'

Although the recordings were never intended for commercial release, in 1998 Tony Barrett, founder of Rockstar Records, a British label set up specifically to release rare Cochran recordings, secured the rights to release the surviving tapes from these sessions with Chuck Foreman. Originally recorded over a period of eighteen months, they provide a remarkable insight into the most important stage of Eddie's musical development. As Chuck mentioned, their initial efforts were based around Eddie's vocals and rhythm-guitar playing, but towards the end of the period a dramatic rise in his standard of musicianship can be heard. These recordings by Chuck and Eddie chronicle a period that saw a fourteen-year-old schoolboy evolve into a highly skilled, professional musician.

The surviving tapes of these sessions were in a very poor condition but the sound quality, surprisingly, is excellent. The vast majority of the tracks are instrumentals but the songs that feature Eddie singing show that, even at the age of fourteen, he displayed a great deal of maturity and confidence. His vocals on songs such as *Hearts Of Stone*, *Candy Kisses*, *Gamblers Guitar* and *Live Fast, Love Hard, Die Young* have all the trademarks of later Cochran recordings – his deep voice, the little chuckles thrown in from time to time and the effortless phrasing of words.

His guitar playing is incredibly advanced, highlighting his ability to impersonate guitarists such as Chet Atkins and Merle Travis with their unique thumb-picking technique, on numbers such as *Poor People Of Paris*, *Cannonball Rag* and *Blue Gypsy*.

Chuck Foreman's influence on Eddie cannot be underestimated: 'I had a tendency to be a bit on the snobbish side. If people weren't shooting high, I couldn't get along with them. Some people were satisfied in thinking that what little they had learned made them great, but other people, like Eddie, were shooting a lot higher. The more you learn, the more you realise you didn't know. We were all shooting for the top, not necessarily for money or fame but for ability. Learn more, know more.'

It seems obvious that Chuck's encouragement and acceptance of Eddie, who was so much younger than him and many of the musicians around him at the time, were crucial in developing his musical knowledge and confidence. Working alongside older, experienced, even semi-professional musicians meant Eddie was able to learn a lot. His maturity and desire to learn were obvious to all those around him, and it was this attitude that allowed him to advance a lot further than his peers.

Throughout the latter half of 1953 and into early '54, as well as his forays into home recording, Eddie continued to play with a variety of bands, turning up with his guitar and jamming with other local musicians. His musical education was provided by artists such as the hugely influential trio of Merle Travis, Chet Atkins and Joe Maphis, along with country singer Marty Robbins, as well as by absorbing the West Coast R&B scene. According to Chuck, 'It was one of Eddie's desires to be able to sit down and play with anyone from BB King to Chet Atkins to Joe Maphis. People would laugh – but listen to his work and you'll find it's true. You don't just sit down and play like that unless you've spent a lot of hours working on it. He wanted to be the complete musician. He was very impressed by the fact that most of the jazz artists were trained in classical music. It's not just being fast, clean and accurate, it's what you're saying at the same time. The notes matter and the chords matter.

'Maphis was always interesting because of his country licks and his wild guitar playing. That "mean thing" that some people associate strictly with Eddie is very similar to a very famous Joe Maphis lick. Maphis was always a wild-hot guitar player but his stuff was very simple. Good technically, but very simple.'

Eddie's only distraction from his music appeared to be Johnnie Berry, his first serious girlfriend. They began dating at junior high, although, as Chuck remembers, Eddie's music still took priority: 'We used to double date together. I had an old '42 Oldsmobile and we used to go to drive-in movies. We were pals despite the five-year age gap but Eddie was a very serious guy – he was no dumb kid, he had quite a brain in his head. Eddie was just obsessed with music and the instrument – it was his primary interest in life in his early days. He was inseparable from the guitar: "What are you bringing that for?" I would say, "We're going to a drive-in movie!"

'Johnnie was rather mature and cool and understanding, so maybe that's why they lasted as long as they did. A steady relationship in those days usually only lasted about five weeks, but she understood that half the time Eddie wanted to plunk the guitar instead of hold her hand. On many of their dates, they just ended up in my living-room, playing music.

'Eddie was pretty serious about Johnnie Berry – well, as serious as you can get at fourteen or fifteen. She was the main girl. One of the things that Johnnie understood was that he loved the guitar more than her. I can distinctly recall looking in the rear-view mirror while taking Johnnie Berry home and seeing her on one side of the seat and Eddie on the other side, playing the guitar. Johnnie was cute – she had a dark pageboy haircut and she was as cute as you can be.

'Altogether we were a pretty clean troop – there weren't any drugs, and we wouldn't get roaring drunk. We'd have the odd beer once in a while, but not much, because it got in the way of the music, and the music was always first. It even came before the girls.'

None of us in those days were into partying. The party
had to have all the instruments and we had to be
playing something and working out harmonies and
parts.

Chuck Foreman

Eddie began to spend more time at the Bell Gardens Music Centre.
Owned by Bert Keither, the place had become a hangout for local
musicians. It was here that Eddie first met guitarist Ron Wilson who
in turn introduced him to Warren Flock, who had also moved to
California from Oklahoma. 'It was around 1954 when I first met
Eddie,' Warren recalls. 'I ran across Ron Wilson who was a good
singer and a rhythm-guitar player. He didn't have a car, and I did, so
he asked me over to Bell Gardens where he was going to introduce
me to a friend of his. We went over to Eddie Cochran's house and we
got to know one another as time went by. Eddie was still going to high
school, but he also worked at the music store in town where I bought
a mandolin, which I saved my paper-round money for. I still have that
mandolin today.

'I played country music and so did Eddie. He was interested in
Chet Atkins – in fact, he was his idol. Eddie would hear a song and
after a little bit he could play the song by ear and could be very close
to every note that Chet Atkins played. As time went along, I married
and moved to Bell Gardens. I lived next door to Eddie's mom and dad
who lived in a trailer in a vacant lot right next to my apartment house.
I was working for the Lincoln and Mercury agency and when I would
come home, or on the weekends, Eddie and I would get together and
I would go over his mom and dad's trailer where we would play music.
Eddie used to play a blond Gibson cutaway. He had his brother's Kay
guitar first.'

Joined by bass player Dave Kohrman, Eddie and Warren formed a
band called The Bell Gardens Ranch Gang. This ensemble played
locally as well as featuring on several local television and radio shows.
Joined by fiddle player Forest Lee Bibbie and by Clete Stewart who
sang and played guitar, they headed north towards Bakersfield to find
work playing on radio stations.

As Warren remembers, however, the venture proved unsuccessful and the group disbanded and headed back to Los Angeles: 'I was playing with The Carlton Brothers, two Italian brothers, and Eddie played with us at Knott's Berry Farm in Buena Park. I met Forest Lee and Clete Stewart on *Squeakin' Deacons Amateur Hour* when I left high school. Eddie and I, along with Don Carlton, Clete and Forest, took off and went to northern California in a '53 Ford. We were hitting the radio stations and trying to get on playing music up there. One radio station told us they didn't have anything but sent us over to a big house in a field where, on Saturday nights, everyone would come over for a television show there. They invited us back to play that evening but that's about as far as we went with that band.

'Eddie fitted in really well. We were all into country then, but we needed singers. Bob Denton was a good singer and Ron Wilson was good too, so we had those guys around. Eddie was four years younger than I was, so he was just like my younger brother, but we stayed in contact and became real good friends. He loved to play guitar and he was eager to learn – he picked up little tricks and techniques from other players.'

At the close of 1953 Eddie and Chuck were working and jamming with a variety of local musicians such as guitarists Don and Tony Carlton, and Billy Earl Galven, known as 'Fireball' because of his red hair.

They met Richard Rae and his band The Shamrock Valley Boys in October 1954 when they turned up for the band's gig at the American Legion Club in Bell Gardens and asked to sit in during the break. Apparently the pair performed so well that The Shamrock Valley Boys were quite intimidated, but despite his initial resentment towards the duo, the group's guitarist Bob Denton went on to become one of Eddie's closest friends.

Bob Denton (whose original name was Bob Bull) was born in Illinois and raised in Phoenix, Arizona, before settling in California with his family in 1950. Bob had already started playing country music in Phoenix and he continued with it following his move to the West Coast. 'I didn't live too far from Bell Gardens and I played some jobs over at some of the clubs over there,' says Bob. 'That's how I got to meet Eddie. I was around eighteen, I guess, and he was very young and still going to school in Bell Gardens. I was working with Richard Rae and The Shamrock Valley Boys and Eddie came and sat with us a couple of times. When he and Chuck Foreman came by the first time, Eddie just kind of rubbed me the wrong way. They acted as if they were above us, but when I got to know Eddie I found that wasn't like him at all.

'One time he called and asked me if I wanted to do a Knott's Berry Farm gig because he couldn't make it. Eddie didn't want to sing so I sang all the time and they offered me a job, but I wouldn't take it cos it was Eddie's job. Anyway, we were friends ever since and we would hang around together all the time. He called us the Brew Brothers as we always had a beer in our hands. Those were the good days.'

The Shamrock Valley Boys occasionally featured Hank Cochran as a guest singer. Bob assumed Eddie and Hank were related, although Eddie had never heard of him. It was Bob's suggestion that the two of them should meet as Hank was looking to form his own band.

'Hank was in our group,' Bob explains. 'We had a little country music group and I got to know Eddie so I introduced him to Hank. Eddie was just playing guitar then, he wouldn't open his mouth – you couldn't get him to sing. He just wanted to be a guitar player and he was good even then.'

Born Garland Petty Cochran in Greenville, Mississippi, on 2 August 1935, Hank was orphaned at a young age. After fleeing the orphanage in Tennessee, he moved to Hobbs, New Mexico, to be near his family. His uncle taught him to play the guitar, which led to his passion for country music. Hank moved to California in 1951, and by 1953 he was appearing on KXLA Pasadena on *The Riverside Rancho* radio show which was hosted by country DJ Squeakin' Deacon.

The Shamrock Valley Boys were also making appearances on local radio and television, including *The Hometown Jamboree* and a regular Saturday radio show which was broadcast from a second-hand car lot in Long Beach, California.

'Half the stuff that was popular at the time was things like *The Hometown Jamboree*,' Chuck remembers. 'It had Jimmy Bryant, Speedy West and they were playing western swing. There's nothing wrong with western swing. Jazz *aficionados* of today can marvel a little bit at it. We called it "flop-eared" music – don't ask me where the term came from. We were always accusing each other of being "flop-ears", adding extra chords or a few extra passing chords. It gave it a modern flavour, which was one of the problems when Hank came into the picture. Hank was a purist and he wanted it as pure country as you could get it, but country wasn't really what we were listening to.

'Hank was fun, and, because he could sing, when we were trying to find some places to play it gave us a good broad range of tunes that we could do. It didn't matter if someone asked for a classic Ernest Tubb tune because Hank would know it and he could sing it with great style. When you're that young and struggling to find any place that will let you play, you want to please the crowd and give them what they want to hear.'

In June 1954 Eddie graduated from junior high. Although music was already taking precedence over his studies, it certainly didn't show in his exam results, which were all highly commendable A and B grades. In a range of subjects that included algebra, agriculture and physical education, his highest grades were in English and, more obviously, Boys Glee, a singing class. By the end of the year, however, the sixteen-year-old, already playing regular local dates, was seriously contemplating a full-time career in music. According to Chuck, 'Eddie aspired to be a very knowledgeable, very capable and very professional musician when he was fifteen years old. When most guys were polishing their bicycles, dreaming of their first car, or which girls they could impress, all Eddie could think of was "What was that chord change? Where did they go to there?"'

Eddie had made a lasting impression on Hank Cochran who asked his younger friend to be his lead guitarist. 'I was looking for a guitar player,' Hank explains. 'He was fifteen at the time and I was seventeen and we were both working in veterans' halls around there. We couldn't play any real clubs until we were both eighteen. Everybody knew Eddie; they said he was young, but he played really good guitar. My first impression was that he was fantastic.'

A decision had to be made, so in January 1955, the sixteen-year-old left Bell Gardens High School. Eddie's family were certainly proud of his musical achievements, but his decision to quit school, just months before graduation, brought mixed reactions from his family, as his brother-in-law Hank Hickey recalls: 'We'd always try and watch Eddie play. We saw him play Knott's Berry Farm and again over in Paramount. In fact the whole family went over to that one time and we all went over to Long Beach too. But Patty wanted him to stay on at school, to continue his studies. Of course, a couple of months later she changed her mind, but Ed's mind was made up from the start.'

The minute he was away from school he was with older people. There wasn't anybody his own age who had that kind of dedication, or interest, or even expertise in what he was doing. Ed was getting a pretty good education hanging around with people that were five years older than he was. I remember once an old blind musician told me always to play with people who play better than you do. You won't shine and you can't impress them but you're gonna learn and they are gonna pull you up to their level.

Chuck Foreman

Through his friendship with Bob Denton, Ron Wilson and Richard McCullough (aka Richard Rae), Eddie formed another band called Eddie Garland And The Country Gentlemen, which also featured Carl West along with Guybo Smith on double bass. There is not a great deal of documented information about this band but it's well known that Eddie worked with and formed a variety of different groups throughout his early career. A few photographs of Eddie Garland And The Country Gentlemen exist, showing the group on stage. Probably performing at Knott's Berry Farm, Eddie is dressed in a fashion typical of country singers at the time and is playing his newly acquired Gretsch 6120.

He worked with so many different musicians that it's impossible to document every one of them, but the one true turning point was his alliance with Hank Cochran. Together they formed The Cochran Brothers (their identical surnames being nothing more than a coincidence) to capitalise on the success of country music and, in particular, the success of other country duos. Their partnership, performing a set inspired by Hank Williams, Ernest Tubb and Lefty Frizzell among other country giants of the time, led to immediate bookings. As Hank explains, 'We started off doing real country stuff like The Wilburn Brothers and people like that, then we wrote our own stuff which we later recorded for Ekko. Eddie was real easy-going and would run with just about everyone – he was easy to get along with. The girls all screamed and hollered and I just pushed him out there and let him have all of that.'

Country music, growing in popularity during the post-war boom years, was originally associated with rural hillbilly communities in the south-eastern states. Although based on European folk music, it borrowed heavily from black blues singers, taking on a different identity in each locality. Aided by radio, it was popularised from the 1920s onwards. Travelling artists absorbed other influences, including cowboy music from the south-western states, creating country and western.

Bob Denton agrees that from the onset The Cochran Brothers were a successful live partnership. 'Eddie and Hank were pretty hot for a while in California and they were good friends, too. I used to go with them on the road once in a while when they were singing together, and we would have a ball. They were doing country rock and I guess they were one of the first to do that kind of stuff. They would jump around and put on one hell of a show. They were something different to the usual stand-up country music singers.'

In those days, if you were going to sing country and western music you had to have the fancy duds. Some guys had enough money to pay for it, but you're talking about sequined materials, fringes and all this stuff, so Gloria had to make a couple of those costumes for them. She was really a very good seamstress. The minute Eddie went into rock'n'roll, there was really no need for it.

Hank Hickey

In early 1955 the Gretsch company began manufacturing the 6120, a guitar that was designed and endorsed by Chet Atkins. In early publicity pictures featuring The Cochran Brothers, Eddie is seen still with a Gibson semi-acoustic guitar, one that he had used exclusively throughout the previous couple of years. As Chuck Foreman explains, however, Eddie made a decision to acquire the new Gretsch. 'One of the big reasons Eddie chose the Gretsch was that it was the Chet Atkins model, and a new model, too. Chet was always very big. *Country Gentlemen* was a big hit record at the time and, let's face it, the Gretsch was a pretty darn good-feeling guitar. It was a much faster, easy-playing guitar with a very bright sound. A little too bright – that was one of the reasons why he changed the front pickup. I don't remember if the old Gibson pickup was out of an L5 or an ES153, but it was one of those oldies, and the whole idea was to be able to throw that switch and get a mellow sound. A lot of this was due to the sound of old Johnny Smith records. Those early 78s that I had of Johnny Smith were of absolute wonderment to most guitar players. We could not believe the triads the man played. Everyone said he was using gimmicked tunings and I thought so, too, but the guitar was tuned properly.

'The Gretsch would have been a real status symbol, especially for a young guy to pull out a top-of-the-line guitar. Then the next question was "What can he do with it?" and that was a driving force. When I'd drive him home after we'd been up all night doing our numbers, he'd just sit on the other side of the damn car with the guitar in the passenger seat, plucking away. He would practise all the way home. It didn't get out of his hands, I'm not kidding you. One of the great guitarists, I can't remember who, was asked if he practised every day. He replied, "Well, if I miss a day, I can tell it, and if I miss two days, the critics can tell. Then if I miss three days, the conductor and the orchestra can tell, and if I miss four days, the whole world knows I haven't been practising."'

Eddie purchased his Gretsch from the Bell Gardens Music Centre shortly after the 6120 went on to the market and, according to Bill Cochran, Eddie's parents helped with the payments. He made two adjustments to his new guitar; the first, as Chuck explained, was changing the neck pickup. The second alteration centred on the gold-painted scratch plate with Chet Atkins' signature emblazoned on it. In early pictures of Eddie playing the guitar, he was using a piece of tape to cover the signature, but finally decided to remove the signature permanently using sandpaper.

Two of Eddie's associates at the time were the legendary rockabilly singer Glen Glenn and his guitarist Gary Lambert. This duo had already established themselves on the Californian country music circuit and frequently crossed paths with The Cochran Brothers, quickly befriending them.

Gary Lambert, a good four or five years Eddie's senior, was already an accomplished country guitarist playing in a style similar to his two great influences, Chet Atkins and Merle Travis. Eddie and Gary would jam together, swapping techniques and organising impromptu home recording sessions. The two guitarists shared a love of country music and, especially, the desire to learn more and better themselves as players. Gary was one of many guitarists Eddie would regularly spend time with in order to improve his own standard of playing.

'I had the 6120 that Eddie Cochran ended up buying,' Gary remembers. 'Glen and I had been on this television show and the guy who was on there taught guitar down at Bell Gardens Music Centre. His name was Red Merle and he was a friend of Merle Travis. Red asked me if I wanted a guitar like his – he had a big old Gretsch with his name inlaid in the neck. He said, "I'll get you one for three hundred and ten dollars." So I asked him to order me one. In the meantime, he called up the Gretsch distributor who said I could have the 6120 to use until mine came in. I had that guitar for four or five months before the distributor called and said, "Your guitar's here, so you have to let me have that other guitar back." He was about sixty miles away, so I said, "Where's it going?" He told me it was going to Bell Gardens Music Centre, so I said, "That's where mine's coming in, I'll take it down there and you can call and verify that it's there." So I took it down there and Eddie bought it. I didn't like the 6120 because it had all that western stuff on it. I bought a Country Club, which was a Sunburst-type guitar. It had my name inlaid in the neck and I thought it was the cat's miaow.'

Gary also explains Eddie's decision to remove the Chet Atkins signature from the scratchplate: 'Eddie put tape over the signature because he didn't like Chet's name being there. He ended up taking the pick-guard off and scraping all the paint off the back so he wouldn't have it on there.'

The Chuck Foreman recordings prove that Eddie was already quite capable of imitating the styles of Atkins and Travis prior to his involvement with Hank Cochran. As Glen Glenn recalls, Eddie was beginning to make quite an impression on the West Coast country scene as a guitar virtuoso: 'He was getting so good. He was a good country session player – he played Joe Maphis-style – and then when he went into rock he came out with his own style. He would have to be considered one of the top session guitar players. He could play everything. I guess his style started on Merle Travis and Chet Atkins, and he always liked Marty Robbins singing. He had one of Marty's first albums, a real country album, and it was scratchy because he played it so much. In fact, he said that was his favourite album – I think it was called *The Song of Robbins*.

'I met Eddie around 1953 or '54. I was playing out at a place called the County Barn Dance and working for a television show in Baldwin Park, about thirty miles east of Los Angeles. We had a television show in LA on Channel 13 every Saturday – Skeets MacDonald was on there and Les "Carrot Top" Anderson was the MC. We played every Friday and Saturday night in this dance hall that held about a thousand people or maybe as many as twelve hundred. Eddie and Hank would come out to the Barn Dance on Friday night and they would get up and play. They were never regulars, though. During that time Hank was doing most of the singing and Eddie was playing the guitar. They had an outfit like Gary and me – I would do the singing and Gary would play the guitar, and that's how Hank and Eddie were doing it. Back then, Eddie had a Gibson – I remember, because Gary had a guitar just like Eddie's.

'Gary and I were doing the same thing they were doing. We were going around playing any place we could play. We'd go to *The Town Hall Party* which was going on during that time and *The Hometown Jamboree* in El Monte, and we ran into Hank and Eddie all the time. I knew all the people who were running around with Eddie – Bob Denton was a real good friend of mine and he was in the army with me later. I guess Bob would be Eddie's best friend, although he had a lot of good friends like Richard Rae and Warren Flock. Warren played mandolin; he was in those early groups before Eddie ran into Hank. They had a little country band and Eddie played guitar; it was Richard's band, Richard Rae And The Shamrock Valley Boys.

'I ran into them in northern California when they were playing up there for a few months. They were playing with Cottonseed Clark and Black Jack Wayne around the San Francisco area where they lived for a while. Black Jack Wayne was booking them around in different clubs and we played some dates with The Cochran Brothers up there too. The Cochran Brothers played with whatever band was there, just like me and Gary – we would play with the house band. They would play mostly uptempo songs – early Faron Young songs.'

Gary Lambert takes up the story: 'Playing was Eddie's main thing in those days. Everyone wanted to be a Jimmy Bryant or a Merle Travis or a Joe Maphis out here because we saw them every week on television and heard them every day on KXLA. In those days The Cochran Brothers were doing what The Wilburn Brothers tried to do and what early Ray Price was trying to do. Pure, pure country – there was no doubt about that.

'They went to northern California later in '56, then Fred Maddox got us a booking up north and we all played in some little place in Salinas. The Cochran Brothers and Glen and I along with a couple of band members from northern California meant that there was six or eight of us there. We outnumbered the crowd!

'In those days Eddie was progressing and was trying to dabble in a little bit of this and that, but because of the difference in our ages I treated him as if I was a senior in high school and he was a freshman. He was a good player. He played everything correctly once he learned it and he was very quick at learning things, and he would never forget.'

Glen Glenn eventually signed with Era Records, one of the many independent labels starting up on the West Coast in the mid-1950s. Along with Gary on guitar and Guybo Smith on upright bass (who would regularly work with the duo when he wasn't touring or recording with Eddie), Glen went on to record some of the most influential and sought-after rockabilly records of the decade. Songs such as *Everybody's Movin'*, *One Cup Of Coffee*, *Blue Jeans And A Boy's Shirt* and *I'm Glad My Baby's Gone Away* are now regarded as classic examples of this music.

Eddie had it all. He could write songs, he could play the guitar and he could sing, too. He could do it all, and everything he did was great.

Glen Glenn

The Cochran Brothers made regular appearances in country music dance halls and local jamborees as well as appearing on two of the most influential television showcases on the West Coast: *The Town Hall Party*, a three-hour country television show broadcast from Compton town hall, just south of downtown Los Angeles, and *The Hometown Jamboree*, a television show broadcast by KXLA every Sunday from the legion stadium in El Monte.

Eddie and Hank appeared as guests on *The Town Hall Party* alongside Merle Travis, Joe and Rose Maphis, Tex Ritter, The Collins Kids, Johnny Bond and Lefty Frizzell. *The Hometown Jamboree* was hosted by Cliffie Stone, a shareholder in American Music Corporation, which was a booking agency run by Steve Stebbins, one of the leading promoters of country music on the West Coast. Steve added The Cochran Brothers to his books in April 1955, which led to a substantial increase in the duo's bookings, as well as arranging an audition with Ekko Records.

Ekko was a tiny independent record label which specialised in recording western swing artists from the 1940s such as Johnny Tyler and Al Dexter. They had two offices, one in California and a head office based on Union Avenue in Memphis, and the label was run by chief A&R man Charles 'Red' Matthews. (Union Avenue was also home to the legendary Memphis Recording Service where, in July 1954, nineteen-year-old Elvis Presley cut the historic *That's All Right*.) Ekko actively sought to nurture new local talent, and in May 1955 Eddie and Hank recorded four songs for the label at Sunset Recorders in Hollywood. These made up The Cochran Brothers' first two releases for the label. The first single was *Mr Fiddle* backed by *Two Blue Singin' Stars*. Released the following month, and with both tracks written by Red Matthews, the A-side featured famed session violinist Harold Hensley together with Eddie and Hank's strong harmonies.

The reviews were promising; one, dated 18 June, read: '*Two Blue Singin' Stars* – A tribute to two popular hillbilly stars now deceased, Jimmy Rodgers and Hank Williams. Nicely harmonised and full of sincere devotion to the memory of these two men, this side could spark a lot of deejay play – and, perhaps, good sales. *Mr Fiddle* – Lest the title mislead, this is not a copy of *Mr Banjo*. While there is little to the lyric, the instrumental sections, particularly those featuring fiddle solo, are good. An excellent dance number.'

Ekko Records had faith in the recording and placed full-page advertisements in a variety of music publications to promote the single.

In keeping with Hank's personal tastes, the two tracks were recorded in a traditional country style, which even by 1955 was becoming somewhat stale, and although the performances showed maturity and confidence, the single bombed.

The final two songs from the session, *Guilty Conscience* (written by Eddie and Hank) and *Your Tomorrows Never Come*, were coupled as their second single and released during the latter part of the year. *Guilty Conscience* enabled Eddie to show off his skills as a guitarist and made this particular song perhaps the strongest of the four recorded during the session. The B-side was closer to the slow, weepy ballad style of *Two Blue Singin' Stars* but, again, Eddie and Hank's harmonies were strong and gave a clear indication of how good their partnership really was. Even at this early stage in their careers, both sang with skill and demonstrated expert musicianship, particularly Eddie, who was already showing signs of developing a unique lead-guitar style. *Guilty Conscience* backed by *Your Tomorrows Never Come* fared as badly as the duo's initial release, failing to chart.

They played an increasing number of live performances and even though their lack of chart success proved to be a major problem for the duo later on, the prestige of having released two singles at such an early point in their career gave them a credibility that many of their contemporaries lacked.

Eddie joined the Musicians' Union on 4 June 1955. With Red Matthews as their first manager, The Cochran Brothers continued to play throughout California and in venues as far away as Dallas, where, in the autumn of 1955, The Cochran Brothers appeared on *The Big D Jamboree*.

Drawing acts from *The Grand Ole Opry* and *The Louisiana Hayride*, *The Jamboree* was a showcase for aspiring local performers, plus a valuable opportunity for both regional and national touring acts. Broadcast from the Sportatorium wrestling arena (the original Sportatorium burnt down in May 1953), *The Jamboree* also gained local television coverage on KRLD-TV and a national slot on CBS radio's *Saturday Night Country Style*.

Early stars of *The Jamboree* included Bill and Joe Callahan, Riley Crabtree, Dewey Groom, Gene O'Quin and Billy Walker. From the start, the show regularly attracted big names like Hank Snow and regional stars such as Hank Locklin.

Grand Ole Opry stars rarely made an appearance – their fees were too high – but acts from California or Louisiana, known to the organisers as Hollywood or Shreveport 'Hillbillies', regularly appeared on the show. As *The Jamboree's* popularity grew, its airtime gradually increased, and by September 1952 KRLD was airing the entire show.

By the mid-1950s, however, acts were moving away from country music as rock'n'roll gained popularity. One particular hillbilly, Elvis Presley, often touring with Hank Snow and a regular on *The Louisiana Hayride*, made four dynamic appearances on *The Big D Jamboree* in 1955 and it was these controversial performances that drew increasing crowds of teenagers to such venues and helped shape a dramatic change in popular music.

At first, rock'n'roll was considered nothing more than a novelty, a passing fad, but its initial impact was powerful enough to alter shows like *The Big D Jamboree* for good. Country music was later eclipsed by rock'n'roll, and at the close of the decade this explosive new musical form inevitably led to the demise of many country shows.

Eddie and Hank arrived to play *The Big D Jamboree* just days after Elvis had performed there. They heard many reports from eye-witnesses of the pandemonium that had ensued. As Hank recalls: 'We played *The Big D Jamboree* in Dallas and met this policeman who was scratched all over. I asked him what happened and how he got all of these scratches. He said that some guy by the name of Elvis Presley played there and the girls tore him to pieces just trying to get to the singer. He only had one record out, *That's All Right Mama*, I think. That was hard for us to believe; young as we were, we weren't too much younger than Elvis.

'We came to Memphis and Nashville promoting our record, so we went out and met Elvis in Memphis. It was just a quick handshake and a "Hi, how are ya?". It was at a radio station – I think it was WMPS. For some reason they had a big gathering there, and the star of all of it was Elvis – from just one record. Everyone knew how big he was going to be.

'Well, Red Matthews was supposed to be managing us, but when the money got tight and he didn't have any, he went off and left us there. So Eddie and I decided to go back to the West Coast and just go home. So we hawked his amp and carried our guitars and hitch-hiked back to California.'

A lot of Jerry Capehart rubbed off on Eddie. Every place you'd go, Jerry Capehart would be there. There was an old show called *The Squeakin' Deacon Show* and that's where everyone hung out who was interested in playing. Jerry Capehart was always there – I think he was there every Sunday. He was a very pushy individual – he knew what he wanted and he went after it, and some of that rubbed off on Eddie, I'm quite sure.

Gary Lambert

Back in Los Angeles, Eddie and Hank continued their work in the recording studios backing Ekko artists such as Riley Crabtree, Jess Willard and Al Dexter. In October 1955 Bert Keither introduced Eddie to Jerry Capehart at the Bell Gardens Music Centre. Capehart, an aspiring songwriter, had recently sent some of his songs to the publishing firm American Music Corporation and had been rewarded with a contract, so he was constantly looking for local musicians to demo his compositions.

Born in Goodman, Missouri, in 1928, Jerry Capehart had moved with his parents to California in the mid-1930s along with millions of other migrants looking for work. After short spells living back in Missouri and Arizona, the Capehart family finally settled in the Los Angeles suburb of Bell Gardens in 1940. After leaving the US Airforce in 1953, where he served in the Korean War as a pilot, Capehart thought about becoming a lawyer but decided against it when he realised how much studying for a degree would cost.

Although Capehart was to become a central figure in Eddie's career, Hank doesn't remember Jerry being particularly important in the duo's development: 'We were doing really well when Jerry Capehart came along. He didn't make much of an impression on me. None at all, in fact. I don't think he helped The Cochran Brothers in any way.'

In a small demo studio in the backroom of the Bell Gardens Music Centre, Eddie, Hank and Jerry began to demo Jerry's songs using direct-to-disc recording facilities. This process bypassed costly studio expenses and enabled musicians to record their tracks directly onto disc in acetate form. It meant, in effect, that any budding musician could walk out of the studio with a one-off record in his hands.

Only a small number of recordings made by Eddie, Hank and Jerry using this process have survived. In the late 1970s Rockstar Records' Tony Barrett discovered three of these Bell Gardens recordings, although the acetates had seriously deteriorated over the years. Of the three tracks, *A Healer Like Time* (a melancholy ballad sung by Hank) and *Closer, Closer, Closer* (an uptempo novelty song about alcoholic beverages, with fantastic country-picking by Eddie) were released on the Rockstar EP *More Sides Of Eddie Cochran*. The third track, *My Honest Name*, remains unreleased.

The latter two songs featured Capehart's vocals supported by Eddie's lead guitar and Hank's acoustic rhythm. All three would have been recorded for the sole purpose of sending the finished product to American Music.

Jerry also began to use The Cochran Brothers as an occasional backing band in the studio and for live performances, as well as taking more of an interest in promoting the duo.

Hank and Eddie were constantly in demand, proving to be a popular live act and making appearances on local television and radio, but their record sales did not reflect this popularity. The poor sales of both singles can mainly be blamed on poor promotion by Ekko, allied to the fact that by late 1955 rhythm and blues, rock'n'roll and western swing were already driving out traditional country and western. The Cochran Brothers' first two singles were pure country, a form of music rapidly becoming unfashionable with record buyers. The lack of success might also have been due to Ekko's financial problems – this small company was already showing signs of being in difficulties before The Cochran Brothers were even signed, and in fact folded shortly after their contract expired.

On top of all this, Red Matthews was spending more time in Memphis, having lost interest in The Cochran Brothers once Capehart got involved. Matthews had initially shown a great deal of faith in Eddie and Hank. He rehearsed them extensively, recorded them and groomed them into professional entertainers capable of holding their own against any local rivals on the Californian country scene, but he eventually tired of the constant interference from Capehart and later blamed him for his loss of interest in The Cochran Brothers' career.

These obstacles severely hindered the duo's progress as recording artists and it became inevitable that The Cochran Brothers would have to look further afield if they were to advance professionally.

Eddie and Hank remained under contract to Ekko but in November 1955 Capehart negotiated a one-off deal with John Dolphin, who ran two tiny independent labels, Cash and Money Records. Based in the Watts district of LA, Dolphin ran a record shop with a small demo studio in a back room of the premises. Recording acetates during the day, he would employ a DJ to play them from a small booth in the shop window. They were then broadcast live onto local radio and through loudspeakers directed at any passer-by on the street. It meant a brand new song would receive instant airplay, reaching a good-sized local audience and, if the response was favourable, Dolphin would press the song immediately, releasing it on either the Cash or Money label.

Capehart managed to convince Dolphin, a tough black business-man with a preference for R&B, to record white hillbilly acts using Dolphin's in-house studio band, a black four-piece R&B unit featuring Ernie Freeman on piano, to provide the backing.

'John Dolphin had some kind of a deal set up in the back of his record store and we would record back there with different people,' Hank remembers. 'Eddie would play lead and I would play rhythm guitar and it was just a way to make another dollar or two. I remember one of the singers, Ernie Freeman, turned out be one of the biggest there in LA. In fact, when they were cutting two of my songs for Dean Martin, I went to the session and he was doing the arranging. He ran over and hugged me saying, "Goodness gracious, what are you trying to do? Take over the country?" But he still remembered back to us all working for Cash Records.'

Their initial effort featured two Capehart compositions, *Walkin' Stick Boogie* and *Rollin'*. Along with the band, Hank Cochran strummed acoustic rhythm while Eddie performed some tough-sounding lead-guitar work. Jerry Capehart's off-tune vocals gave the songs a rather amateur sound, however, spoiling a fairly good performance by all the musicians involved.

One music writer wrote a fair review for this poor release: '*Rollin'* – Guitar backing by The Cochran Brothers is a help to warbler Capehart on this rhythmic tune. Shows the Presley influence. *Walkin' Stick Boogie* – Not much to this side.'

Eddie and Hank were rewarded with a label credit, the record being released under the name 'Jerry Capehart Sings . . . Featuring The Cochran Brothers'. When the single was eventually released on Cash Records, a certain J. Grey was listed as composer of both tracks. This was actually a pseudonym for John Dolphin; losing recognition as the songwriter was one of the prices that Capehart had to pay for the deal. John Dolphin paid a heavier price: this practice eventually led to his early demise when an irate songwriter looking for royalties shot him dead in the booth of his record shop.

Rockin' And Flyin' was recorded in June's living-room in Bell Gardens – that was June Cochran, Bob's wife. We'd take the recorder in and set up the instruments and play for an hour or two. When they stood up and started the tune it was such a wild sound! 'Hey, guys, that sounds like you might make some money from it.'

Chuck Foreman

Another session was booked for Cash Records at Capitol Studios, on 16 February 1956. It featured Eddie and Jerry Capehart on vocals along with top country session guitarist and Cochran hero, Joe Maphis, together with Ernie Freeman and his band. For some reason Hank Cochran did not seem to be present, which may be an indication of his reluctance to get involved in the many enterprising schemes Capehart was trying to initiate at the time.

The songs recorded that day included *Rockin' and Flyin'*. Eddie and

Hank had already produced a demo for this song in late 1955 when Chuck Foreman taped a rehearsal in Bob Cochran's home. The original demo survived and was eventually released on the Rockstar CD *Rockin' It Country Style* in 1997. It features Eddie and Hank only, no other musician, and it was obviously intended to allow rock'n'roll to infiltrate their set. This may have been Eddie and Hank's first attempt at recording a rock'n'roll song.

Even though the backing is fairly sparse, the track rocks pretty well and allows Eddie to develop his trademark rolling technique on the guitar. It was a technique that would also emerge on other Cochran Brothers recordings such as *Tired And Sleepy* and *Slow Down*.

The new Capitol Studios version of *Rockin' And Flyin'* differs considerably. The lyrics are slightly different, perhaps rewritten by Capehart, and, with the added bonus of the Ernie Freeman band and Joe Maphis on second lead guitar, the song takes shape. The backing is superb and Eddie and Maphis swap great solos, but ultimately the finished product is let down by Capehart's vocal performance. The band did record a backing track of the song without the vocals, however, and it was released on a couple of small independent labels.

Mary Jane, an awful song set to a Latin beat, was also recorded at the session. Eddie's guitar playing cannot save this poor effort and thankfully it was never released. Again, Capehart took over the vocal duties but the band sound disjointed and confused with the changes in tempo from Latino to uptempo country.

Eddie and Hank continued to record together throughout the first half of 1956, backing Don Deal on *Cryin' In One Eye* and *Broken Hearted Feller* for Cash Records as well as recording *I'm Ready* for Hank, featuring Jerry Capehart slapping a box to provide the percussion. *I'm Ready* was one of the best-loved rockers recorded by The Cochran Brothers during this period. It is possible that it was recorded as a single for Cash Records but, due to the lack of success the label was having with Capehart's gamble of incorporating hillbilly and country music in a black R&B-based independent, John Dolphin quickly decided to stop issuing records in this style. *I'm Ready* features the prominent slap-bass playing of Guybo Smith and Eddie's forceful rhythm mixed with his intricate two-string melody lead work. Hank, for his part, sounds comfortable with this new genre of music, turning in a great vocal performance to match the musicianship of Eddie and Guybo.

In the early part of 1956, The Cochran Brothers made appearances throughout northern California and further up the West Coast to Oregon and Washington State. The duo were booked as regulars on KVOR-TV's *California Hayride*, which was broadcast from Stockton, just inland from San Francisco, and the pair lived in this area throughout the early part of the year.

'We backed Jess Willard, whom we worked and went on tour with,' Hank explains. 'We went up north with him and we were working the *California Hayride*. We got caught in a bad flood up there and we were all covered up in one room for about two weeks just trying to live.'

While they were staying in a motel in Napa, Eddie and Hank got to know Jack and Chuck Wayne, brothers who worked as DJs for KVSM. By this time a popular live act, The Cochran Brothers also made several appearances at a dance hall called the Garden of Allah which was owned by Jack and Chuck, and they reportedly backed several local musicians in the studio for Jack Wayne's small record label.

Nearer to home, The Cochran Brothers appeared on *The Hollywood Jubilee* on 10 March 1956 at the El Monte stadium, alongside many of their contemporaries including Tom Tall, Don Deal and Jimmy Merritt.

Eddie was a fun guy to be around. We liked the same things. He liked to drink beer and chase women – although the women chased him when he had all the hit records. He had a lot of friends. Elvis was just the opposite, he was a lonely guy. He was so big that even big stars couldn't get in to see him. Hank was more country, he was a straight country singer, but Eddie and I wanted to be like Elvis.

Glen Glenn

'Rockabilly' – a term coined by reviewers at *Billboard* and the plethora of other weekly musical papers that reviewed new releases – was used to describe a type of rock'n'roll music that leaned much more towards country and hillbilly than most rock'n'roll artists, who took their influences from black music such as R&B and blues.

Elvis Presley's début single for Sun Records in 1954, *That's All Right Mama* backed with *Blue Moon Of Kentucky*, is widely regarded as the first rockabilly record.

Using the bare essentials in terms of musical equipment, Elvis and his two band members, lead guitarist Scotty Moore and double-bassist Bill Black, created a sound that was unique. Elvis would drive the song with a forceful acoustic guitar rhythm assisted by Bill Black's percussive slap-bass playing, while Scotty Moore filled out the sound with a guitar-playing style that was heavily influenced by country guitarists Chet Atkins and Merle Travis. Moore adapted their complex thumb-picking technique by simplifying it and adding tough-sounding two-string blues riffs to create a blistering array of solos which punctuated the rockers that Elvis recorded throughout his time with Sun Records.

Proof that Presley's singles for Sun were different to the country, R&B and rock'n'roll music most DJs were used to dealing with was shown by the reluctance of certain radio stations to play his records. While country-orientated radio shows felt that Presley's records sounded too 'black', black stations refused to play his records, as they deemed them too 'white'.

Although the radio stations' reluctance to broadcast Presley's Sun recordings initially hindered his chart status, his music proved immeasurably influential to countless young singers and bands who instinctively felt that this new music was the breath of fresh air they had been waiting for.

Bill Haley had been recording rock'n'roll since the beginning of the 1950s but with little commercial success. In 1954, the film *The Blackboard Jungle* featured his recording of *Rock Around The Clock* as the title track, and the reaction from teenagers was overwhelming. From that moment on, rock'n'roll became the music for the youth of America and, later, the world.

Although Haley's rock'n'roll was musically superior to most of his later rivals, it lacked a certain rebellion that the younger rockers later injected into their music. Here, Elvis Presley became the musical equivalent of James Dean. Presley was the first artist to match rock'n'roll with teenage rebellion and thus became the leader of a generation of singers and musicians who regarded him as the main source of their musical influence. Presley's initial singles for Sun Records earned him a credibility that many artists never achieved and he was regarded as an innovator right from the very beginning of his career.

Eddie Cochran was one of the many young musicians who kept a close ear on the music coming out of Memphis. He was able to adapt to rockabilly with ease – he recognised its country roots and saw making it as a natural progression. Other young country singers around the US also made the transition. Artists such as Buddy Holly, Gene Vincent, Johnny Burnette and Conway Twitty would later use this influence to create their own unique brand of rockabilly, along with countless other lesser-known artists who were responsible for making some of the finest records in this style of music. Singers such as Charlie Feathers, Mac Curtis, Joe Clay, Andy Starr, Eddie Bond, Billy Lee Riley and Warren Smith all made high-quality, powerful rockabilly recordings which would help to create and influence the next generation of rockabilly rebels when, in the late 1970s and early '80s, the music made a welcome return to the pop charts around the world through the recordings of contemporary artists such as The Stray Cats, The Jets, Matchbox and Shakin' Stevens.

Rockabilly's strength was its raw, rough-edged, aggressive approach. As with Presley's Sun recordings, all that was needed was acoustic rhythm, slap bass and lead guitar. Drums were later added, but were never particularly necessary as the overall feel of the performance needed to be one of raw energy. Rockabilly was very much the unhinged, slightly deranged side of rock'n'roll that did not possess the slick, well-produced, high standard of musicianship that rock'n'roll took from its main influences of country swing and R&B. Its major strengths also contributed to its commercial downfall, therefore, and rockabilly never became a chart force for a sustained period. Presley's Sun recordings never broke into the national pop charts and the same is true of nearly all the music's main originators and champions. Only Carl Perkins enjoyed a massive hit with the original version of his self-composed *Blue Suede Shoes*, recorded by Perkins as pure rockabilly, then turned into a rock'n'roll standard by subsequent cover versions.

As the rough edges of rockabilly's originators were smoothed out, the majority of these artists moved towards rock'n'roll, which had maintained its chart success by constantly changing and adapting to suit its audience. The softer, more commercially acceptable side to rock'n'roll for many more conservative teenagers appeared in the form of artists such as Pat Boone, Charlie Gracie, The Everly Brothers and later in the decade with the teen-idol brigade of Fabian, Bobby Rydell and Frankie Avalon among others, and this lighter side of rock'n'roll certainly helped keep the music in the charts. Rockabilly never had a softer side, which is perhaps why the music was doomed to commercial failure, but it is for this reason alone that rock historians today regard rockabilly as perhaps the purest form of rock music ever created.

Hank Cochran, had he wanted to, could have become a great rockabilly artist. His flirtation with the music lasted only a short time, though, certainly shorter than Eddie's perseverance with it. Hank's recording of *I'm Ready* proved that he could rock with the best of them, and later Cochran Brothers recordings also identified his willingness to go along with the musical flow, even if he did not particularly enjoy himself in the process.

It's a strange fact, but many of the greatest rockabilly recordings were made by country artists desperately trying to adjust to rock'n'roll by trying to create black-based rock'n'roll music. In failing dismally, they instead made music that let their country-music roots shine through the heavy backbeat needed for rock'n'roll.

Hank Cochran was not much older than Eddie, but he had a far greater maturity and respect for country and western music as created by his heroes Hank Williams and Jimmy Rodgers. Although he felt uncomfortable with this new music, he at least understood its origins.

Rock'n'roll was barely starting over here – it wasn't really off the ground. We were all into western swing because every club in town and all the television shows were western swing. If you weren't a cowboy you weren't pickin' in this town! I used to wear blue suede loafers but I still had to wear cowboy pants!

Chuck Foreman

Country music underwent a radical change during the course of the 1940s. As the decade progressed, western swing gradually became less influential and was replaced by the music played by smaller, more authentic hillbilly combos. The rise in popularity of honky-tonk artists such as Hank Williams, Ernest Tubb and William Orville Frizzell (who was apparently nicknamed 'Lefty' Frizzell due to a legendary left hook) meant that major record labels were constantly making changes to accommodate the new trends in country music. On a parallel course, R&B also enjoyed an increasing popularity and the two musical styles would often borrow from each other in order to cross over their respective markets.

During this period, several influential music publishing companies were formed in order to help the major record labels find the material needed to meet this demand. Two of the most important during this transitional period in country-music history were Hill and Range, based in New York, and American Music on the West Coast. Formed in 1946 by businessman Sylvester Cross, American Music was initially responsible for helping Capitol Records break into the lucrative new country market by supplying most of their best-selling material.

One of the first signings to American Music was guitar legend Merle Travis, who had just finished serving in the Marines through-out the Second World War. Upon his discharge, Travis had settled in California and was appearing in a number of cowboy movies, as well as recording for a number of small local independent labels. A brilliant songwriter, Travis was signed to Capitol Records shortly after his initial release, *Cincinnati Love* backed with *No Vacancy*, became a double-sided hit, reaching number 2 and 3 respectively in the country charts in the summer of 1946. Other hits by Travis followed. *Divorce Me C.O.D.*, his second release, reached number 1 and even crossed into the pop charts, reaching number 25 a few months later. For the next three years, Merle Travis was practically a permanent fixture in the US country charts.

In 1954, with a back-catalogue brimming with hit songs, Sylvester Cross decided to form Crest Records and use it as a vehicle to record local talent and showcase new songwriters signed to American Music. Cross planned to use two of his staff writers, Dale Fitzsimmons and Ray Stanley, to act alongside Jack Lewis as A&R men for the label and scout for local songwriters and musicians to demo and release their material. It was hoped that by using Crest Records, new releases could be picked up by local DJs or covered by well-known artists, ensuring that their newly acquired copyrights would become regional or even national hits.

Cross's good business sense often paid dividends. One example of this was the Ray Stanley composition *Glendora*. Originally recorded by Crest's Jack Lewis, the song was covered by 1950s pop giant Perry Como on RCA and became a Top 10 hit in the summer of 1956.

That same year, however, the onslaught of rock'n'roll created a drop in fortune for American Music. Fitzsimmons and Stanley had, since the birth of the label, been concentrating on outdated western swing, novelty pop tunes and the occasional half-hearted attempt at recording R&B. Despite their clever marketing ploys, including using coloured vinyl on certain releases, Crest did not achieve a great deal apart from the odd regional success, so the two A&R men decided to adopt a more modern approach and concentrate on rock'n'roll.

The label's policy of offering one-off deals to songwriters and recording cheap demo versions – which often ended up as the actual release – ensured that Crest Records released a surprisingly large amount of rock'n'roll and rockabilly music, with varying degrees of quality, throughout the decade.

Fitzsimmons, an ex-western-swing bandleader with a long history in the music business, arranged the sessions using Master Recorders on Fairfax Avenue or Goldstar Studios on Santa Monica and Vine. These were both within a mile of Crest Records' headquarters at 9109 Sunset Boulevard, and Fitzsimmons would often participate in the sessions by playing drums or bass.

Pianist Ray Stanley (born Stanley Ray Nussbaum on 24 July 1924 in Dermott, Arkansas) was encouraged by his mother to take up the instrument. Along with Fitzsimmons and Stanley's best friend, singer and guitarist Jack Lewis, they created the first two releases for Crest by forming a fictional group entitled The Ragtime Rascals, which included Bill Dane and Lynne Marshall on vocals.

By 1955 Lewis and Stanley had formed Jack Lewis And The Americans using various Crest employees to record their compositions. The musicians involved included mailing clerk Carl Tandberg on bass, Mitchell Tableporter and Ray Stanley on piano, Jack Lewis on guitar and Biggie McFadden and Jesse Sailes on drums.

Jack Lewis And The Americans recorded *My Honest Name*, written by Jerry Capehart. Jerry, along with The Cochran Brothers, had produced the original demo for the song at the Bell Gardens Music Centre, and the track, a bluesy tale of farmers working hard all day in the fields, became the next release on Crest for Lewis.

Stanley and Fitzsimmons decided to arrange a recording session for Capehart, who was under contract to American Music, to demo more of his songs at Goldstar Studios. On 4 April 1956, Capehart, backed by Eddie and Hank and possibly Guybo on bass, entered the studio to record five new songs.

Ray Stanley recalls his initial meeting with Eddie, Hank and Capehart. 'I first met Eddie in the early 1950s. He was with Hank Cochran at the time and lived in Bell Gardens. I said to Eddie, "Are you and Hank brothers?" and he said, "No, we just perform together."

'Jerry Capehart became Eddie's manager and I was writing for American Music. I wrote lots of things during that era and Eddie did many demos for me. I always thought his guitar playing was the greatest – Cochran played the guitar like nobody could. We recorded loads of demos at Goldstar. Most were destroyed, but they were great.'

Once Elvis came out we changed our style of music overnight. Over on the coast we didn't hear any of his Sun Records stuff, but we would read about Elvis and we heard about him. Then, when *Heartbreak Hotel* came out, it went to number 1 in about a week, and once we saw him it changed everything.

Glen Glenn

Goldstar Studios became a focal point in Eddie's future recording career. The Hollywood-based studios offered a high standard of recording at inexpensive rates and was often referred to as 'The King of the Demos'. Co-owner Stan Ross, who engineered the sessions at Goldstar, explains the history behind the studio and its connection with Eddie Cochran: 'I was born and raised in Brooklyn and came to

California with my parents at the age of fifteen. In high school I used to have a music column and I used to write reports called "Musical Downbeat" and "Surfers Noise". I would review records and, coincidentally, I got a job working in a recording studio after school and then I worked in another recording studio for about four years.

'In 1950 Dave Gold and I opened up Goldstar. We built our own equipment and found our own location and expanded our location over the years and then stayed out at Santa Monica Boulevard and Vine Street in Hollywood until 1984 – that's thirty-four years.

'From 1956 onwards we had two studios. One was a simple mono demo studio at a low price range for people to do demos, and the other was where we did the Phil Spector "Wall Of Sound" in and also Sonny and Cher. It was the one with the big echoes and everything – studio A.

'All the consoles in Goldstar were built by my partner Dave Gold and we were using Dave's console in studio B along with Ampex tape machines. It was mono for the most part. Last year I went to the Rock'n'Roll Hall of Fame Museum in Cleveland and they showed Elvis's Sun Studio and, lo and behold, it looked just like my control room in studio B at Goldstar.

'I first met Eddie before he became a recording artist. He was doing a lot of demos with Jerry Capehart for American Music. As far as I remember, he was not a record star at that time. We used to do a lot of Eddie's stuff in studio B because they were demos and it was a little cheaper in the price structure. We didn't charge too much for that stuff. When we did a demo session for American Music I think it was $25 an hour, in that one studio, and they'd book it every Wednesday for ten hours. They would come in and say, "What can we do to this song to embellish it?" and we'd spend some time on the song. We'd overdub and overdub and add this and that. Before you knew it, the thing was bristling with sound and we'd say, "Wow, this is more than just a demo, this is a record!"

'Well, don't forget, the public doesn't know what a demo is. A demonstration record was used to take around and play to Merle Travis or Dean Martin or whoever at Capitol, who would record the song. We did the demo for *Jezebel* for Frankie Laine using Freddie Darien singing it. Frankie Laine said recently, "If Fred Darien had released *Jezebel* I would never have recorded it, because the record was so terrific."

'We had two mono machines – one which we used for tape reverb and one that we cut on and then we'd go back and forth from mono to mono. We never had two-track and it was easier that way, because what you heard was what you had. Two-track would have meant too many decisions – put the voice on one track and put the band on the other and mix it later – and we didn't have time for that. These were demos – they had to walk out of there with eight songs all done.'

The tracks recorded during that first session at Goldstar were *Pink Peg Slacks*, *Latch On*, *Heart Of A Fool*, *Yesterday's Heartbreak* and *My Love To Remember*. The songs were written by Jerry Capehart and The Cochran Brothers (with the exception of *Latch On* which was composed by Dale Fitzsimmons and Ray Stanley). *Latch On* was covered later that same year by MGM artist Ron Hargrave.

This session marked the first step in Eddie becoming a solo artist: he sang lead vocals on *Pink Peg Slacks* and the two ballads, *Yesterday's Heartbreak* and *My Love To Remember*. Listening to these early recordings, Eddie's vocals seem hesitant and unsure, but his understanding of the new rock'n'roll genre is certainly evident. *Pink Peg Slacks* is certainly a great rocker, displaying copious amounts of youthful frustration with its tongue-in-cheek lyrics.

Hank's role in this session seems to be relegated to lead vocals on the two versions of *Latch On*, with Capehart taking lead vocals on *Heart Of A Fool*. Both songs feature superb rockabilly guitar playing by Eddie. This entire demo session was eventually released by Rockstar Records in 1982 on the vinyl LP *The Young Eddie Cochran*.

It was these demos that brought Eddie to the attention of Stanley and Fitzsimmons, and American Music was to feature prominently in Eddie's career as the year developed. Knowingly or not, Capehart had presented them with a good-looking teenage singer and guitarist, possessing an understanding of rock'n'roll that they themselves did not and never would possess. His musical abilities were beyond question. Even if his vocals were still rather unsure at the time, his interpretations of rock songs were filled with a vast amount of enthusiasm.

Also in Eddie's favour was his dedication and open-minded approach to music – qualities that made him the ideal vehicle for Sylvester Cross, Ray Stanley and Dale Fitzsimmons to use as one of their main rock'n'roll contributors to both Crest and American Music. Before too long, the two A&R men were regularly throwing work in Eddie's direction.

Many of Eddie's musical associates from this time have commented on how easy he found rock'n'roll music to play on the guitar. Chuck Foreman mentioned earlier that Eddie's broad musical tastes from jazz to country, through to blues and classical, gave him more versatility as a guitarist. As his reputation grew, Eddie was guaranteed a place as a regular musician, not only for American Music and Crest, but also for the growing number of local independent labels experimenting with rock'n'roll.

Stan Ross remembers every American Music demo session as being a very casual, laid-back affair for all the musicians involved. 'Ray Stanley was on the piano usually, and Dale Fitzsimmons would play the box or the drums depending on what sound we were going for. Guybo played the bass and Eddie played the guitar. If Connie couldn't get the bassline, a guy called Carl who worked for American Music played bass also. It's an amazing situation. Dale Fitzsimmons was also a piano player at American Music and Carl was also a bass player at American Music, working in the library or something, so these were not professional musicians, they just came to the studio and jammed. The chemistry all happened because they were having a day off. Every Wednesday they came to Goldstar to have a day off from work and they were having a ball.

'Guybo's trademark was the slap-bass sound. We didn't over mic him. We used one microphone for everything – even the drums only had two mics, one for kick and one for overhead. In those days, the musicians played to the microphone and not the microphone to the musicians. Today, you try to pick up every sound a musician has got coming out of him, and sometimes that's not a good idea.

'Eddie became what they called "a performer", and he was not a performer when he started out – he was a recording artist or a studio artist. He was not a studio musician, he was a studio *artist*, and he could do anything in the studio. He didn't know if he was good or not, but when he went on the road and started appearing in concerts with other people, he realised that they were important and, as he was on the same bill, he must be important too. That helped his ego and that helped his sound. Eddie was more interested in his guitar work than thinking of himself as a star. Everybody else did, but he didn't.'

By 1956 rock'n'roll was more than a limited regional success and the twenty-one-year-old Elvis Presley, now signed to RCA Victor, had taken teenage America by storm. His début single, *Heartbreak*

Hotel backed with *I Was The One*, sold 300,000 copies in the first three weeks of its release (it went on to sell over a million copies), turning the regional star into an international sensation. His first album, *Elvis Presley*, which was released in March, also sold over a million copies, and the following month negotiations began for a seven-year movie contract with Paramount Pictures.

Politically, these were also changing times for America. In the south, Dr Martin Luther King, Jr, was gaining national prominence in his fight for racial equality, while black artists such as Little Richard and Chuck Berry were starting to enjoy huge successes in the charts with a more R&B-orientated rock'n'roll. Although their images were certainly in keeping with the music they were performing, race-conscious middle-class America was still not ready to give black artists such a high profile.

Rock'n'roll was branded as the devil's music. It created divisions between generations, classes and all aspects of American and Western culture, and inevitably caused a difference in musical direction between Hank and Eddie Cochran.

Eddie was a straight-ahead kid. He didn't mess around with drugs – I don't even remember him smoking. He might have smoked out in the parking lot! Eddie was a very clean, candy-bar-and-juice or soda-pop kid. He didn't mess around with too many things, he was straight ahead, like the kid next door – or how the kid next door used to be!

Stan Ross

The Cochran Brothers' second and final session for Ekko, completing their contractual obligations, took place shortly after their initial demo session for American Music. In the autumn of 1956 the duo returned to Sunset Recorders in Hollywood and recorded four new compositions all written by Eddie, Hank and Jerry Capehart.

The influence that rock'n'roll was now having on Eddie and Hank could not be better illustrated than by this session. Gone were the novelty country tunes and the slow weepy ballads. Also absent were the steel guitar and fiddle, which had been replaced by pianist Les Taylor and drummer Roy Harte – members of the local television *Hometown Jamboree* band – and together they created four of the most boisterous, enjoyable rockabilly tracks ever to be recorded by a supposed hillbilly duo.

Tired'n'Sleepy kicks off proceedings, and, right from Eddie's opening guitar riff – a kind of double-string pull-off on the top strings – this potent mix of teenage jive talk, heavy drumming and wonderful slap bass work perfectly with Eddie and Hank practically shouting the lyrics at each other as they trade verses.

Fool's Paradise, although slightly slower in tempo, repeats the same formula, Eddie and Hank sharing the vocals while the band keep up a relentless enthusiasm.

The third song, *Open The Door*, features an unknown bass vocalist who manfully joined in to beef up what was already an extremely powerful performance by the duo, who managed to save the song from becoming a predictable novelty number. Again the piano and drums drive the song, and special mention must be given to both Taylor and Harte for the obvious abundance of energy they brought along to the session. At times, Taylor seems to be thumping the piano keys with all his might. The piano sounds almost like an early electric model, as the sound often comes across as very clean, with little sustain, and does not have the soft acoustic tones of a normal upright. It has been suggested over the years that this may indeed have been the case – although, as Chuck Foreman stated earlier, he and Eddie experimented heavily with microphone placements during their home recording session in order to create different sounds for various instruments. It's a good argument to suggest that this may be a normal upright mic'd up in such a way to cause this unusual sound.

When listening to these recordings, the band members seem a little uncertain with their arrangements at times, suggesting a lack of rehearsal before the session took place. It's likely that Taylor and Harte quickly went over the tracks on the day of the session, but this looseness only adds to the overall performance and does not detract from what today sounds like a recording session that everyone involved with enjoyed tremendously.

The final track, *Slow Down*, is arguably the superior rocker cut that day. Again, the song possesses a strong resemblance to *Tired'n'Sleepy* as Eddie and Hank share the vocals and use similar jive talk for the lyrics, but this song really does rock along superbly with Eddie and Les Taylor trading licks during an extended solo. Taylor almost steals the show with a frantic display of pounding piano and Guybo shines with some fantastic slap bass.

All in all, it represented a good day's work for the duo, and the only problem left was to choose two tracks for the final single release on Ekko. The decision went to *Tired'n'Sleepy* backed with *Fool's Paradise*, leaving the other two tracks to languish unheard for over twenty years until they were discovered by Tony Barrett in the early 1980s. *Open The Door* and *Slow Down* eventually saw the light of day in the Rockstar release *The Young Eddie Cochran* in 1982.

When *Tired'n'Sleepy* was released in 1956, it was described by the music press as 'a tantalising, quick-paced jolter earning The Cochran Brothers an entry in the rock'n'roll honours', while *Fool's Paradise* was reviewed as 'slightly slower than its A-side although remaining a driving, rhythmic ditty'.

Unfortunately this final release, although far more contemporary than The Cochran Brothers' previous two singles, was doomed to failure due to the label's imminent demise. This single, the product of their last session for Ekko, also marked the final collaboration on vinyl between Eddie and Hank recording as The Cochran Brothers.

I still listen to those old Cochran Brothers recordings now. I thought Eddie was a great guitar player even then. If he'd had a couple more years there's no telling what kind of guitar player he'd have turned out to be.

Hank Cochran

After the hectic recording schedule of April, early May saw The Cochran Brothers supporting country legend Lefty Frizzell in Hawaii and playing to some of their largest ever audiences. The duo nearly met an untimely end during rehearsals for this show. 'We went over to rehearse and work with Lefty Frizzell,' Hank recalls. 'I had an old Nash car. We got a flat tyre going over there, which we changed and on the way back we had a flat again. So we called Eddie's brother to come and get us and we left the engine running because it was getting cold. By the time he got there he had to revive us because the fumes had knocked us out. That's how close we both came to getting it.'

Returning to the mainland, Eddie and Hank worked for a while in a small club in Escondido, near San Diego. Although The Cochran Brothers proved to be a popular act in such venues in and around the California area, the failure of the Ekko singles as well as their musical differences proved to be too much for the partnership to continue. Hank, already a married man with two children, wasn't interested in making rock'n'roll a career, whereas the seventeen-year-old Eddie, encouraged by an ambitious Jerry Capehart, was ready to embrace and conquer this new musical form.

Gary Lambert has another, more plausible, explanation for the duo's eventual demise: 'Hank had a burning desire to do one thing and Eddie had a burning desire to do another. What they were doing together wasn't really working out because they weren't making any money at it.'

Warren Flock also adds that: 'The duo act was very good back then but with a duo you have to work together all the time, which was all right, but Eddie always wanted to do more work. He hung around the studios all he could because there was more work along with the job he had.'

After Eddie's initial introduction to American Music – through the demo session of 4 April at Goldstar – it is almost certain that he signed a publishing contract with the company. Although there is very little evidence of this, as no contracts have ever surfaced, American Music together with Cross Music, another publishing company owned by Sylvester Cross, would play an extremely important part in the development of Eddie's career.

By all accounts, Eddie had a very good working relationship with Sylvester Cross and would often drop by his office on Sunset Boulevard for social visits. In return, Cross took an active interest in the development of Cochran's career and gave Eddie as much time in the studio to work on his own compositions as he needed. Eddie returned the favour by playing on as many demo sessions for American Music as Stanley and Fitzsimmons required, an arrangement that suited all the parties involved.

Eddie and Jerry Capehart began to spend more time collaborating on their songwriting and experimenting with the end results at Goldstar whenever studio time was allotted to them by Fitzsimmons.

As Stan Ross explained earlier, Goldstar was booked every Wednesday for many years by American Music for the sole purpose of creating demos for their compositions. The results were often good enough to release immediately on Crest Records, and this situation continued throughout the 1950s and into the next decade.

Eddie and Jerry now had the perfect foundations on which to build Cochran's already growing reputation as a budding rock'n'roll artist.

Eddie came on the scene around the same time that Elvis came over very big. I remember recording Eddie and he was doing the same reverb sounds that Elvis came out with, and I said, 'Hey! We've got our own Elvis Presley here on the West Coast.' But it didn't happen that way, unfortunately for him.

Stan Ross

Through their strong connections with American Music, Eddie and Jerry were given a one-off deal with Crest Records. In July 1956, a split session was booked at Master Recorders on Fairfax Boulevard for Eddie and another newcomer to the label, Gene Davis, to record two solo tracks each.

It was not unusual for small labels, working to a tight budget, to cut costs and have two artists share the same session using one band to provide the backing. The musicians for this particular session were Ray Stanley on piano, Jesse Sailes on drums and Guybo on slap bass.

The Cochran and Capehart composition *Skinny Jim*, backed with *Half Loved* (which was probably recorded at an earlier date), became Eddie's first solo release, on Crest 1026, that same month.

The A-side, a manic rocker featuring the wonderful slap-bass playing of Guybo Smith and a thunderous guitar break from Eddie, races along with Eddie's coarse vocals shouting out the lyrics to great effect. *Skinny Jim* is today regarded as a rockabilly classic and is still a standard feature on many bands' live sets around the world. The B-side, *Half Loved*, does expose Eddie's limitations as a balladeer, but despite this it is a well-structured song with good performances from all the musicians involved. Ray Stanley later took the song to his connections at RCA where it was covered by Janis Martin, Milton Allen and Osie Johnson.

(It has been long speculated that Hank Cochran used the pseudonym Bo Davis to record the final two tracks of the session. However, it has recently been discovered that *Drowning All My Sorrows* and *Let's Coast A While* were recorded by Gene Davis as Bo Davis, an artist in his own right.)

After completing his own solo tracks Eddie returned to the role of session guitarist, accompanying Gene on his two songs. Although Eddie's remarkable guitar-playing skills quite literally stole the show, special mention must be given to Guybo on bass, particularly on the driving *Drowning All My Sorrows*. Collectors and rockabilly historians regard this particular single as one of the finest double A-sides for this genre of music.

Both Crest singles were released in August 1956 but failed to make any chart headway. Even so, this was a giant step forward for Eddie recording as a solo artist.

One final song recorded at this session was *Latch On*, which had previously been recorded as a demo by Hank Cochran on 4 April at Goldstar. This time the Stanley and Fitzsimmons composition was given a greater rockabilly treatment by the band. According to Gene Davis, he played lead guitar with Jerry and Eddie providing lead and harmony vocals respectively. It is probable that Eddie gave his Gretsch to Davis and told him to play lead so he could concentrate on singing, but on aural evidence it seems possible that Eddie may be playing lead and singing harmony vocals at the same time.

The end result was a great jiving rocker, with Guybo giving it his all. The recording remained unissued until it was included on the

Rockstar LP *Eddie Cochran – Words And Music* in 1982.

Musical differences and the lack of any real success finally caused The Cochran Brothers to split, although Hank remembers the parting as being extremely amicable. 'Eddie got a throat problem and I told him: "Nothing against rock'n'roll, but I would rather be in the country end of it." Eddie said he was going to give it a break for a while to see what happened. I had a family by then, so I guess Capehart just moved in from there.

'Eddie showed that he had country in him and it was still in him by some of the things he did later. But with rock'n'roll and country, the only thing different is the arrangement – the words are mostly the same. You can listen to Chuck Berry's *Memphis Tennessee* and it's about as sad a love song as you've ever heard. If you listen to some of those songs that people write, the only thing they ever do differently is the arrangement.

'We weren't any different from everyone else. We would go hunting together, but we just loved music and tried to write about whatever we thought about. We didn't do it for the money then. If we had any, we certainly wouldn't have been hitchhiking around the country. We were just jumping from one thing to another. Anything to see what happened first. I think that if you believe in something enough it will happen.

'When I wrote *Make The World Go Away* the publisher told me it was the worst song I had ever written when I played it for him. Just because someone turns you down or doesn't agree with you, don't quit. Believe in yourself and keep at it.'

Finally moving to Nashville in October 1959, Hank decided to pursue his ambition in country music. As well as *Make The World Go Away*, his legendary songwriting successes include *A Little Bitty Tear*, *I Fall To Pieces* and *Funny Way Of Laughing*.

Step Two . . .

We all realised that to make it you had to do what was
popular. What was popular may not be exactly what
you wanted to do, but at least it was something. At
least you're working, at least there's money and at
least you're a musician.

Chuck Foreman

Throughout 1956, the enormous popularity of rock'n'roll was
proving increasingly lucrative with the teenaged record-buying
public. The effect that this music had on its two main influences,
blues and country, was to prove almost disastrous. It would take both
musical styles almost a decade to recover before they were able to
reinvent themselves and become a chart force again. While many
younger artists embraced rock'n'roll, older, more established artists
resented moving in this direction in order to sell records.

One advantage Eddie Cochran had over his contemporaries was his
knowledge and understanding of the recording studio and techniques
of the time. As Stan Ross explains, 'Eddie Cochran became an artist
because of all the chances he had to make demos of quality tunes.
American Music was basically a Merle Travis label and Eddie was able
to interpret country tunes and country lyrics.'

'Eddie did a lot of sessions,' Bob Denton recalls, 'a lot of which had
to do with Capehart too. Actually it was Capehart that got Eddie and
Hank to split up. Hank was country and Eddie was a country boy too,
but he was looking where the money was and I don't blame him. If
you want to get into the music business you should go in it for the
money. I don't know what he promised Eddie but he got Eddie into a
lot of recording sessions and things, then later after Eddie's death,
Jerry did the same with Glen Campbell. Glen was one of the highest-
paid recording studio musicians in LA at one time – all that twelve-
string stuff coming out of LA was all Glen Campbell.'

It's impossible to determine just how many recording sessions
Eddie worked on for American Music and Crest Records, not to
mention the assortment of other small independent labels that
Cochran was associated with throughout his career. For many of these
sessions, he would have been paid cash in hand, eliminating the need
for paperwork to be completed and sent to the Musicians' Union. On

receiving session details, the union would expect the responsible party to pay the musicians used a set rate. This was a legal requirement but one that many small labels chose to ignore and use as a cost-cutting measure to ensure their survival in difficult times. Throughout LA, record companies were forming and dissolving virtually overnight as the music business grew during the 1950s, and it was rare for session details to be kept detailing the musicians involved in each recording.

This has meant that a tremendous amount of detective work has to be done to ascertain a link between Cochran and a recording that is rumoured to feature him in some capacity. Eddie created a highly distinctive guitar sound and style which can be easily recognised, but his enthusiasm to be involved in the recording process throughout his career meant that he could be playing bass, drums, acoustic rhythm, or even appear as a backing vocalist on a variety of recordings. His versatility as a studio musician now means that the full extent of his recording output will probably never be known.

Although rock'n'roll was the music of the moment, from a session musician's point of view, it would have been impossible to make a living solely in that genre. Eddie's country-music background and appreciation of jazz, classical and R&B proved invaluable to him, increasing his versatility as a musician and allowing him to work in a variety of different musical styles.

Rock'n'roll was, however, becoming a key factor in Eddie's development as more and more country artists began to experiment with this new musical style. As a teenager, Eddie would have instinctively known how rock'n'roll should be presented, and as a musician, he would have been able to relate this to the artists now employing him on their sessions.

One example was a split session for Capitol Records at Western Recorders in Hollywood on 26 July featuring Wynn Stewart and Skeets MacDonald, two prominent country artists. During Stewart's session, recording *Keeper Of The Keys* and *Slowly But Surely*, Eddie drew inspiration from Chet Atkins and Merle Travis, while the Skeets MacDonald tracks *You Oughta See Grandma Rock* and *Heartbreakin' Mama*, two of the wildest and most outrageous rockabilly tracks to emanate from a middle-aged country artist, enabled Eddie to take centre stage and personalise these two songs with his unique and aggressive style of playing.

From April 1956 throughout the summer of that year, Eddie and

Jerry Capehart spent a great deal of time at Goldstar recording demos of their own songs and working on various sessions for Crest records. Eddie, Guybo and Jerry re-recorded *Pink Peg Slacks* and *My Love To Remember* (originally recorded on 4 April) plus a new song written by Dale Fitzsimmons' wife Jaye and Ray Stanley, entitled *Half Loved*, prior to the *Skinny Jim* session. *Pink Peg Slacks* became a much tougher-sounding rocker compared with the initial demo, whereas the latter two – both ballads – were fleshed out with more instrumentation, assisted by Stanley on piano, Jesse Sailes on drums and Carl Tandberg on bass.

Eddie undertook a great deal of experimental work to develop his vocal abilities and gain the confidence he needed in order to become a solo performer. Although he made tentative steps in this direction early on in his career, with Eddie Garland And The Country Gentlemen for example, by mid-1956 he was still regarded by the local music fraternity as one half of The Cochran Brothers, even though that partnership had dissolved during the summer.

Maybe as an afterthought, following a long day at Goldstar working on his own demos, or perhaps as a deliberate move to incorporate more contemporary rock'n'roll material into his already impressive recorded repertoire, Eddie decided to cover *Blue Suede Shoes*, *Long Tall Sally*, *I Almost Lost My Mind* and *That's My Desire*, four songs that by mid-1956 had already proved their status as classic recordings following a variety of cover versions by different artists. *Blue Suede Shoes*, originally a Top 10 hit on Sun Records for its composer Carl Perkins, had also charted, with varying degrees of success, for Boyd Bennett, Pee Wee King and Elvis Presley. The Little Richard hit *Long Tall Sally* had also proved popular for Marty Robbins and Pat Boone. *I Almost Lost My Mind* by Ivory Joe Hunter, was also destined to be covered by Pat Boone.

There seem to be three reasons for recording these songs, in May or June 1956. Firstly, although Eddie and Jerry had written some good rockers up to this point, they needed instantly recognisable material to showcase Eddie's new musical direction. *Blue Suede Shoes* and *Long Tall Sally* would perfectly provide this aspect. Secondly, Eddie still needed to stamp his own authority on material that he had not written. All four songs gave him the opportunity to develop a style he felt comfortable with. Thirdly, and more importantly, it was hoped that the demos would portray Eddie as a confident, professional artist, thus elevating him from his status as a musical sideman into a solo performer capable of handling any material handed to him.

On the two rockers, the lack of instrumentation – due mainly to Capehart on cardboard-box duties trying to make up for the lack of drums – does tend to give the impression that they are slightly underplayed. If you listen closely, though, Eddie and Guybo are providing just the right amount of attack and enthusiasm to justify what, in reality, is a credible performance from the pair.

The two ballads once again expose Eddie's lack of technical ability as a vocalist. To his credit, both tracks do show his attempts at adapting his deep breathy vocals into a style that would later prove to be a capable and effective way of handling this type of material.

It's also important to note the balance of rockers and ballads that Eddie was concentrating on during this period. It indicates a deliberate and carefully thought-out plan to portray him as an artist who could mix both styles with ease, thus making him a more commercially viable prospect to tempt major record companies into offering a deal.

As Cochran and Capehart edged closer to achieving their ultimate goal, they continued with their obligations as session men on a variety of recording dates put together by Dale Fitzsimmons for American Music. Prior to Eddie's first solo release, *Skinny Jim*, he had worked with Jack Lewis as a backing vocalist on a track entitled *Butterscotch Candy And Strawberry Pie*, which was released as a single on Crest 1025. Their next collaboration was a split session between Lewis and Lynn Marshall which produced two singles for Crest – Jack Lewis And The Americans' *Someone to Love Me* backed with *I.O.U.* and Lynn Marshall's *Borrowed Love* backed with *You'll Find Out* – both of which were released in autumn 1956 on Crest 1033 and 1034 respectively.

Someone To Love Me, written by Dale Fitzsimmons, was a song that American Music obviously had a certain degree of faith in, as Eddie later recorded the song with Paula Morgan. This later version coupled with *Only A Fool*, was released on the Demon label in April 1958. The Jack Lewis version showed his ability to croon a pop song to great effect, whereas *I.O.U.*, a rather half-hearted rocker penned by Ray Stanley, exposed his inability to adjust to rock'n'roll. Both tracks, although marred by what sounds like a lack of rehearsal, feature strong guitar work from Eddie – de-tuning his Gretsch to good effect on *Someone To Love Me* – and Guybo once again pounding the bass to compensate for the cardboard-box-playing Capehart.

Lyn Marshall – daughter of Jack Marshall, a Hollywood musical arranger who worked with Peggy Lee on her classic cover version of Little Willie John's *Fever* – lent strong, if not particularly interesting, vocals for the two songs she contributed to. *Borrowed Love*, written in typical fashion by Dale Fitzsimmons, is a good bluesy effort featuring great guitar work by Eddie with sterling support from Guybo. The Ray Stanley song *You'll Find Out* is a toe-tapping track which again features prominent bass along with a very loud backing-vocals group to provide the necessary 'Oohs' and 'Aahs'.

It is probable that another song, *Tood-A-Lou*, was put down on tape during this session but deemed unworthy of release and eventually discarded. Discovered by Ray Topping from the UK's Ace Records at the home of songwriting team George Motola and his wife Ricki Page, the track was eventually released by Rockstar in the late 1980s on the album *Eddie Cochran – Thinkin' About You*. Despite Jack Lewis's rather stilted vocals, *Tood-A-Lou* is a great rockabilly record. Driving slap bass, a great Scotty Moore-style guitar solo from Eddie and Goldstar's trademark slap-back echo turn this into Lewis's finest moment in rock'n'roll.

American Music maintained their connections with Capitol Records which commenced in the late 1940s and well into the next decade. This proved fortunate for Ray Stanley as he was offered a one-off record deal with the label on the strength of two songs he had written and recorded as demos at Goldstar. The two songs, *Let's Get Acquainted* and *Commonsense*, were recorded with Eddie on guitar, Stanley on piano and vocals, and the usual assortment of American Music employees on bass and drums. Stanley hoped that Capitol would use the finished masters and release them as a single but it soon became clear that, although they were impressed with the songs and Stanley's efforts on vocals, Capitol felt the songs needed to be re-recorded as the backing singing was not up to standard.

On 2 May 1956 Stanley went into Capitol Tower to re-record the two songs using an in-house studio band. The finished product was released shortly afterwards. The single failed to chart, thus ending Ray Stanley's brief career as a Capitol recording artist, but he made enough connections to ensure that, in the future, he would be able to get more of his compositions to the right people in order to get the songs recorded by other artists on the label.

Eddie was not really a singer. He became a singer later. He just wanted to do the lead and harmony work. Later, Eddie could see that with rock'n'roll and a little more work, he could have the freedom to be a little more inventive. Liberty [Records] got him singing because he was a very good-looking man. Like today, the young entertainers are good for the women and keep the record sales going.

Warren Flock

As well as being the capital of the motion picture industry, Hollywood was also home to many influential recording and publishing companies. It was the ideal place for Eddie to meet influential people who might be able to further his career. One such person was Boris Petroff, with whom Jerry Capehart had a vague acquaintance, and meeting him during a hectic recording schedule in the summer of 1956 dramatically changed the course of Eddie Cochran's solo career.

Born in 1894 in Saratov, the Russian had a long and distinguished career in movies. As a writer, director and producer, his career spanned four decades, starting in 1937 with his directorial début, *Hats Off*. Petroff's other credits include *Red Snow*, *World Dances*, *Arctic Fury* and *Two Lost Worlds*. By the mid-1950s, however, he was stuck in the B-movie horror-flick circuit, directing *Anatomy Of A Psycho* and *The Unearthly* under the pseudonym Brooke L. Peters.

His final film was *Shotgun Wedding*. According to Jerry Capehart, he and Eddie wrote and recorded the theme tune along with incidental music for the score, including the instrumental *Country Jam*. (As *Shotgun Wedding* is documented as not being released until 1963, however, it is difficult to ascertain whether Eddie was involved in this particular movie or one of the director's earlier productions.)

Boris Petroff reportedly asked Eddie if he would be interested in making an appearance in the film *Do-Re-Mi*, which was being directed by one of his colleagues. Apparently Eddie initially took the whole idea as quite a joke, still regarding himself as a studio musician and a sideman rather than a solo artist.

In an interview during the latter part of 1957, Eddie described his initial meeting with Petroff: 'I was a guitar player and I was playing, you know, record dates out in Hollywood and I moved out there from Oklahoma City. I was doing one of those record dates one day and a fella walked in there. It was just in between takes so I was just sitting there picking on my guitar to my own *amazement*, and he walked in and wanted to know if I wanted to make a movie as a singer. I told him "Yeah I'll do it." I never had done too much singing, really, you know, but I went out and cut a dub of *Twenty Flight Rock* and I took that out to 20th-Century-Fox and they put me in *The Girl Can't Help It*, just over that dub.'

Although Eddie's account is somewhat lacking in detail, mainly in order to keep a long story short, it is essentially correct. *Do-Re-Mi* was later retitled *The Girl Can't Help It* to match the Little Richard song featured in the movie, and in the best tradition of fairytale rags-to-riches storylines, Eddie obtained his part in the movie by simply being in the right place at the right time.

Cochran's next stop was American Music in a bid to find a suitable song for the movie. He had obviously been told that his appearance in the film would be as a new rock'n'roll singing sensation, so a song in the appropriate style was needed. After listening to a dozen or so possibilities, he chose *Twenty Flight Rock*, composed by staff writer Nelda Bingo who wrote under the pseudonym Ned Fairchild. It was decided that if 20th-Century-Fox agreed to go with the song, Eddie would receive co-writing credit, but all royalties would revert back to Nelda Bingo.

A recording date at Goldstar was scheduled for late July and Eddie, assisted by Guybo on bass and Jerry on cardboard box, went into the studio to record the song along with three other Cochran and Capehart compositions, *Completely Sweet*, *Dark Lonely Street* and *My Love To Remember*. Eddie had already produced one demo of *My Love To Remember*, yet he still didn't feel that he had a satisfactory version of the song. He would record it again on two further occasions during his career.

Eddie's performance of *Twenty Flight Rock* at this session was quite a revelation. Until this point he had displayed a great understanding of rock'n'roll as a musician, but his few attempts at performing the music vocally had met with varying degrees of success. He was still finding his way as a solo vocalist and relied on enthusiasm to make up for his lack of technical ability. But *Twenty Flight Rock* was tailor-made for him. His urgent hiccuping delivery of the lyrics, mixed with an effective use of that Goldstar slap-back echo, belied his inexperience as a soloist and produced a masterful performance. A manic, triplet-flavoured guitar solo together with Guybo's driving slap bass also contributed to the finished product, which today is regarded as a rock'n'roll classic.

Following Eddie's film performance of the song, the waves created by *Twenty Flight Rock* spread far and wide. According to legend, John Lennon only agreed to allow Paul McCartney to join The Beatles on the strength of McCartney memorising the lyrics to *Twenty Flight Rock*. To this day, McCartney often uses the song during his live set. The Rolling Stones have also performed the song on tour, as have The Stray Cats. It has been covered by a wide range of rockers and pop stars including Cliff Richard, Vince Taylor and Alvin Stardust among others.

Although the song's storyline is fairly inane – telling the story of a broken-down elevator, and having to climb twenty flights of stairs (hence the title) to meet his girl – it is Eddie's performance, both lyrically and musically, that has inspired countless cover versions over the years. The song will forever be associated with Eddie Cochran, and it is against his original version that all others are judged.

With a screenplay written by Herbert Baker and Frank Tashlin, *The Girl Can't Help It* was a satire exposing Hollywood's perception of the rock'n'roll industry. Tashlin also produced and directed the film, which had been afforded a generous budget incorporating all the usual latest cinematic advances, including CinemaScope – featuring 'glorious color by Deluxe'.

Starring Tom Ewell, Edmond O'Brien and the blonde bombshell Jayne Mansfield, *The Girl Can't Help It* would later be regarded as one of the best rock'n'roll exploitation movies ever made – if not *the* best. Featuring a vast array of musical talent, *The Girl Can't Help It* boasted cameo performances from some of rock'n'roll's finest exponents, including Gene Vincent, Little Richard, Fats Domino, The Platters and, of course, Eddie Cochran. Also lined up for appearances were a host of one-hit wonders, obscure pop singers and would-be rockers such as Eddie Fontaine, The Chuckles, Abbey Lincoln, Nino Tempo, Johnny Olenn and The Treniers.

The main musical artist featured in the film was Julie London. By 1956 she had already featured in the movies *Jungle Woman*, *Nabonga* and *A Night In Paradise*, but she was better known for her superior singing talents on her classic recordings such as *Cry Me A River*.

The plot centres around faded press agent Tom Miller (Tom Ewell), who is hired by former gangster Marty 'Fats' Murdoch (Edmond O'Brien) to turn the stunning Jerri Jordan (Jayne Mansfield) into a recording star. According to Murdoch, Jerri deserves to be a star, regardless of the cost, as he cannot afford to be seen in public with a nobody, in case it damages his already battered image. Miller attempts to teach the musically challenged Jerri to sing but finally abandons his efforts when he realises that her sole ambition is simply to settle down and become a housewife. Needless to say, just as Miller gives up on his endeavours to turn Jerri into a starlet, the pair fall in love and live happily ever after.

Of course, *The Girl Can't Help It* is not regarded as a classic for its plot. There are fine performances from all the actors involved, but it is the brief clips of the rock'n'roll artists involved that have given the film the status it enjoys today.

Gene Vincent's incredibly intense performance of his classic *Be Bop A Lula* is an absolute stand-out, as are the performances by Little Richard singing *Ready Teddy*, *She's Got It* and the film's title track, *The Girl Can't Help It*. Fats Domino sings *Blue Monday*, Eddie Fontaine delivers his fine jazz-influenced rocker *Cool It Baby*, The Platters perform their hit *You'll Never Know*, and even famed band leader Ray Anthony makes an appearance helping out with the suitably awful *Rock Around The Rock Pile*, a song written by the Fats Murdoch character while serving time in prison. This song appears in the movie as Jerri Jordan's musical début, and her character's lack of talent is made more than evident in the tuneless, piercing screams she emits throughout the performance.

Arguably the two finest musical performances in the movie belong to Eddie Cochran's energetic Elvis-inspired *Twenty Flight Rock* and to Gene Vincent, whose deathly white face framed with dark unruly slicks of hair falling down over his eyes would later be cited as influencing a whole generation of would-be rockers.

As television was still in its infancy, the cinema was often the only place teenagers could see their favourite artist perform. All the performances in *The Girl Can't Help It* made an unprecedented impact on the teenage audience that flocked to the cinema, eagerly anticipating their first look at the rock'n'roll artists whose records they were buying by the million. With this in mind, a rash of rock'n'roll films appeared overnight, usually filmed on a shoestring budget and with little or no plot. Using actors as wooden as the film sets they were appearing in, the only saving grace for the audience was that more rock'n'roll than acting was required.

The Girl Can't Help It proved to be an exception. A mixture of fine acting performances with the right amount of humour and visual gags – many aimed at Mansfield's more obvious assets – helped make the film hugely enjoyable. Despite the predictable storyline, the movie deserves the recognition it receives today.

Eddie's cameo was filmed at the Fox studio on West Pico Boulevard on 14 August 1956. His appearance in the film is less incidental than many of those featuring his fellow rock artists, who were mainly performing their songs in the environment of club scenes or rehearsal rooms. Cochran is introduced into the film for a purpose, and in doing so he is given a far bigger build-up than many of the other performers.

Fats Murdoch has just received the bad news from Tom Miller that Jerri cannot sing a note. As Miller walks Jerri back to her apartment, Murdoch thinks this over and by the time the two reach Jerri's home, the former gangster is on the telephone with an answer. He orders the pair to turn on the TV where an up-and-coming rock'n'roll artist is preparing to perform his next song. As they watch in complete bewilderment, fictional TV host Peter Potter introduces a new rocker, 'Eddie Cochran, one of America's top rock'n'rollers' to wild studio applause.

Standing on an empty stage with only an amplifier for company – a band was obviously deemed an unnecessary expense – Eddie springs into action with a little half-turn jump and launches into *Twenty Flight Rock*. Right from the onset of his performance, it is obvious that he has been asked to do his level best to imitate Elvis Presley and to his credit he enthusiastically applies himself to the job in hand. His heavy use of the trademark Elvis leg-shaking, shoulder-twitching and lip-curling all help to give Eddie's performance a great deal of street cred. He was also made up to resemble Elvis as much as possible, with baggy pegged pants, sports coat – borrowed from his Cochran Brothers stage act – and a heavily greased pompadour with long sideburns.

His only prop was his flame-red Gretsch 6120 guitar. Looking resplendent on the big screen thanks to 'color by Deluxe', the Gretsch also conveyed the message to moviegoers that Eddie was no mere

Elvis clone, and it would go a long way to present a strong image of him as a musician in the eyes of the public. Here was an artist who, despite his blond hair, resembled Elvis with his good looks and his stage mannerisms, but who could also play his own lead guitar, something of a rarity in those days. In this one clip, Cochran also elevated the Gretsch 6120 to the lofty heights of legendary status, ensuring the guitar would forever be regarded as one of the ultimate rock'n'roll instruments.

Eddie's performance of *Twenty Flight Rock* was as exciting and energetic as the song itself. It is easy to forgive him for his awkward attempts to mimic Elvis's stage movements, which his inexperience seemed to magnify. Overall his brief appearance, which was made even shorter by an executive decision to edit out his fantastic guitar solo in the film's final cut, left a lasting impression on its teenage audience. The combination of Eddie's strong visual image, good looks and the status of *Twenty Flight Rock* as a powerful rock'n'roll classic, ensured Cochran a healthy following – not to mention an army of female admirers guaranteed once the film began showing throughout the country.

Following an appearance in a major film, the next logical step for Eddie was to knock on record-company doors. He already had a healthy collection of self-penned songs, as well as cover versions of current rock'n'roll hits, to take to all the major labels in and around Hollywood. His part in *The Girl Can't Help It*, albeit a brief cameo, was an excellent promotional tool for his solo career and guaranteed interest in his commercial capabilities.

I never looked at Eddie as a rock'n'roll singer to begin with, but you could call him our first successful one.

Si Waronker

Now owned by EMI, Liberty Records was originally founded in Hollywood by Simon Waronker in 1955. Born in 1915, Si was a child prodigy. Starting high school at eleven and graduating at thirteen, he received a scholarship to study violin in Philadelphia and then in France. Ending up in Germany during the rise of Hitler, the Jewish Waronker was forced to return to the United States after barely escaping from a Nazi youth gang that was pursuing him. Back in Los Angeles, he worked for 20th-Century-Fox from 1939 until 1955, playing musical scores for movies.

In 1955 his cousin, Herb Newman, suggested that the two of them should start their own record company. After a lot of thought and discussion with his colleagues, Si left his highly paid job at 20th-Century-Fox to start Liberty Records. Although the intention was to be in partnership with his cousin, Herb Newman backed out of their agreement and started his own record company, Era.

The first release on Liberty was *The Girl Upstairs* and *Conquest* by Lionel Newman. This recording indicated that Waronker was continuing to work with the music he knew best: big band music, movie music, orchestral music and some jazz. Waronker contacted jazz artist Bobby Troup and tried to sign him to Liberty in 1955. Still under contract to another label, Troup declined, although he talked Si into signing his girlfriend, Julie London. Julie, as mentioned earlier, immediately had a hit with *Cry Me A River* and became the 'Liberty Girl' as she went on to make a string of successful records for the label.

In 1956 Liberty signed Henry Mancini, a staff writer of soundtrack music for Universal Studios. Liberty issued two singles by Mancini, *Main Theme* backed with *Cha Cha Cha For Gia* from *Four Girls in Town*, and *Hot Rod* backed with *Big Band Rock And Roll* from the teenage rock'n'roll flick *Rock Pretty Baby*. Mancini also recorded several albums for Liberty, but unfortunately for Waronker, he soon became hot property and moved to RCA in 1959.

'It was a terrible struggle in the 1950s,' Si Waronker explains. 'The company was started with practically nothing and we had some financial troubles. I take the blame for most of it only because I hired the wrong people. I found out later that they didn't like to pay artists, they didn't like to pay publishers and I had to get rid of them. After that we did very well and I finally left the company in 1963 because we were too big for our own good – and when you get so top-heavy something has got to fall.

'There was a big investigation of Payola [a notorious scandal where record companies bribed DJs to play their records] at one time and practically all the companies – every one of them – had to take some sort of consent agreement whereby they wouldn't admit anything but they promised that they wouldn't do it again. All, that is, except Liberty. To my knowledge, we were never involved in any Payola but I do know how it worked, of course, and we were approached many times. You'd give free records for it and then the free records – or dollars or whatever the DJ wanted – would be taken, usually by the distributor, to give to the DJ. As far as I was concerned, I wanted no part of it.

'I don't think Payola had anything to do with the artists' success. Maybe I'm wrong but I wouldn't use a Payola bid for anybody. If you got ahead on Payola, you couldn't last; you had to able to deliver and if you couldn't deliver the goods then you couldn't last in that business.'

Throughout the label's lifetime, Liberty's many signings included the sisters Patience and Prudence McIntyre (who had hits with *Tonight You Belong To Me* and *Gonna Get Along Without Ya Now*), Margie Rayburn, Billy Ward And The Dominos, Martin Denny, Bobby Vee and Willie Nelson, a cousin of the great teen idol Ricky Nelson.

In 1958 the idea of speeding up the tape of the human voice created novelty records such as *Witch Doctor* and *The Chipmunk Song*. The Chipmunks, 'Alvin, Simon and Theodore', were wryly named after Liberty executives Alvin Bennett, Simon Waronker and Theodore Keep, and their success produced a long-running series of singles and albums for the label.

Between 1959 and 1961 Liberty also acquired bandleaders Si Zentner and Felix Slatkin, and entered the folk-music scene by signing Bud And Travis and later Jackie DeShannon. Their country roster included Floyd Tillman, Ralph Emery, Bob Wills, Tommy Duncan and June Carter. They sometimes also made deals with smaller labels to distribute hits that had become too big for their original labels to handle, an example being the 1959 number 1 single *Come Softly to Me* by The Fleetwoods.

Other artists recording for Liberty in the early 1960s included Johnny Burnette, television star Walter Brennan, Gene McDaniels, Gary Miles, Buddy Knox, Timi Yuro, Vikki Carr, Ernie Freeman, Ed Townsend, Nick Noble, Gary Paxton, Dick And Dee Dee, The Johnny Mann Singers, Van McCoy, Matt Monro, Billy Strange, the post-Buddy Holly Crickets, Eddie Heywood, The Mar-Kets, and P.J. Proby.

By 1963 the vice-president of Liberty, Al Bennett, was responsible for the business side of things. Si Waronker was in poor health, so he and Bennett agreed to sell the company to Avnet, an electronics company, for twelve million dollars.

EMI/Capitol now own the Liberty and Sunset along with United Artists, a label that briefly took over Liberty in the late 1960s. Sunset was started by Si Waronker as a budget label specialising in albums from artists once connected with Liberty or one of its subsidiaries.

EMI have resurrected the Liberty label many times, initially as a vehicle for their back catalogue and then as a country label that primarily featured Kenny Rogers. It was discontinued in 1984, although in 1990 EMI announced they were renaming their Capitol-Nashville division Liberty. The biggest artist currently recording on this new label is Garth Brooks.

Most pundits looking into music think that rock'n'roll started with The Beatles. Well, it didn't. It started in the States and that's never going to change. The history books will show that people like myself were introduced to it by the American artists. The funny thing is, if you watch people in a stage show and they do a rock medley they go way beyond The Beatles. I never think of doing a Beatles song actually, but I'll go back and I'll do *Jailhouse Rock* or *Twenty Flight Rock*. You have to go back to that era to get the feeling of basic rock'n'roll because that's where it all started.

Cliff Richard

The first major rock'n'roll artist signed to Liberty Records was Eddie Cochran. Although Si Waronker had strong ties with 20th-Century-Fox, Eddie, surprisingly, did not come to his attention through his involvement with *The Girl Can't Help It*, even though Liberty Records had a vested interest in the film. The label's biggest star, Julie London, had a major part in it, of course, and other artists in the movie such as Johnny Olenn, Abbey Lincoln and Nino Tempo were already signed to Liberty or signed shortly afterwards. One of the main links between Liberty and *The Girl Can't Help It* came with the film's musical supervisor, Lionel Newman. A former member of 20th-Century-Fox's orchestra, he was the first artist to release a single on Liberty. It's also probable that Newman, a trusted friend and confidant of Waronker, used his influence to help Liberty place so many artists in the one film.

It is not unreasonable to assume that Newman may have been impressed enough with Eddie Cochran's performance in the film to inform Liberty of his existence, but, according to Simon Waronker, it was the seventeen-year-old Cochran that took it upon himself to arrange an audience with the label boss.

'I don't even remember *The Girl Can't Help It* at all,' Si explains. 'Eddie just came to my office and sat there until I had to see him. He was very persistent. I hadn't heard of him or the movie. In fact, I had to ask him what his name was.

'Eddie was just this little kid of seventeen with his guitar who wanted to audition for me. There were so many people who tried to get into the business that way and tried to sing for anybody that would listen to them, so I wasn't happy about anybody just walking in to my office and trying to gain an audience. Finally I couldn't do any better than let him in, for the simple reason that he was there for days and he insisted. He came in, played his guitar and sang at the same time, and I knew, right there and then, there was something.

'I asked him if he had any material and he said, "Oh, yeah, I have a lot of stuff." So I said, "Okay, let's hear it." I knew immediately he had a great talent, but to put the tune, the singer and the production together was not going to be easy.

'When Eddie first came to me, Elvis Presley was just beginning and he was very popular, but we didn't see Eddie as an answer to Elvis Presley because nobody could answer that at the time. But we wanted to take that whole way of thinking, and as far as records were concerned, Eddie was going to be our number-one star in that type of music. As far as rock'n'roll goes, I didn't care what it was, I signed him as an artist, but I never try to put a title on an artist to say what they could or couldn't do. If he could sing a ballad, that was great. In those days we didn't look upon it as rock'n'roll, we just heard a rhythmic thing that he could do great. The image had to come from him. As far as manufacturing an image goes, I didn't have any idea of how to do that at the time.

'I don't think we signed him for the full seven years, I think we signed him for three or five years. However, I signed all the contracts in the same way – all my artists received 5 per cent of the suggested retail price, and the cost of recording was always deducted from their royalty. A good artist didn't have to worry about it because he knew how successful his records were. The reason that I gave 5 per cent was only because that would keep them from going overboard on the recording costs. In those days, we could record a single for a thousand dollars. Today you can't even go into a studio for a thousand dollars.'

On 8 September Eddie signed a recording contract with Liberty Records. Shortly afterwards, the New York booking agency, General Artists Corporation, took over his touring schedule. Before the end of the year and before any release on the Liberty label, though, Eddie was signed to appear in another movie, the Warner Brothers production *Untamed Youth*.

Meanwhile, Eddie spent every spare moment in Goldstar recording as many songs as he could in order to find his initial Liberty release. Although *Twenty Flight Rock* was an obvious choice for his début single, he still needed as much new material as possible. Much of his recorded output at this time was still regarded as demo material and not up to release standard. Between September and December 1956, it is possible that songs such as *Teenage Cutie*, *Never*, *Sweetie Pie*, *Mighty Mean* and many instrumentals that are Cochran classics today were experimental recordings to enable him to develop a unique style and one that he was comfortable performing. With his combination of rockers and ballads, Eddie was certainly conscious of Waronker's decision to portray him as an all-round entertainer.

Teenage Cutie, a rockabilly classic in the hands of Eddie and Guybo, was probably recorded for inclusion in a film soundtrack, either *The Girl Can't Help It* or *Untamed Youth*. However, Nick Todd eventually covered the song for the Dot label, and his version was used in the obscure film *Rockabilly Baby*.

Throughout this three-month period Eddie continued with his session work, recording with Ray Stanley, Lee Denson and The Holly

Twins. The novelty single *I Want Elvis For Christmas* backed with *The Tender Age* was released on Liberty as a yuletide single in December 1956. It featured the typical musicianship from Eddie and Guybo with the added comical bonus of Eddie's impersonation of Elvis at intervals on the A-side.

Si Waronker sums up Eddie's recording activities during this period for Liberty: 'I had him up in the studio trying different tunes. Not very many of them, so he didn't do very much. He hung around the office and went up to the studios and if he had any ideas he'd put them on tape. He didn't do very much at all in those three months.'

They used my guitar for the movie *Untamed Youth* and took it on location up in the valley, in the cotton fields where they shot the movie. Ed didn't get it back right away, so he went back to get it and they already had it stamped 'WB'. It was ready to be sent off to Africa for another movie so he caught it just in time.

Bill Cochran

Untamed Youth was a typical teenage exploitation movie, with a plot that centred around violence, sex, corruption and, of course, rock'n'roll. The story was originally written by Stephen Lonstreet, then adapted for the screen by John C. Miller. Distributed by Warner Brothers, *Untamed Youth* was directed by Howard W. Koch and produced by Aubrey Schenck, a partnership that also made films on the Bel-Air label for United Artists.

Untamed Youth was shot on location twenty miles south of Bakersfield in California over a two-week period. It starred the queen of the B-movie, Mamie Van Doren. Billed as 'The Platinum Powerhouse', Mamie was reportedly paid $15,000 for her part, while Eddie received a modest payment of $350 per week.

With a host of unknowns in the supporting cast, the film opens as Mamie Van Doren and her screen sister, played by Lori Nelson, are arrested for vagrancy and sentenced to thirty days on a correctional farm. Along with an assortment of juvenile delinquents, the duo rock'n'roll and calypso their way through the plot, seeking justice for the mistreatment the teenagers receive from the corrupt farm owner played by John Russell. As well as working the poor teenagers half to death, some of his tricks include feeding the young offenders canned dog food as a clever cost-cutting measure.

Eddie, who had been drafted into the movie to play a character curiously known as Bong, does his best to look both cool and menacing throughout the film. The few lines of jive talk he is allowed to utter are presented well, but he still looks awkward while performing his one song, *Cotton Picker*. In fact, he decides to use his picker's bag as a makeshift guitar halfway through the performance in an attempt, no doubt, to find some way of covering up his embarrassment at having to imitate Elvis yet again on the big screen.

Prior to filming, Eddie was introduced to Mamie Van Doren by director Howard Koch. As Eddie and Jerry had written material especially for the soundtrack, he often spent time at the home Mamie shared with her husband Ray Anthony, performing his work for her. Mamie Van Doren has often stated that she took an instant liking to Eddie. On one occasion, while Ray Anthony – a popular big band leader with a well-known hatred for rock'n'roll – was away rehearsing, Mamie and Eddie ended up in a passionate embrace, abruptly halted when Ray arrived home earlier than expected.

The movie soundtrack was produced by The Les Baxter Orchestra, with incidental music for the dance sequences recorded by a fictional group billed as the Hollywood Rock'n'rollers. In reality they were probably members of Baxter's orchestra featuring Eddie on lead guitar. The four main tracks used in the film and performed by Mamie Van Doren were *Salamander*, *Go Go Calypso*, *Rollin' Stone* and the Cochran and Capehart composition *Oo Ba La Baby*, which on its release added the names Baxter and Adelson as co-writers.

In December 1956 Eddie recorded these songs with Mamie Van Doren and Les Baxter at Capitol Studio in Hollywood. The end results were released on an EP and sent to DJs to help promote the film. For some unknown reason, Les Baxter re-recorded the songs again without Eddie, and it was these later recordings that finally appeared in the movie soundtrack.

According to sources involved with the movie, Eddie fell for one of his co-stars, Jeanne Carmen, who played the character Lillibet. During filming, the pair had to be very discreet with their liaison for fear of upsetting Mamie Van Doren. It is said that Eddie later recorded his Liberty songs *Jeannie, Jeannie, Jeannie* and *Pretty Girl* especially for her.

After the movie's release, the teen magazine *Dig* ran a cover story linking Eddie to Yvonne Lime who also had a small role in *Untamed Youth* playing a character called Baby. Eddie and Yvonne also recorded together and, although only one song has ever surfaced – *Ting-A-Ling Telephone* – more may have been put on tape. *Dig* speculated on their friendship, publishing pictures of the pair in a recording studio with Eddie surrounded by members of his fan club as he recorded his new single for Liberty. The article seemed to be engineered to promote Eddie's career rather than any supposed romantic involvement with Lime.

Yvonne had briefly dated Elvis after meeting him on the set of his second film, *Loving You*, in which she had a small role. She later appeared in numerous teenage B-movies as the decade progressed, including *Teenage Werewolf, High School Hellcats, Dragstrip Riot* and *Speed Crazy*.

Untamed Youth was previewed by critics in March 1957. One described it as being 'an artless melodrama compounded of sex, swing and sadism. Rock'n'roll numbers are introduced with the slightest excuse, the heavy gyrating of Mamie Van Doren somewhat belies the title.' Another wrote highly of Eddie, stating: 'There's a guy who worked with Mamie whom I've never heard of – one Eddie Cochran, who writhes through *Cotton Picker* in a manner that could make Elvis envious. Real frantic, this boy.'

On its release in the spring of 1957, *Untamed Youth* – all 79 minutes of it – served its purpose and did well with the teenage audience it was aimed at, becoming a popular drive-in movie of the time.

Eddie was fantastic. When I saw him in *The Girl Can't Help It*, he kind of had an Elvis look about him, although he sounded very different. He sang *Twenty Flight Rock*, and to me that's still a classic. It rates along with *Heartbreak Hotel* in terms of a classic rock song. He had a massive effect on me.

Cliff Richard

Liberty decided that Eddie's first release would be *Twenty Flight Rock* backed with a song written by Jerry and Eddie entitled *Dark Lonely Street*. This beautiful ballad was recorded at the same session as the A-side together with two more Cochran and Capehart songs, *Completely Sweet* and *My Love To Remember*. All four songs were intended as demos, as *Dark Lonely Street* features only Eddie's vocals and guitar along with Guybo's bass, although the sparseness of instruments adds to the song's haunting quality. *Completely Sweet* is similar in sound and performance to *Twenty Flight Rock* but has a slightly slower pace, and again features great guitar and powerful bass playing by Guybo. *My Love To Remember* is a fairly standard ballad, but is obviously a song Eddie had a certain amount of faith in – he recorded it on no fewer than three separate occasions during his career.

Twenty Flight Rock was scheduled for release in December 1956, but before the song was pressed it was shelved when a twist of fate totally disrupted Liberty's plans and changed the course of Eddie's solo career.

Waronker had tried to purchase a song entitled *Sittin' In The Balcony* from Jack Bentley, owner of the Colonial label based in South Carolina. The song had been written and recorded by John D. Loudermilk under the pseudonym Johnny Dee and was eventually sold by Bentley to ABC Paramount. At the time the song came to Waronker's attention, it was still only a regional hit and, as Waronker had failed in his bid to purchase the original master, he decided that Liberty would issue a cover version.

As Waronker explained earlier, he did not sign Eddie to be solely a rock'n'roll artist. His intention was to mould Cochran into an all-round performer who could incorporate rock'n'roll into his repertoire. On his suggestion, *Sittin' In The Balcony* was to become Eddie's first release on Liberty and on hearing the Johnny Dee original, the young singer agreed with Waronker that it was a potential hit.

At the close of this hectic year – a year that started with the success and then break-up of The Cochran Brothers – Eddie's new career could not have begun in a better way. With two movie appearances ready for release in the new year, plus a recording contract with a major independent record label, Eddie Cochran now had the perfect opportunity to realise his potential as a solo artist.

They had to hate me for what I did with *Sittin' In The Balcony*. I copied that song. I was always very hungry for hits, I guess we all were. We were honest in most things but we wanted hits so we covered each other. I was covered so many times it hurt, and when I say covered I mean copied.

Si Waronker

The new year, 1957, began with Eddie recording *Sittin' In The Balcony* at Liberty Custom Recorders in Hollywood. According to Si Waronker, Eddie was not the first choice to record the song: 'A very good friend of mine called and said, "I've found a tune that you've got to record, I'll send you a copy of it." So he sent me a demo of this tune called *Sittin' In The Balcony*. I thought, "Great, I think it's a hit!" I had one or two people on the label that could do a great job of it. One was a boy by the name of Johnny Olenn. I called Johnny in Las Vegas and played *Sittin' In The Balcony* to him on the telephone but he said, "That's okay, I pass." Now, in the meantime, Eddie was in the front office, so I called him in and asked him if he thought he could record it. He said he would, so I told him that I would have the lyrics typed up so he could learn the tune and words and be ready to record that night and he just said, "Okay, fine," because he wanted the chance to break in. Anyway, we recorded all that night and finally got the tune. I copied that record and I'll take all the blame on that. If you put them together you'll hear that everything is identical. Even the ending, the echo – the "reverse reverberation" as I call it. I just overdid the reverb, but that's the only difference.

'We released it almost the following day and sent the final copies to the distributor, and I'll be damned if it would turn out to be a hit. From that point on I knew we had something. I always felt that Eddie had the ability to go very far because when you heard him you knew that the kid had something more than just a voice – he had a style.'

Backed with The Johnny Mann Singers and accompanied by Guybo on bass and probably Jerry Capehart on percussion, *Sittin' In The Balcony* was typical of the teen-orientated pop songs that were proving popular in the mid-1950s, a happy pop song with nonsensical lyrics, more akin to the type of material recorded at the time by artists such as Pat Boone or Perry Como.

Vocally, this is a good performance from Eddie. He sounds very confident, even to the point of chuckling his way through some of the lyrics. A tremendous guitar break, midway through, lifts the song and manages to add a little rock'n'roll credibility to the process.

Bob Denton, however, remembers that *Sittin' In The Balcony* proved to be a difficult song for Eddie to record: 'I was at that recording session. It was a brand new recording studio and very experimental and they had nothing but trouble at that session – it took all night to do that song. Eddie liked the song, but they just couldn't get it right for some reason, but they finally got it. In those days recording studios were very different. Nowadays you just put it on another track, but back in those days you had to do it over and over until you got it right. Once he got that record out and got moving, he was gone.'

Waronker also agrees that the session was long and difficult, but believes that if he had rush-released Eddie's version the song would have been a hit. 'We started that record at seven o'clock that night and ended at five o'clock the next morning,' he recalls. 'I shipped the same day. So the Loudermilk record developed into a cover of Eddie's record! And it's dirty, I know it is, but that is the way the business was in those days. But I admit it. Loudermilk never called, and I never even knew him. He was good; as a matter of fact, I think that his record was better than ours – except we shipped faster, and I called every one of the distributors and said, "Let's lay on this record because we do have competition."'

Although Waronker may have felt that Johnny Dee's original was better, Eddie's version certainly benefited from a higher standard of musicianship and from Waronker's production. 'I always recorded the songs at a higher level. I did that purposely and I also insisted that we pressed the records higher than any of the pressing companies were doing at the time. That was because the people who had to use the needle on vinyl would not have to turn up the volume as high and consequently it got rid of a lot of the scratches that were so prevalent in those days – on a 45 especially. If I had the level up high, the volume could be turned up high and you would still hear everything on that record.

'Eddie was very easy to work with. He was very co-operative. He would put his own input in often, and I'd listen very carefully to what he had to say. It's different to how it is today. In those days, my job as a producer was to sit in a booth, listen, and know when it was good or bad – or we had to redo it. Sometimes we would record one tune in hours, and other times we were lucky enough to do it in one take. Also in those days we didn't have multiple-track recording and we had to do everything on one track. If we were lucky we were able to record in stereo, which was nothing more than two-track recording. Eddie was very good at that. I would work with other artists all day and we'd never get one take, but Eddie was very good.

'I did a lot of experimentation in those days – in fact we built our own two-track machines because we couldn't afford to buy the two-tracks that were available, they were so expensive. Even when we were lucky enough to have the three-track, I used to record two tracks on the outside and feed them into the third track. In other words, when you had eight violins and put the entire three-track on those violins I could make them sound like twenty-four. We had a lot of fun with the recordings in those days. Today, when you have 24- or 48-track, you don't need it. We used to have to work like hell to get an artist to be perfectly in tune, but today they do it automatically and it frightens the hell out of me. That's one reason I'm happy to be out of the business.'

In March 1957, *Sittin' In The Balcony* backed with *Dark Lonely Street* was released on Liberty 55056. That same month saw the release of *The Girl Can't Help It* which, along with Waronker's fierce promotion, helped to push Eddie's version of the song further. Entering the Billboard Hot 100 on the 23rd, *Sittin' In The Balcony* peaked at number 18 and remained in the charts for thirteen weeks, eventually reaching the bestsellers chart at number 22. *Billboard* reviewed the single on 2 March, stating that: 'This one has plenty of teenage appeal and could move out with the right exposure. Cochran warbles with sock showmanship – *à la* Presley. Flip is a moody ballad, *Dark Lonely Street.*'

The track also proved popular on other charts such as the Disc Jockey and Jukebox charts, reaching numbers 18 and 20 respectively.

Johnny Dee's original only just managed to get inside the Top 40, peaking at number 38. Obviously the potential of both these versions was hampered by the fact that they were competing against each other, one of the risks that Waronker took in producing the cover version.

When the movie *The Girl Can't Help It* came out, all the girls in high school were just swooning and raving about this guy that looked just like Elvis – Eddie Cochran. We didn't have the money to see the movie so I went down to the theatre and looked at the posters to see what the guy looked like. I saw Eddie on the poster and it was just love at first sight. I looked at my little sister and said, 'When I grow up, I'm gonna marry him.'

'Yeah, right,' she replied, 'you and all the other girls in the world.'

But that became my mission. How to get to Eddie, how to meet Eddie, and I had to be in the music business to meet him.

Sharon Sheeley

In April, in the wake of his new success, Eddie began touring, accompanied by Guybo Smith on bass and Jerry Capehart as his manager. Spending a week on a package show at the Mastbaum Theatre in

Philadelphia, Eddie met Gene Vincent for the first time, cementing a friendship that would last throughout his lifetime.

Born Vincent Eugene Craddock in Norfolk, Virginia, on 11 February 1935, Gene Vincent scored a hit in 1956 with *Be Bop A Lula*, the B-side to the single *Woman Love*. With his band The Blue Caps – comprising lead guitarist Cliff Gallup, rhythm guitarist Willie Williams, bass player Jack Neal and drummer Dickie Harrell – 1956 had been an unprecedented year for the singer.

In 1955 Vincent had been forced to leave the US Navy after sustaining a serious leg injury as a result of a motorcycle accident. Spending several months in hospital, he wrote *Be Bop A Lula* with fellow patient, Donald Graves, who later sold his share of the song to Vincent's manager, Sheriff Tex Davis, for twenty-five dollars. After performing it on his local radio station, Gene was offered the chance to make a demo and in April 1956, he was signed to Capitol Records and shortly began making public appearances with The Blue Caps.

Before the end of the year The Blue Caps' line-up changed dramatically. Rhythm guitarist Willie Williams left the group in September and was replaced by Paul Peek; then, in December, lead guitarist Cliff Gallup left the band. Throughout their professional career The Blue Caps' personnel changed frequently, but Cliff Gallup's departure came as a huge blow. This highly skilful guitarist is now regarded as perhaps the finest player of the rockabilly genre and had a huge influence on Vincent's first 35 recordings for Capitol. When he left, a large part of The Blue Caps' sound went with him. However, it was not long before a new band was formed, which again featured a highly imaginative guitarist – Johnny Meeks. This new line-up helped create a different sound for Vincent which was best portrayed in his next big hit following *Be Bop A Lula – Lotta Lovin'*. The new-look Blue Caps had a new sound which included backing vocalists, hand-claps and an overall more restrained approach to playing rock'n'roll compared to the unhinged, manic and unbelievably wild rock'n'roll of the original Blue Caps.

Other performers joining Eddie and Gene in Philadelphia included Nappy Brown, Al Hibbler and George Hamilton IV. Eddie also appeared on a bill at the Chicago Opera House alongside the Everly Brothers, Tab Hunter, Charlie Gracie and Chuck Berry. In August a promotional tour was set up with the main purpose of meeting key disc jockeys such as Bill Randall in Cleveland, Joe Smith in Boston and Barry Kaye in Pittsburgh. It was a perfect networking opportunity in the music industry, with Eddie meeting and thanking the DJs for playing his records, thanking the stations' listeners for buying, and hopefully securing their interest in any future releases.

One person who well remembers the hectic touring period following Eddie's initial success was John Rook. Born in Ohio and raised in Nebraska and South Dakota, Rook's early interest in the music business led him into local radio. He moved to LA in 1953, finally graduating from high school two years later. His involvement in local broadcasting blossomed into a highly successful career which saw him become one of the most powerful men in American radio throughout the 1970s and 1980s.

'California was a totally different world then,' John Rook explains. 'We had Pat Boone and Elvis and everyone was so refreshing and new. I remember meeting Eddie on the lot at 20th-Century-Fox doing *The Girl Can't Help It* and from then on we became very close for two or three years. We didn't know at that time what his career meant.

'Eddie had literally no one doing any promotion for him, he was just an artist. In the 1950s record companies didn't have any promotion set up. They just mailed records out to radio stations and asked DJs to play them. So having been in radio I said I'd do some promotion for him, back before there were really any promotion men. In those days you turned on *Dick Clark's Bandstand* to find out what you should play. Dick Clark broke a lot of acts in those days.

'Eddie was doing everything. He had to go out on tour and do DJ tours back in a time when everyone was doing their own promotion. He'd call disc jockeys and have to introduce himself and ask them to please play the record they'd received, and that took up a lot of his time. By the time he did his own music and his own production, as well as television coming in and then the motion pictures, he was pretty busy.

'I remember a three-day tour with Eddie. I went back to Ohio where he was doing a concert. All I could do was make sure that his things were collected and ready to go to the next step while he was doing whatever he had to. I thought the road manager was a bellman!

'He was just on tour to promote his record. I didn't go on a concert tour with him. I've seen Eddie live on stage three times. I think it was all in one year, really, and I was impressed. I remember watching and thinking it didn't seem like he was Eddie.

'Sometimes, I would drive him up to Hollywood for his appointments. He was in and out quick and then back home. He did not like spending time in Hollywood – it was fake to him, and Eddie was what he was. He was very funny with his dialects and he'd take off The Coasters, or he and Bob Denton would sit and take off Fats Domino singing *Sick And Tired* and do it better than Fats Domino. They were some fun times. We would sit and play poker for a penny a piece. Television was only just coming in so we didn't sit around and pay attention to it, except for *Bandstand* maybe, and when it came to anything else, the radio was it.'

Dick Clark's American Bandstand was one of the USA's most influential pop music television shows of its time. Dick Clark took over the reins of the Philadelphia-based show in July 1956 and turned the local show into a national institution when it began showing coast-to-coast on ABC from 5 August 1957.

Airing every weekday afternoon, dancing was a major feature of *Bandstand* and it also became a showcase for rock'n'roll's early stars, including Bill Haley And The Comets, Buddy Holly, Connie Francis, Bobby Darin, Fabian and Ritchie Valens. Regular dancers on the show, known as The Committee, were real kids from Philadelphia who became almost household names as Americans followed their dance steps on TV and their personal lives in teen magazines. Every day hundreds of hopefuls would line up, hoping to join these unpaid regulars and dance alongside them to the Slop, the Hand Jive, the Bop, the Stroll, the Circle and the Calypso.

Eddie's appearance on *American Bandstand* in 1957 came at a time when, as a new movie and recording star, he was at the forefront of the media. Eddie's recording of *Sittin' In The Balcony*, and its release, timed perfectly to coincide with the release of *The Girl Can't Help It*, established him as an exciting newcomer, a new teen idol. Surprisingly, when interviewed for the *New Musical Express* in the UK, he described the track as his biggest disappointment: 'I cut *Sittin' In The Balcony* and didn't like it at all,' he told the reporter, 'but it went on to sell a million and I was the most surprised of all!'

Although Eddie was concentrating on his busy career, he still found time to continue his role as session guitarist, helping out old friends in the studio. In April of that year, he arranged a session at Goldstar Studios featuring Guybo on bass and Capehart on percussion. The end result was a recording which, as Bob Denton explains, kick-started his own career. 'Eddie was on the road and he came back and said, "Bob, I've got this song that's just right for you." I wasn't on a label or anything. So we went down to Goldstar and Capehart played a cardboard box for a drum and we hired these three guys to sing behind it, and we recorded *On My Mind Again*. The next day I was over at Dot Records signing up, and they released it and it got to number 14. Back in those days you would do singles until you had enough to make an album, but nowadays you do an album and take the records off the album. It's a lot different.'

I wanted to get on Liberty. Eddie had already recorded *Sittin' In The Balcony* and he always liked [my song] *Everybody's Moving*. He wanted to cut it and his manager wanted to do it, but that was my only song. I've always said that I wish Eddie had cut it because he would have sold a lot more records than I did. That was my first record; Bob Dylan, Bruce Springsteen, Neil Young all covered it and The Stray Cats did it too.

Glen Glenn

During the second half of 1956, songwriter Ray Stanley left American Music to start his own publishing company. Forming a partnership with Billy Sherman, the pair set up Sherman Publishing, opening offices in Hollywood's Melrose Avenue, an area that was already home to a number of publishing companies.

Stanley's first move was to arrange a session at Goldstar to record a clutch of self-penned rockers to build up his new company's catalogue. Eddie, Guybo and Jerry provided the backing, while Stanley took responsibility for the vocal and piano duties. Only a handful of titles now survive from these sessions; many years later, Stanley threw out a whole batch of acetates from this period after deciding that he had no further need for them.

Initially intended as demo recordings, the enterprising Stanley leased six of these titles to a couple of small independent labels in early 1957, and saw three releases under his own name. *Market Place* backed with *Pushin'* and *My Lovin' Baby* backed with *Love Charms* were released on the tiny Zephyr label, while *Over A Coke* and its B-side *I Can't Wait* were released by Argo.

Stanley came into contact with Zephyr via Lester Sill, an influential figure who worked for Modern RPM Records in the early 1950s and eventually progressed into management with the highly successful R&B group, The Coasters. By early 1957, The Coasters had broken through into the pop charts with the double-sided hit *Searchin'* and *Young Blood*. The songwriting team responsible for both of these tracks, Jerry Leiber and Mike Stoller, were in partnership with Lester Sill in a business venture comprising the small independent Spark Records label and a publishing company, Quintet Music, which were both operated from Sill's offices on Melrose Avenue.

It was in these offices that Lester Sill came into contact with Ray Stanley. Following the success of Perry Como's *Glendora*, Stanley's reputation as a songwriter had grown considerably, and while out canvassing his songs to record companies along Melrose Avenue, he secured Sill's interest in his material.

Along with his other musical activities, Sill was also involved in production deals for a variety of artists and labels in the Hollywood area, and proved to be a useful contact for the ambitious Stanley. From the batch of acetates comprising demo recordings made by Stanley, Eddie, Guybo and Jerry at Goldstar Studio, Sill selected the track *Market Place*.

Along with his production partner, George Motola, Sill arranged for the song to be recorded by Modern RPM artist Etta James, with Motola and Sill producing the resulting single and releasing it in March 1957. As well as Etta James, *Market Place* was also covered by UK rocker Terry Dene in 1957 and included on his Decca EP release *Terry Dene No.1*.

George Motola, who worked in an office nextt to Sill, started his career as a second-hand car salesman. Another musical entrepreneur, Motola specialised in involving himself with as many different areas of the local music business as possible. Co-writing songs with his wife Ricki Page, a recording artist in her own right, the pair later formed a social relationship with Eddie which often resulted in Cochran helping out, on a casual basis, with demo sessions for their compositions.

Motola had been approached by local businessman Geordie Hormell to head an independent label that he was considering forming. Small record labels were springing up and disappearing virtually overnight throughout this period, and it was not unusual for a wealthy man like Hormell, who made his fortune through a meat packaging company, to branch out into the music business in order to avoid his next tax payment. Consequently, Zephyr Records served its purpose in its brief life by releasing several singles and albums that consisted of demo recordings or material thrown together for songwriters to showcase their music on behalf of small-time publishers.

Songwriters Leiber and Stoller, for example, put together a band of studio musicians that featured top saxophonist Plas Johnson and drummer Earl Palmer to record an album of their own R&B material. It was released on Zephyr under the fictitious name, The Scooby Doo All Stars. Through his connection with Lester Sill, Ray Stanley also got in on the act, leasing the four titles that made up his two singles to the label.

Although Stanley was never likely to challenge Mario Lanza in terms of vocal ability, he was more that capable of writing catchy rock'n'roll tunes. Of the four songs he leased, *Pushin'*, *Love Charms*, *My Lovin' Baby* and *Market Place*, three were covered by various artists, with the exception being the instrumental *Pushin'*. *Love Charms* was recorded by Phoenix rockabilly singer Sanford Clark on Dot Records in 1958; Nick Greene covered *My Lovin' Baby* for Capitol in 1957 and this song was also picked up in 1966 by a group called The Stacy's Fifth for Jubilee records.

On the original Ray Stanley demos, it is the performances by Eddie and Guybo that make the songs worth a closer listen today. Eddie, in particular, seems to be enjoying himself enormously on these recordings, performing one magical guitar break after another. Employing his now regular trick of detuning his guitar so that the top and bottom E strings were in D, with the others detuned accordingly, he was able to create a deep twangy bass sound. This was used to great effect on many of the recordings that he took part in during this period, and shows his obvious desire to develop a unique style of playing – far removed from his earlier influences such as Chet Atkins, Merle Travis and Joe Maphis. By now, Eddie's style and sound could only be described as tough and aggressive, perfect for rock'n'roll. The blistering guitar solo on *My Lovin' Baby*, added to Guybo's heavy slap bass, turns the record into a minor rockabilly classic. *Love Charms*, played in a minor key which increases its appeal, is another toe-tapping slice of rockabilly with surprisingly clever lyrics. Buried deep in the mix of this song, and barely audible, is a guitar overdub that features Eddie using the old Les Paul trick of slowing down the track by using the vary-speed control on the tape machine. When the overdub has been added, the track is then played back at normal speed with the guitar overdub sounding less like guitar and more like a harpsichord. It was a clever use of studio technique that Eddie had experimented with back in his home-recording days with Chuck Foreman.

The haunting *Market Place*, described on the Zephyr record label as 'a Cajun blues original as sung by the composer', is another fine song that prominently features both Guybo and Eddie. Its B-side, *Pushin'*, is a funky piano-led instrumental that today is regarded by many as something of a Cochran masterpiece.

As Stanley hammered out the melody on the piano, Eddie played a simple blues riff in the background. It was helped to sound a little more distinctive through the use of Eddie's fixed-arm Bigsby tremolo unit on his Gretsch guitar. Halfway through, however, he launched into a typically aggressive solo that transformed *Pushin'* into a much tougher-sounding rocker, before allowing Stanley to finish the song the way he started.

Two more instrumentals with a similar feel and approach have been discovered in recent years by Tony Barrett at Rockstar Records. *String Fever* and *Nice'n'Easy* were found at the Cochran family home in Buena Park, California, in 1993. Discovered in acetate form by Eddie's nephew, Ed Julson, Rockstar released them on two CDs: *Mighty Mean*, released in 1995, featured *Nice'n'Easy*, while the 1998 release *Don't Forget Me* contained *String Fever*. Both of these tracks are almost identical to *Pushin'* and prove that Eddie's experimentation with rock'n'roll instrumentals helped him to discover his own niche as a rock guitarist.

Several more instrumentals were found at the same time: *Jungle Jingle*, *Guitar Blues* and *Meet Mr Tweedy*. *Jungle Jingle* displays a definite Bo Diddley influence whereas *Guitar Blues* has an almost Link Wray feel. *Meet Mr Tweedy* is a tongue-in-cheek reworking of the Les Paul song *Meet Mr Callaghan* and uses all the same vary-speed overdubs again, with Eddie playing all the guitar parts himself.

Jungle Jingle and *Guitar Blues* probably date from a similar period to *Pushin'* and both show Eddie's awareness of other guitar styles that were starting to become prominent in rock'n'roll. *Meet Mr Tweedy* may date from 1958 as it is not dissimilar to another Cochran instrumental favourite, *Scratchin'*, which first saw release as the B-side to the novelty single *I Hate Rabbits* on Dot Records in August 1958.

Kiss And Make Up and *Equator* are two more Ray Stanley compositions that were recorded at Goldstar featuring Eddie and Guybo. The sound and performance on both songs indicate that they were recorded during the same period as the two Zephyr singles. It seems that Stanley rejected *Kiss And Make Up* as there is no evidence of a cover version or a release for the demo recording in its own merit. However, Stanley sold the rights to the song to RPM, and a slightly modified version was recorded by The Teen Queens as *Let's Make Up*. With hindsight, Stanley's original rejection was a wise decision, as it is a rather ponderous effort, and one of the rare occasions where even Eddie's guitar work or Guybo's bass playing could not salvage any plus points for the recording.

Equator ended up in the hands of Louis Prima, who released his own version on Capitol Records. Stanley had used his connections at Capitol wisely, and saw a handful of his compositions recorded by various artists associated with the label, including *Mississippi Dreamboat* by Dean Martin, *How About You* by The Four Preps, *Good Luck Good Buddy* by Jack Jones and *Kissin' On* by Alicia Adams – all through the efforts of Capitol producers Voyle Gilmore and Lee Gillette, who were the usual recipients of Stanley's songs.

Stanley's sole single release on Argo, a small subsidiary label connected to the legendary R&B mainstay Chess Records, was again made up of two Goldstar demos, *Over A Coke* and *I Can't Wait*. According to Stanley, they were recorded at different sessions. Eddie was present for the recording of the A-side *Over A Coke*, a rock ballad featuring some typical Cochran guitar work that brightens up what would be an otherwise dull song. Jack Lewis provided lead guitar for *I Can't Wait*, a novelty rocker with prominent slap bass and jazz-influenced guitar riffs. The latter song was covered by Pearl Wood for Dot Records shortly after Stanley's Argo single was released.

As the decade progressed, Stanley flitted from one independent label to another, drafting in Eddie again and again to help out on sessions. During March and April 1957 Stanley moved into production, arranging a session for a young singer-songwriter by the name of Lee Denson. The resulting single for RCA subsidiary Vik Records was a combination of the Denson song *Climb Love Mountain* backed with the Stanley composition *New Shoes*.

Growing up in Memphis, Denson had befriended the young Elvis Presley and the Burnette brothers, Johnny and Dorsey. His first single for Vik featured a reworking of *Heart Of A Fool* (a composition by The Cochran Brothers and Jerry Capehart) backed with *The Pied Piper*. Stanley brought in Eddie for the *New Shoes* session and his guitar work for this slap-bass-led rockabilly song features one of Eddie's toughest solos. Stanley signed Denson to his Sherman Publishing company on the strength of *Climb Love Mountain*, but no hit records were forthcoming. Denson later found fame as a songwriter, penning the gospel classic *Miracle Of The Rosary*, recorded by, among many others, his childhood acquaintance Elvis Presley in the early 1970s.

In 1957 Ray Stanley worked briefly as a label manager at Liberty Records, producing and promoting new releases on radio and television. He also assisted on sessions for Liberty artists Julie London and Jack Costanzo before moving on to the label's first subsidiary, Freedom Records, which was set up in 1958.

At Freedom he worked with Jimmie Maddin (writing his single release *I'm Studying You*), The Upper Classmen, Jay Johnson and Barry Martin, as well as Sherman Scott on the single *How Dja Do?* backed with *Way Out Far*. Many of these featured Eddie on guitar along with Capehart's involvement with the production.

The last time I saw Eddie was over in his house in Bell Gardens about the time when he was filming *Untamed Youth*. I went over and Jerry Capehart was there and there was a whole bunch of people in there hassling him about something. He motioned towards his bedroom door, so I just went on into his bedroom and sat down. He came in and collapsed on the bed, saying, 'Man, this isn't what it's all cracked up to be.'

'What do you mean?' I replied, 'you've got records out. You're getting rich and famous.'

'Brother, Dad,' he said, 'I've got 'em all fooled. I go
out there, I grab one string and pound the crap out of
it, wiggle my ass and they go nuts. I'm not playing a
thing!'

Chuck Foreman

In May 1957, as *Untamed Youth* reached cinema screens, Eddie's
second single, *One Kiss* backed with *Mean When I'm Mad*, was
released. Optimistic that this record would follow the success of
Sittin' In The Balcony, Si Waronker produced a full-colour picture
sleeve for the single, a luxury usually only afforded to artists of a
greater magnitude. 'I came up with all kinds of merchandising,' he
remembers. 'We found that spending a couple of extra cents here and
there for a record was a very good investment. Eddie was a very good-
looking boy and we wanted to show that as much as we could. In those
days, television was just starting to be something but it wasn't that
important yet. So you couldn't get anybody on television. The only
place we had any luck was on *Ed Sullivan* and anybody would take
anybody who had a hit on the label and put them on. But Eddie never
did *The Ed Sullivan Show* as I remember.'

Despite Waronker's promotional endeavours, *One Kiss* failed to
reach the Hot 100. Jerry Capehart regarded the release as a disaster,
as its lack of success brought Eddie, Jerry and Liberty Records
crashing back down to earth. *One Kiss* was perhaps too close to *Sittin'
In The Balcony* in concept. It certainly employed all the echo gimmicks
and even lyrically was not dissimilar.

Although the B-side, *Mean When I'm Mad*, identified Eddie's talent
as a rock'n'roll artist, *One Kiss* is more teen-orientated pop. It does
include a typical Cochran solo, however, and is very reminiscent of
Sittin' In The Balcony in that the guitar break lifts the song and stops
it becoming another mundane run-of-the-mill teenage pop song.

In May 1957 Eddie started work on his début album, *Singin' To My
Baby*. The album contained a mixture of ballads and rockers and was
representative of Eddie's style at the time and consistent with
Liberty's plans to mould him as a cross between Pat Boone and Elvis
Presley. The album title alone immediately made the listener aware
that this would not be a record packed with wild rock'n'roll.

Singin' To My Baby has been unfairly criticised over the years, but by November 1957, when the album was released, rock'n'roll's rough edges were starting to be smoothed over and a more commercial aspect was being introduced. As Waronker explained earlier, he wanted to establish Eddie as more than just a rock'n'roll singer. Many in the music business still regarded rock'n'roll as a fad, so Liberty kept their options open by presenting Eddie, through *Singin' To My Baby*, as an all-round entertainer.

Fans often question why *Singin' To My Baby* was the only album released during Eddie's lifetime. 'The single records in those days were the important products of the industry,' Si answers. 'In fact, all the so-called gold records were single records. Today there's hardly any such thing. You never made an album for an artist unless they had a single hit. It was financially impossible to record an album of twelve tunes if the one tune couldn't be heard and bought. As far as doing Eddie's one album, we had greater success with his single records than we had with the one album. Don't forget his career wasn't long at all.'

Waronker also hints at other reasons why *Singin' To My Baby* was destined to be Eddie's only album released during his lifetime: 'The important thing was finding the material for albums. I didn't want to do only Capehart's songs because there weren't that many. Just to do songs that Sylvester Cross or American Music wanted to submit wasn't the way to do it. You had to fill at least half of it with commercial tunes. American Music tried to get most of their stuff recorded, but I had to okay it and I wasn't going to okay anything that I didn't think was commercially feasible.

'I think that by '58 Eddie had just reached the tip of the iceberg with commercial success. Singles were more important in terms of getting the artist heard. Eddie had to keep coming out with singles in order to keep his name rolling. That's how I felt about it, anyway. Make an album as soon as we could put one together. That made sense. Then make it and release it.'

Waronker also believed that at times Eddie tried too hard to be an independent artist. Waronker felt that by writing, producing and playing all of the instruments on some of his later recordings, Eddie was overstretching himself as an artist. Maybe he was losing touch with the business at hand, namely producing commercial songs for a commercial audience. As Si explains, 'I think that a lot of artists in those days held back their chart success by being too self-contained.

A good artist would have one hit and that would be the end of them because they thought they knew what to write and what to do to sell records just because they had one hit. I've always said, "Give me the right material and I will make a hit." '

Although Eddie had the choice of the two Goldstar studios, he still continued to use the smaller Studio B due to its better acoustics. The album was recorded in this studio using Guybo on upright bass, The Johnny Mann Chorus on backing vocals and Jerry Capehart providing rhythm with a cardboard box. Si Waronker was in charge of production and was a huge influence on the overall sound and presentation of the album. 'There was no album that came out with Liberty in the early days that I didn't produce. Then, as time went on, I couldn't possibly do it all. I produced all the important records that we had, with the exception of what Snuffy Garrett did later. Not that I'm proud of it all, but some of it turned out well. Actually, that was my job as the creative end of Liberty. As far as planning is concerned, when I was sent the dub of a record, I heard something on that that made me go for it. I don't want to say I copied or covered it, but I heard enough of the original to give me some idea what to do. For instance, at the very end where we used the tape reverberation: that didn't take planning, it just happened to go that way. In those days, when we didn't have a definite ending to a tune, we'd tail off by repeating the last line of the lyric and let it just tail off. As far as the instrumentals were concerned, that had to fall into place, and very often, not to take anything away from anybody, you'd find that the musicians themselves would lend an awful lot. They had an awful lot to give to a record but very rarely did you let someone just come in and take off on their own.'

Side one of *Singin' To My Baby* opens with Eddie's début single for Liberty, *Sittin' In The Balcony*. Next is a re-recording of *Completely Sweet*, which is far more polished than the earlier demo but still features great guitar and slap bass. A collection of ballads follows with *I'm Alone Because I Love You*, *Undying Love* and *Lovin' Time* which is a wonderfully performed song featuring Eddie playing a ukulele, and the side ends with a typical piece of '50s pop, *Proud Of You*.

Side two starts off with the extremely tough-sounding *Mean When I'm Mad*, which features great backing vocals and lyrics. The gently rocking *Stockin's 'n' Shoes* follows, and ballads in the shape of *Have I Told You Lately That I Love You* and *Tell Me Why*, mixed with pop-rockers *Cradle Baby* and *One Kiss*, close the album.

Of the twelve songs, three are Cochran and Capehart compositions – *Completely Sweet*, *Undying Love* and *Mean When I'm Mad*, with *One Kiss* credited to Eddie in his own right. The album is incredibly well produced and the musicians involved turn in superb performances. Eddie's vocals seem confident throughout, even though his lack of range and technical ability is once again noticeable on the ballads.

Overall, *Singin' To My Baby* was an excellent début album from the eighteen-year-old, who only a year before was limited to singing harmony vocals and lead guitar as one half of The Cochran Brothers.

Drive-In Show backed with *Am I Blue* were also recorded at the same time as *Singin' To My Baby*, although they were omitted from the album to be released as Eddie's third Liberty single.

Drive-In Show – a ukulele-strummed pop song that just managed to grace the lower end of the pop charts, reaching number 82 – turned out to be one of the weakest singles released by Liberty in 1957. Eddie's performance on the single does appear to be mundane, although the odd chuckle does give the impression that he was enjoying himself. *Am I Blue*, in contrast, is a rockabilly classic, complete with machine-gun-style drumming after every verse, reminiscent of Elvis Presley's *Hound Dog*, along with two brilliant guitar breaks from Eddie. A great vocal performance rounds off this superb version of an old classic.

After the failure of *One Kiss* and *Drive-In Show*, Eddie's future as a recording artist may have appeared to be in doubt. However, he still maintained a high public profile due mainly to the popularity of *The Girl Can't Help It* and *Untamed Youth*. In addition, his blond good looks guaranteed him plenty of coverage in teenage magazines. More importantly, Si Waronker's continued faith in Eddie's ability ensured his future at Liberty.

One Kiss and *Drive-In Show* failed because, by comparison, they were poor songs and too obvious follow-ups to *Sittin' In The Balcony*. Si Waronker's vision of Cochran as a mixture of Pat Boone and Elvis Presley was failing, and Eddie would have to be reinvented if he was to achieve any chart success. There was little or no aggression in his stage act and, with a few exceptions, the same could be said regarding his recorded repertoire. Eddie was getting lost among an abundance of would-be rockers. He needed to find his own identity, both as an artist and a performer, and he needed to find it fast.

The young Eddie Cochran

Frank and Alice Cochran, with
Eddie, Patty (kneeling) and Gloria

Eddie about fifteen years old

Eddie and Hank Cochran – The
Cochran Brothers

Signing an autograph for an
admirer, circa 1957

Eddie and fans, circa 1956

At Liberty Custom Recorders, 15 May 1957; from left to right:
Eddie, Johnny Mann (at piano), Jack Ames and Simon Waronker

Taking a break from the
music business

Visiting KCSR DJ Freeman Hover
in Denver, during the Show Of Stars
tour, 1957

A sultry publicity photo, circa 1957

Eddie with Charlie Gracie, circa 1957

OPPOSITE PAGE: On stage in Melbourne, Australia, during his tour
with Gene Vincent and Little Richard, 1957

Dear Patron:

Welcome to the Fall Edition of the "BIGGEST SHOW OF STARS FOR '57."

Once again we have gathered together all the foremost artists in the Popular and Rhythm & Blues music world to entertain you in person. We are proud of the reputation the "BIGGEST SHOW OF STARS" has gained throughout the country . . . the show that brings you more top stars than any other tour package. And, we at Super Enterprises, Inc., intend to maintain the "Biggest Show Of Stars," the biggest entertainment value on the road. You'll find it pays to wait and see the original and only "BIGGEST SHOW OF STARS." Watch for announcements of the next "BIGGEST SHOW OF STARS" coming to your town—it will be another SUPER ATTRACTION.

We have tried to tailor each edition of the "BIGGEST SHOW OF STARS" to fulfill your entertainment wants. We'd appreciate your suggestions on how we can make the "BIGGEST SHOW OF STARS" even better. We'd like to know what artists you would like to see on our next shows. Your opinion is important to us. Just write us at Super Enterprises, Inc., 1110 Seventh St., N.W., Washington 1, D.C.

Yours for the BEST in entertainment,

SUPER ENTERPRISES, INC.

IRVIN FELD, Pres.

Eddie on stage, circa 1958. Guybo can be seen at the far right on bass

Fats Domino signing autographs. Eddie is on the far right

OPPOSITE PAGE: Advertisement for Irvin Feld's
The Biggest Show Of Stars Tour, 1957

A publicity photograph featuring Eddie's prized Gretsch 6120

When Eddie was in Australia he was running around
with some very well-to-do women over there. He said
that he met a wonderful woman and he was very
interested in her. He showed me pictures of her and he
told me he liked Connie Stevens too, but sometimes
things don't materialise like you want them to.

Warren Flock

In October 1957 Eddie toured Australia with Little Richard, Gene
Vincent, Australian rocker Johnny O'Keefe and Alis Lesley – who was
billed as the female Elvis Presley. Promoted by Lee Gordon, 'The Big
Show', as it was named, was only the second rock'n'roll tour to visit
Australia, preceded in January by Bill Haley when he toured Down
Under accompanied by LaVern Baker, Freddie Bell And The Bell
Boys and Big Joe Turner.

Although Eddie would have performed his current Liberty singles,
as a new artist he would have also covered popular hits of the day.
Posters advertising the tour feature Eddie singing the Charlie Gracie
hit *Butterfly*, along with the country standard *Gone* and the pop song
White Sports Coat. Although three singles had been released prior to
his arrival, they had made little or no impact, and Eddie was unknown
in Australia. Therefore, he had to fill his set with contemporary hit
songs, as these cover songs would have been more of a selling point
than his own material.

Opening in Wollongong, New South Wales, the show moved on to
Newcastle, Brisbane, Sydney, Broken Hill, Wayville and Melbourne,
before returning to Sydney where the tour was cut short when Little
Richard turned away from rock'n'roll and found religion.

Night after night, Little Richard caused riots throughout theatres
as he shed his clothing on stage and threw it into the audience. As the
controversial tour continued, the police began to intervene, trying to
break up fights between teenagers battling over the singer's clothes
and eventually forbidding any further striptease acts from Little
Richard, and even banning dancing in some venues.

By the time the tour reached Melbourne, Little Richard had made
up his mind – the world was coming to an end and he was returning
to America to be baptised. In Sydney, he threw four diamond rings

into the Hunter River to prove his faith in God, and the following evening, Saturday, 12 October, 'The Big Show' tour came to a close.

All the members of the tour obviously benefited from the constant stream of press attention that Little Richard drew. Eddie made many radio appearances during the tour, most notably on Stan Rofes's *Platter Parade Show* where the nineteen-year-old singer carved his name on the turntables. Buddy Holly also added his signature to the turntable in February 1958 when he made an appearance on the same show.

By incredible coincidence, as Warren Flock explains, Eddie ran into Flock's brother Bernard, who was on shore leave in Australia while in the US Navy. 'Bernard looked up on a theatre marquee and saw that Eddie Cochran and Gene Vincent were going to be appearing. It was really amazing that they ran across each other. Eddie was glad to see my brother because he could get US cigarettes, so my brother was invited to all the parties and all the shows.'

Eddie flew back to America in mid-October to join Irvin Feld's 'The Biggest Show Of Stars For '57' tour. Travelling across the country by coach, Eddie's fellow performers included Chuck Berry, Fats Domino, Paul Anka, Buddy Holly and The Everly Brothers. Eddie forged a lasting friendship with Buddy, Don and Phil Everly when they all appeared together in the Paramount Theatre in New York during Christmas.

Phil recalls those tours with great affection: 'On those big packages you went out and you did about three numbers, depending on your position in the show. The first big tour we did was a Fats Domino tour. They had a big band and there were 120 people on the tour. There were about ten acts – you name them, they were all there: Frankie Lymon, Buddy, Cochran, Chuck Berry and Buddy Knox had also been in the middle of the tour. Chuck Berry would always open the show in his rock suit to pick up the girls. He would open the show then spend the rest of the night hanging out at the Coke machine to get the girls.

'The longest tour I can recall lasted eighty days. On the big tours with Fats Domino, a guy named Junior ran the band bus. Junior came on the road free with the truck and carried everybody's equipment so that he could gamble, as there was a lot of gambling going on backstage. We played dice and craps, and a thing called 4,5,6 with three dice. If you got twenty people in on the game and if you know how to play 4,5,6 you can pick up a lot of money and it would stack up like you wouldn't believe. Junior would play this every night after the show. He was like a pre-roadie, doing it free for just the gambling rights.

'The timing was real precise on the tours and Eddie would not always be there with all of us, he would come in late. I've seen him come in as they were ready to announce him and we'd all lay money on whether Cochran would make it or not. All of a sudden the door would bust open and Eddie would come in with Guybo following him. He was always wearing his coat like he was a German officer, he had it on over his shoulders. You'd hear the door open and Eddie would drop his coat onto the floor, pick up his guitar and walk straight out on to the stage. I'd see him do this in one sweeping movement without stopping. He would walk straight out, do his thing, walk out the other side and then he'd be gone.'

To coincide with 'The Show Of Stars' tour, Liberty released Eddie's fourth single, *Twenty Flight Rock* backed with *Cradle Baby*. It's quite possible that Si Waronker felt that the version of *Twenty Flight Rock* used in *The Girl Can't Help It* was perhaps a little too rough around the edges, and decided a slicker, more polished version should be issued instead. Whatever the reason, Eddie re-recorded the song around the same time as the *Singin' To My Baby* sessions.

By the time *Twenty Flight Rock* was released it was already too late. The single failed without ever entering the charts, ending Eddie's first year as a solo artist on a sour note. It must have been extremely frustrating for the singer as a great deal of 1957 had been spent on the road, as well as constantly promoting his new releases on radio and television. The realisation that his image and style of music were not proving to be a commercial success certainly began to hit home as the year drew to a close.

Eddie's re-recording of *Twenty Flight Rock* was every bit as exciting and energetic as the film version. It features the heavy backing of The Johnny Mann Chorus on backing vocals, but on this occasion their presence enhances the song, which cannot always be said for the majority of the songs on the *Singin' To My Baby* album. Once again, Guybo shines with a wonderful series of slap-bass runs and Eddie gives a great performance, although he holds back on the guitar solo, the only drawback on a fine version of the song.

Cradle Baby is fairly similar to *One Kiss*. Although it does rock along a little better, the recording is essentially the same as other Cochran failures and even a great guitar solo could not push the single into the charts.

Despite these setbacks, Eddie enjoyed full backing from Liberty and was given assurances from Si Waronker that he was regarded as a priority artist and would be treated as such. He still continued with his role as a session guitarist but had ample opportunity to record his own songs and ideas in the studio.

Liberty Records had their own problems, however. By late 1957 the company was virtually bankrupt.

Al Bennett was a super salesman and a first-rate businessman with an unbelievable personality. He could sell a burnt match. He was exactly what was needed to bring Liberty to its full potential.

Simon Waronker

Corrupt sales managers and bad bookkeeping left Liberty Records with debts that totalled almost $800,000, with $167,000 owing to the government in taxes.

Si Waronker was totally unaware of what was happening to his business. It only came to light when Randy Wood, who was running Dot Records, put in a bid to buy Liberty. Together Wood and Waronker agreed a price of one million dollars, but after auditors were called in to look over Liberty's finances, the trouble was discovered.

Jack Ames, Waronker's partner and sales manager at Liberty, had altered the figures representing the number of records that distributors were buying from the company. When asked for ten records, Jack Ames would add two zeros to make it appear that one thousand records were ordered.

To Simon Waronker, it looked as though Liberty were selling huge amounts of records, only to discover later that distributors were returning vast amounts unsold. Also, pressing plants that were owed hundreds of thousands of dollars by Liberty, in particular the RCA pressing plant, were refusing to manufacture further releases.

Waronker was in a mess but he embarked on the task of rebuilding his company with admirable results. 'There were more companies going bust during that time than ever before or after,' Si explains. 'Nobody got paid and the cashflow made it hard to stay afloat.'

So did this affect the artists on the label? 'Very much so,' Si continues. 'If the company is only getting paid on 40 per cent of the returns of the sales, you can only pay the artists on 40 per cent of the sales. Consequently a lot of artists would come in and say, "Where's our money? We understand we're number 4 in *Billboard* and we only got paid on 40,000 records. Where's the rest of the money?"

'Well, you'd try and explain, "You got paid today, next month when we get the money in that's owed, you'll get more."

'You never knew what the complete sales were until after a year had gone by because the distributors had to be paid every month. It was rough, but all the artists got their money. Eddie got paid because I made sure he did while I was there anyway. I made sure the artists under my control were paid. I was able to have these artists flock to help me when I needed them, because I did pay them.'

Waronker fired his bookkeeper and purchased his sales manager's 20 per cent stake in the company. He contacted a few distributors that were close to him and asked for an advance of $10,000 and in return they could pay thirty-five cents a record instead of forty-five. In three days he collected $80,000. After meeting with executives at RCA they agreed that he could clear his debt over an eighteen-month period, while the IRS agreed to give him a one-year extension on his tax debt.

Si Waronker hired Al Bennett after hearing that this astute businessman had left Dot Records. Bennett was instrumental in turning around Liberty's fortunes by going to all the distributors and persuading them to stick with the label, and then he set about the task of selling records – with spectacular results.

Liberty's second release of 1958 was the novelty tune *Witch Doctor* by David Seville, alias Ross Bagdasarian, a close friend of Simon Waronker. Bennett, who had to be convinced himself that this was a hit, arranged for the pressing plants to produce the record even though Liberty were out of credit. Bennett's hard work paid off: *Witch Doctor* sold 2.8 million copies within the first six weeks, wiping out the company debts and becoming Liberty Records' first number 1 single. Al Bennett became the new president of Liberty with a 35 per cent share of the company before 1958 was over. It was also Al Bennett that single-handedly turned around Eddie Cochran's career.

I pretty much try to find anything I can on Eddie. It's his whole persona that speaks to me. It's his song-writing, his guitar playing, his look and his attitude. I think something that I've indirectly adopted from Eddie is his laidback, kinda carefree attitude about the music business. I hear little stories from people that I kind of act the same way towards it, and I think that's an indirect adoption of Eddie's attitude.

Brian Setzer

Twelve days into 1958 and Eddie returned to the studio to find a song capable of getting him back into the charts. Accompanied by top session drummer Earl Palmer and the redoubtable Guybo on upright bass, Eddie went into Liberty's studio on North La Brea to record *Jeannie, Jeannie, Jeannie* and *Pretty Girl*.

Written by George Motola and his wife Ricki Page, who was a Liberty artist in her own right, *Jeannie, Jeannie, Jeannie* has a colourful history. It was originally entitled *Johnny, Johnny, Johnny* and was recorded by a couple of female artists, one of whom was Kay Cee Jones on Imperial Records. Apparently Eddie helped to record the backing track for one of these versions, but it was later turned into *Jeannie, Jeannie, Jeannie* by DJ Jimmy Maddin. Then, according to co-writer George Motola, after Eddie heard Maddin's version, he decided to cover it himself.

Marilyn Smith, Guybo's fiancée at the time, remembers this as a very long, difficult recording session: 'That was one I don't think they practised on very much. They went over and over that song. I finally had to go and sit in the car.'

Jeannie, Jeannie, Jeannie was a complete contrast to the material Eddie had been recording throughout the previous year. Vocally, he was developing a style reminiscent of one of his favourite rock'n'roll singers, Little Richard, and this gruff style – one he used to great effect on his later classic recordings – could be heard on this track for the first time.

Eddie was also looking to create a harder edge to his music, and the addition of Earl Palmer, a top session drummer who had worked with Little Richard and Fats Domino among others, was a considerable help in achieving this.

As Si Waronker explains, 'I hired the musicians, as I happened to know the musicians that were good for that type of work, or rock'n'roll if you want to call it that. I would hire them, and later on Jerry got to know them himself and he would hire the same musicians whenever he wanted to. Plas Johnson was one of them and the drummer that did practically all of our work was Earl Palmer. I used him on practically every date I had. He had a lot to do with many of the hits than came out of Los Angeles.'

By early 1958 Waronker and the Liberty executives started to give Eddie and Jerry Capehart more freedom and creative control over their recording sessions – due mainly to the limited success of Eddie's last three singles. The image that Liberty had so carefully created, along with the music that Eddie was recording, failed to excite record-buying teenagers.

Something radical had to be done, but Si Waronker still had a great deal of faith in Cochran: 'I wasn't concerned, because I knew the kid had talent and it was just a matter of time before we could actually make the happy transition of a tune and an artist, and sales would fall into place – I had faith in him. I would never have allowed him to leave if I had any say in the matter, and he never wanted to, because we recorded almost anything that he came up with.

'Although I chose the singles for release, Eddie would come to me and tell me what he wanted or liked, and nine times out of ten I would agree with him. I gave him the benefit of the doubt practically every time. If he wanted to do something I'd say, "Great, let's do it." I had to give him a great deal of respect for his judgement and his judgement was usually right.'

Jeannie, Jeannie, Jeannie backed with *Pocket Full Of Hearts* became Liberty's first single of the year when it was released in January 1958.

The B-side was very much a pop-styled rock ballad and would not have sounded out of place on the *Singin' To My Baby* album as it was recorded around the same period. Although Liberty were happy to go along with Eddie's ambitions to become a tougher-sounding rocker, they would continue to keep their options open, for the time being at least, by ensuring that one of the two sides maintained the sound and feel of his previous singles.

'This is a powerful side by the artist who hasn't clicked recently. Exuberant delivery on this catchy rockabilly could put him back on top,' wrote one reviewer.

Another mentioned the similarity between the vocal styles of Eddie and Little Richard: 'Eddie Cochran, an exciting rock'n'roll performer best remembered for his big-selling rendition of *Sittin' In The Balcony*, has a torrid new release that should burn up the charts. A wild and woolly rocker with Cochran wailing in an exciting manner, Cochran's delivery on this side could be described as a subdued Little Richard style.'

Although the reviews were very promising, this radical change in style for Eddie failed to entice the record-buying public and *Jeannie, Jeannie, Jeannie* only managed to scrape into the charts at number 94.

Days after completing *Jeannie, Jeannie, Jeannie*, Eddie started work on a song entitled *Ah, Pretty Girl*, not to be confused with the previously recorded *Pretty Girl*. The song had originally been recorded at Goldstar during the previous year, when some thirty-two takes were laid down, before the masters were taken to Liberty Custom Recorders for overdubs with The Johnny Mann Chorus. The results were still unsatisfactory, so Eddie and Jerry decided to persevere with another session.

Recording at Liberty Custom Recorders in April 1958, Eddie added a superb guitar solo, very reminiscent of the one in Elvis Presley's *My Baby Left Me*; but for all his time and devotion, *Ah, Pretty Girl* did not see the light of day until after Eddie's death. This gentle rocker was probably looked upon as an experiment rather than a potential single release.

Also in January 1958 Eddie recorded a demo version of a song entitled *Little Lou*, written by Jerry Capehart along with singer Eddie Daniels. The song was intended for John Ashley, under contract to Capehart, and his version of the song was released later that year. Eddie drives this Chuck Berry-inspired rocker along with his acoustic guitar and, although intended as a demo, *Little Lou* stands up well today mainly as a result of Eddie's fine performance.

Recorded on 3 March, Eddie's second release in 1958 was *Teresa* backed with *Pretty Girl*. It is possible that Si Waronker chose the A-side for Eddie, thinking that it was strong enough to enjoy commercial success. Unfortunately, it wasn't, and *Teresa* soon joined the ever-growing list of Cochran singles that were failing to get anywhere in the charts.

In fairness, *Teresa* is not a bad song, but Liberty's gamble of portraying Eddie as a balladeer proved time and time again to be the wrong choice. The song is a bright-sounding ballad and Eddie does his best to add all the gimmicky vocal inflections, but once again only manages to highlight his inability to deal with this style of song with any conviction. On top of that, the annoying female backing vocals quickly convince the listener to lift the needle off the record before the song ends.

Pretty Girl, by contrast, is a fantastic rocker. Almost from the same mould as *Jeannie, Jeannie, Jeannie*, this track has the added bonus of coming from the pen of Cochran and Capehart, the first time one of their collaborations had been used on a Cochran single since *Mean When I'm Mad*, almost a year previously.

The lyrics to their compositions were often humorous. Eddie's friends and family remember that he had a dry, well-developed sense of humour, which often centred around practical jokes played on unsuspecting band members. His sense of fun would often surface on many of his songs and enhance the overall performance. As mentioned earlier, Eddie would often laugh between lyrics to let the listener know that he was having a good time and enjoying himself. In later recordings, especially the heavier rockers, that chuckle developed into a more menacing snarl, fitting in perfectly with his change in style. Cochran was very aware of his image and worked hard on it, but if it was not working and not selling records, he would change it and start again.

On invitation, Eddie helped Gene Vincent work on his album *A Gene Vincent Record Date*. The two had remained friends since their first tour together the previous year, along with Gene's band The Blue Caps, so Eddie was certainly not seen as an outsider at these sessions. Recording between 25 and 29 March at Capitol Records studio in Hollywood, Eddie added bass vocals to the album as well as providing valuable production advice and ideas. He assisted in building a sound-proof structure within the larger studio to separate the sound and is reputed to have arranged a lot of the material. Although The Blue Caps remember this as a friendly involvement, in later years Jerry Capehart regarded it as professional only, with Eddie simply attending the sessions because he was paid to do so.

Although Eddie was always in demand as far as studio work was concerned, Capehart's scenario is unlikely. It is just as possible to assume that Eddie and Gene had discussed the idea of recording together during their long tours over the previous year. In The Blue Caps, Vincent had a group of highly skilled musicians, especially with guitarist Johnny Meeks, so Eddie would not be needed on a Gene Vincent recording session in his usual capacity as a musician. He did possess another quality that would allow him to fit into the band, though: his voice.

Eddie Cochran's voice may not have been one of the most techni-cally versatile in the history of rock'n'roll, but his harmonising was incredibly adept. From his days with Hank Cochran, Eddie proved he could handle the high harmony, but on the recordings with Gene Vincent, his ability to imitate the bass vocal parts, normally associated with black R&B groups, is uncanny. At this time in The Blue Caps' history, Paul Peek and Tommy Facenda were employed by Vincent to sing back-up harmonies, but neither could provide the bass vocal. Eddie fitted in with ease and contributed to one of the most unique and underrated of Gene Vincent's albums.

Of the seven songs that Eddie worked on, the notable contribu-tions are in *Lovely Loretta*, *Somebody Help Me* and *Git It*. All three are fantastic rockers and feature Eddie's vocals to the fore.

Git It, in particular, has achieved almost legendary status with rock'n'roll fans over the years. Eddie starts the record with a deep 'Well-o, well-o, wop, wip, wip, wip' phrase, then the band joins in at a frantic pace, joined by the high harmonies of Peek and Facenda with a high falsetto from Vincent. It is surely one of the greatest intro-ductions to a rock'n'roll record from that era.

The standard of musicianship throughout the whole album is breathtaking, and had the bonus of Gene Vincent's unmistakable and highly skilful vocals, which as well as possessing great technical qualities, could also rock like crazy when the song needed it.

With hindsight, adding Eddie Cochran into the equation as a bass vocalist was a stroke of genius, and it sounds as though everyone on the record was having too much fun to be involved simply for the pay-cheque.

Eddie got involved in rock'n'roll because he wanted to be a star. After Elvis came out and he saw him on television nationwide, this is what he wanted. So if that's what it took, that's the way he was going. Secretly he was yearning to be a star. 'I'm gonna be big,' he would say. 'I can play guitar – he can't.'

John Rook

Meanwhile, Sharon Sheeley, in her quest to enter the music industry, wrote a song called *Poor Little Fool*. Recorded by Ricky Nelson, who at the time was Elvis's only rival as the nation's teen idol, Sharon's first composition turned out to be a huge hit, reaching number 1. It was an incredible achievement for the teenager who, as she recalls, tricked Ricky into believing the song had originally been intended for Elvis. And it was this hit record that led her to Jerry Capehart and eventually to Eddie Cochran, just as she had planned.

'I used to write poems to pass the time walking home from school, and when I was fifteen and a half I wrote *Poor Little Fool*,' she recalls. 'My sister liked it a lot, so I put a little melody to it and that was my first song.

'I told Ricky Nelson that my godfather wrote it for Elvis. After hearing it he told me he had to have that song. He asked me to get my godfather to come along and sign a contract but I showed up and he was furious. I think he died hating that song because a girl pulled one over on him. After it became a hit, all these managers were calling me because at the time it was so unique to have a girl write a song. I was on the covers of all the teen and movie magazines. They all wanted to manage my career but I kept saying no. I didn't care if they were managing Clark Gable, I would still say no.

'Ironically, my sister and I went to see Gene Vincent at a rock'n'roll show and a guy in the audience asked me if I wanted to meet Gene Vincent. He took us backstage and that was the first time I met Gene. He was very drunk and very obnoxious and he scared me. Then, months later when I was in Hollywood, we were walking by a coffee shop and I saw the same guy at the counter. I said to my sister: "Look, there's that guy that introduced us to Gene Vincent." He saw us and motioned for us to come in. He introduced himself as Jerry Capehart and asked what we had been up to. When I told him that I wrote the song *Poor Little Fool*, he said, "That's an incredible song – who manages you?"

'"No one yet," I replied. "Who do you manage?"

'He said, "John Ashley and Eddie Cochran."

'Bingo!

'So Jerry Capehart became my manager. He asked me if I had any songs that Eddie would like. I told him that I had a lot of songs that would be great for Eddie Cochran, but really I didn't have any. I had to run home to start cramming away, writing songs for Eddie. Jerry set a meeting up for me to meet Eddie, although I had met him previously, but very briefly, when The Everly Brothers were in town doing a big rock'n'roll show a few months before. Now I was to meet him again. Eddie didn't remember that first meeting at all – that's how much I impressed him. I was scared to death. My God, I was so nervous! I was supposed to meet him at Jerry's apartment and when I got there Eddie opened the door, as Jerry wasn't there. Eddie said, "I hear you wrote a song for me," and handed me his guitar and asked, "Are you going to play it for me?" Well, I couldn't actually play the guitar. I couldn't sing either – I was so frightened my voice was up twenty octaves. I croaked out a few bars of *Love Again* and it was dreadful, but Eddie could hear it through the croaking and the nervousness. At the time he was teasing me. I remember him saying it was a song for black people and not really his kind of song, and I ran out of there in tears. I passed Jerry in the hall as I ran out crying and I heard him yelling at Eddie, saying, "You just chased a million dollars out the door. You go and apologise." He did, he came out to the parking lot and told me he was just teasing me. He recorded the song two weeks later on the *Summertime Blues* session.'

It's funny, but I have to say that people in America
didn't really know who Eddie Cochran was. They knew
Summertime Blues and that was really the major impact
he had in the States.

Brian Setzer

As the year progressed, Liberty Records began to repay its debts and
re-establish the label's good name within the music industry. Hits by
David Seville such as *Bird On My Head* and *Little Brass Band* as well as
a big seller by Billy Ward And His Dominos entitled *Jennie Lee*
continued to ease the situation with the company's creditors.

Al Bennett, however, was having little success with Eddie's records,
which he considered uncommercial. After the failure of *Teresa*, Eddie's
future looked uncertain until Al heard the B-side to his next single
Love Again. Entitled *Summertime Blues*, Al felt that this time Cochran
had finally got it right and used all of Liberty's promotional resources
to ensure that the record was a huge hit.

Recorded in May 1958 in Goldstar Studio B and engineered by
Larry Levine (a nephew of Stan Ross), *Summertime Blues* is now one
of the most covered records of all time, and, for Si Waronker, a great
success for Liberty Records: 'Eddie came to me one day and said,
"There's a tune that I'm writing with Jerry Capehart called *Summertime Blues.*" So I said, "Fine, let's hear it," and he played it and it was
great, so I asked him to record it. He came up with it, and that was his
first hit for the big time and from that point on it was easy for him to
record. He was very prolific – we would record several tunes in one
session.

'I think *Summertime Blues* broke the ice quicker than any other
thing that he could have done. *Sittin' In The Balcony* was nothing more
than a good way of getting him started, but *Summertime Blues*, which
was his way of performing, did more than anything else. The other
tunes that he did were not as commercially successful. We had limited
sales – that was one of the reasons we had only one album.'

Recorded as a simple three-chord trick – with overdubs of hand-
clapping and driven by Eddie's playing of Bill Cochran's Martin D18
– this rock'n'roll classic was apparently written in half an hour in
Capehart's apartment the previous evening. Assisted by Earl Palmer

on drums and Guybo on bass guitar, Eddie played all the guitar tracks and added the handclaps afterwards.

With its intelligent lyrics, driving rhythm and catchy chorus, Eddie's final masterstroke was adding a spoken lyric at the end of each verse. In typical Cochran humour he used his impersonation of Kingfish, a character from the popular radio show *Amos'n'Andy*.

Destined as the A-side to *Summertime Blues, Love Again*, along with another of Sheeley's compositions, *Lonely*, was also recorded during the same period. However, as Al Bennett predicted, when *Love Again* was released on 11 June, the ballad was rapidly eclipsed by its B-side.

This song is not only important as Eddie's one and only Top 10 hit in America, but it marked the end of his Ivy League image that Si Waronker and Liberty Records had cultivated. Waronker also started allowing Eddie more creative freedom during his own sessions: 'Eddie always had confidence in his own ability. I started to ease off when I realised that he could produce his own stuff as well as he did. I'd say, "Well, go into the studio, Eddie, and let's see what it sounds like." He would bring back an unfinished product, and I'd tell him to go ahead and finish it, and I didn't even have to be there. I would have to okay what he was doing, so very often I'd allow him to be in the studio by himself. As far as his ability went, it was unquestionable.'

Capehart signed Sharon Sheeley on a management contract mainly due to her songwriting success with *Poor Little Fool* for Ricky Nelson. The song she offered Eddie initially was *Love Again* and Capehart obviously felt that the ballad could match the success of Nelson's million-selling single. In fairness, had Ricky Nelson recorded the song, it probably would have sold a million copies, but unfortunately Eddie's version is marred by his lacklustre performance.

Another of Sheeley's compositions, *Lonely*, was also recorded by Eddie during this period. This beautiful ballad had the added benefit of a much more polished performance from Eddie and was eventually released in the UK on a posthumous single as the B-side to *Sweetie Pie*.

As Stan Ross explains, it was not unusual for B-sides to be picked up by DJs and promoted in preference to the intended A-sides: 'We did most of Eddie's records in Studio B, but we always expanded and there was always Studio A. (Apart from the period when we took over the empty building next to us and decided to create another Studio A, or adding on, with echo chambers and a coffee lounge. The echo chambers were our priority.) I did *Tequila* by The Champs around that time. That again was an experimental record and it was a demo that turned out to be a wonderful master. That was the backside, too; *Train To Nowhere* was the A-side.

'When I hear Eddie now, I can close my eyes and think of the studio; it sounds wonderful. Even with Ritchie Valens, *La Bamba* was done live. He stood in the middle of the room while the band was chopping away at that thing. Again this was also the backside; *Donna* was the A-side.'

Summertime Blues was released on 11 June 1958. Not an instant smash as one would have expected, the song eventually entered the charts almost two months later, peaking at number 8 on the Billboard Hot 100.

Summertime Blues came at a time when Cochran's chart career looked almost over. He had not enjoyed a hit record since his Liberty début, *Sittin' In The Balcony*. This convinced Eddie and Jerry that they should go ahead with their planned change in musical direction and elevate Eddie's status to that of a credible rock'n'roll singer. He could write, produce and play his own material and still have the odd huge hit thrown in for good measure. The pressure was lifted from his shoulders with this one hit record, and *Summertime Blues* gave Eddie Cochran a style of music that was finally representative of his ability. No longer an imitator, Eddie Cochran was now an innovator.

Eddie drove me down past Hollywood High. We'd just been down to Goldstar studios and we were listening to some tapes of his multi-tracking – he'd played all the instruments apart from the bass. I can still remember looking up at the palm trees, and in California those days the sky was really blue. I can't believe we screwed it up so fast.

Phil Everly

Firmly established as a new teen idol for the nation, Eddie Cochran was in demand. Fan clubs were forming all around the United States and teenage magazines of the time such as *Dig*, *Teen*, *16* and *Hep Cats*, as well as the movie and music press, were all keen to feature the young artist.

Despite his new status, Eddie's feet remained firmly on the ground. Still a teenager, it's no surprise that he lived at home with his parents where he was still fondly regarded as the Cochran family's youngest son, rather than the pop star that the rest of America perceived him to be.

A new addition to the Cochran family was Ed Julson. Eddie's nephew and son to his eldest sister Gloria and her husband Red Julson, Ed also shared the Cochran home with his parents, grandparents Frank and Alice, and his Uncle Eddie. Although other commitments kept Eddie away from the household for lengthy periods, the times he spent at home with his family are fondly remembered. 'Our home entertainment was based around the TV,' Ed recalls. 'Eddie was home so little, but our family favourites would have been Wyatt Earp and Bat Masterson, all the Westerns of the time. They were very popular.

'Eddie always had presents for people when he came back from a tour. One of the strongest memories I have of Eddie is him coming off of a tour either during Christmas or right after my birthday. Eddie loved his guns and could fast-draw against the best of them. I had gotten a little toy gun in a trick holster and I was sure I was going to beat Eddie for once. You didn't have to pull the gun out of the holster to fire it – the gun and holster were attached to your hand with a string. All you had to do was lift your hand and the holster swivelled up and the gun would fire. Even so, I still couldn't beat Eddie.

'I also remember the time we had a great big cardboard box, like a water heater came in it or something, and I was using it as a tunnel. Eddie and Guybo were just teasing the daylights out of me. They had made some little homemade throwing darts and they were sitting there with those in their hands just begging me to go crawling through that tunnel.

'As soon as he got off his tours he would go out to the high desert for a week and camp and hunt. He usually went out with Bob Denton but sometimes he would go out on his own.'

Eddie's favourite gun was the Buntline Special .45 calibre. With its long barrel, it was certainly a very accurate weapon. Hunting had been a pastime for Eddie for several years and, along with close friends such as Bob Denton and Warren Flock, he often went out to the desert for several days at a time. Eddie was a skilled huntsman and an extraordinarily fast draw, and he was often challenging others to beat him. 'One of the reasons I got my guns was because Eddie had them,' Phil Everly remembers. 'But Eddie was an extraordinarily fast draw. A man can make a move on a gun and it takes the brain 17/100th of a second to register that his hand had moved. Cochran's reaction time was about half of that.'

Eddie's trips to the desert, although meant as relaxation, also proved eventful. As a child he often went shooting with his older brothers and on one such trip with his brother Bob, Eddie was accidentally shot in the leg. 'While Mom and Dad were away in Oklahoma, his .22 misfired,' his sister Patty explained. 'We tried to keep it from Mother because she'd be mad at all of us. I was at the house one day when Mom called and she said she wanted to talk to Eddie. I said I'd go and get him, but he was really limping around and when he eventually got on the phone, she said, "What took you so long to get to the phone?"

'"Oh, I was just slow in getting there," he replied, and she knew something was wrong. When she got back she was mad at us 'cos we hadn't told her.'

Warren Flock also remembers another incident that occurred in the desert. 'We nearly got killed once. We were going hunting and my wife was driving and I was talking to Eddie over in the back seat. Anyway, we came to a right turn and she was doing about fifty, and she turned a ninety-degree turn at that speed. The car went around on two wheels, then it straightened up and rolled across in front of some traffic coming the other way. When I looked around this car was coming towards me doing about sixty-five or seventy, coming down the road. Luckily my car was still running so I reached down with my foot and stomped on the gas pedal and we just jumped out of the way. Nobody got hurt, but it was quite an experience.

'We would go hunting with Bob Denton, and Eddie's brother Bill and myself. About three or four of us went.

'When Gene Vincent was in town, he was staying in a hotel pretty close to Capitol Records in Hollywood and I was interested in going over as I was trying to get a Fender amplifier from them. Fender would supply all their instruments and I was interested in getting one if they could misplace it somewhere. We also went over to Sharon's house one night and while we were there we had a party which many songwriters gatecrashed, hoping to meet singers that would record their songs. The Everly Brothers and Ricky Nelson were there. That was just after Ricky finished *Rio Bravo* with John Wayne and the Nelson family was still on television [in *The Adventures of Ozzie and Harriet*], so I was tickled to meet them.'

Teenage magazines were soon taking an interest in Eddie's social life and were soon romantically linking him to Sharon Sheeley. Jerry Capehart felt that their relationship would prove to be excellent publicity. He had the couple photographed in various locations including a drive-in burger bar, a record shop and on a park bench, and even had some publicity pictures taken at Goldstar, where Sharon and her sister Mary Jo can be seen sitting in on Eddie's sessions. 'It was amazing to watch him,' Sharon recalls. 'Eddie would work on his own arrangements and production. He'd do a take then go in and listen to it and change what he didn't like and everybody took so much credit away from him for stuff that they didn't really do.'

As John Rook explains, 'I remember the period [when Eddie dated] Yvonne Lime and Connie Stevens. I don't think there was any romance involved – it was a studio set-up thing. They were friends but people were just having fun at parties without having to have any relationship. He was seriously involved with Johnnie Berry, he thought she was fantastic, and when that broke off he was on a downer for a while. I don't ever remember him being down on a girl other than her. He thought a lot of Connie, but that wasn't anything serious. Then he met Sharon.'

Si Waronker adds: 'Sharon was a songwriter – that's why I first met her; then she was with Eddie and they were very close for some time. Eddie and I talked about her. He said: "What do you think?" and I said, "Fine, you're young enough to have all the experiences you want, kid, and I'm not going to tell you what or what not to do there." As far as writing with her goes, I told him he could learn a lot. Sharon did a lot of writing at one time and she had her name on songs with Eddie too.'

Eddie began to spend more time in Hollywood, where Sharon was based among a clique of teenage songwriters, singers and performers who would meet in her apartment. Members of this social circle included Don and Phil Everly, Ricky Nelson, Johnny and Dorsey Burnette, and Dorothy Harmony.

Dorothy, or Dotty as she is known, was a dancer who had also been a recent girlfriend of Elvis Presley prior to his temporary exit from the music scene when he was drafted into the army in March 1958. With Elvis out of the picture, Dotty attracted a newcomer to their Hollywood circle, James Marcus Smith (later to record under the pseudonym Jet Powers and who today is known as P.J. Proby). 'After I graduated, I went straight to Hollywood in '57,' says James. 'When I got there I only knew Elvis and Tommy Sands. Tommy was working with Pat Boone and Elvis was busy finishing up some pictures before he went into the army. Tommy sent me to Lillian Goodman, a vocal coach, and after about a week or two she introduced me to a guy named Ray Gilbert, who wrote songs such as *Zip-a-Dee-Do-Dah* and all the music from the movie *Song Of The South*. He became my manager and he took me around various agencies until I was signed. Paul Newman walked in one day needing someone to drive him around, so I became his chauffeur. It was the cushiest job I ever had. We would go to the gym every day, then cruise up and down Hollywood Boulevard looking for chicks.

'When I had just turned eighteen, a friend of mine offered to introduce me to Dotty Harmony, whom I had seen in all the movie magazines and who, of course, used to date Elvis. He said that Dotty was over at his friend Sharon Sheeley's house, the girl who wrote *Poor Little Fool*. I didn't believe him, but I went with him anyway, and he introduced me to Sharon, her sister Mary Jo and her mother. Then, all of a sudden, at the top of the stairs down came Dotty and I just could not believe it!

'Sharon said, "Why don't you come over tomorrow? Eddie's coming over, so we can sit and have some beers." I said, "Yeah, I think I can make it," but I was so determined to be there I almost slept in the flowerbed!

'Eddie and I started doing shows for DJ Jimmy O'Neil who, funnily enough, became Sharon's husband in later years. So Eddie and I would go out and open supermarkets, you know, we would do these little gigs, me and Eddie and Ritchie Valens.

'Sharon used to throw parties. These were parties with her friends who just happened to be The Everly Brothers, Ricky Nelson, Johnny and Dorsey Burnette and Baker Knight, who wrote *The Wonder Of You*. I mean, the list goes on and on. All of us would meet at Sharon's every Friday night – well, every Friday afternoon, but it would last into the night because we were all big beer drinkers. I was there mainly because I had stated dating Dotty right after we first met. She had just broken up with [the singer] Bob Luman. So we all hung around together and it was kind of a little clique. There were songwriters, pop singers and us.

'I was over at Sharon's all the time with Dotty, so I saw more of Eddie than Johnny and Dorsey or Baker, or any of them, because I was with Dotty and he was with Sharon. Eddie was a good old boy. He liked to drink and raise hell, but he was a gentleman. When we were all through drinking and partying we would go back to our hotels or individual apartments, but Eddie would go home to his family, so he still had a lot more values around him. He would not allow anybody to swear around the girls. He would just get up and knock you over. He didn't say, "I'm gonna punch you" or "We're gonna have a fight" or just start swinging, but he would always warn you first before he hit you, saying, "Put your hands up, I'm gonna knock you out!"

'The first time I came across this was when Dotty was dancing at a roadshow. She had left her Cadillac with me, so Sharon, Eddie and I went to pick her up. As I was driving them down there, I can't remember what happened exactly, but it was a red light and someone ran in front of me or something. "You motherfucker, goddamn it!" I yelled.

'Eddie said, "Pull the car over."

'So I pulled the car over and he made me get out, saying, "Put your hands up, I'm gonna knock you out. I don't allow that kind of language around Sharon."

'I talked my way out of it, but he made me sit on the back seat while he drove, but nothing more was ever said. I don't think Sharon even told Dotty.'

Sharon also remembers a wonderful story concerning Eddie and Johnny Burnette. Johnny and Dorsey Burnette moved from Memphis to Los Angeles in 1957 after an unsuccessful period signed to Coral Records as The Rock'n'Roll Trio – featuring Johnny on vocals, Dorsey on upright bass and guitarist Paul Burlison. Although this period wasn't financially rewarding for the brothers, they did create some of the wildest rockabilly ever recorded with songs such as *Rockabilly Boogie*, *Sweet Love On My Mind*, *Baby Blue Eyes* and *Train Kept A Rollin'*.

As Sharon recalls, 'I had a date with Eddie to go to the movies. He was supposed to pick me up at eight o'clock but he called me and said he was stuck on the freeway and there was a lot of traffic. Unknown to me, he was calling from the apartment right underneath me where these two hookers lived. He was there with Johnny Burnette. Johnny had dragged him down there because he wanted company and the girls all loved Eddie. So they were down there drinking with these girls right underneath me! This went on for about an hour and a half and finally Eddie told John that he would have to go up and take me to the movies. They had just run out of Scotch so he said to Eddie, "Just go with me to the liquor store to get another bottle then I'll stay here with the girls and you can meet Sharon and go out on your date."

'So, driving down Fountain Avenue, Johnny crashed right into the side of this brand new Cadillac and totalled it. The old guy driving the Cadillac and Johnny got into a big fight. The guy called the police, and while he was doing that, Eddie and Johnny pushed the car out of the road and down some side street out of view. When the police came and asked Johnny where the car was, he pointed over to a blank space, slurring, "Well, it's right over there."

'"There's no car over there," the policeman replied, so Johnny pointed somewhere else, saying, "Well, then, it must be right over there," and they said, "There's still no car there either." Johnny pointed to another spot and the police said, "No! There's no car!" Finally, Johnny looked over at Eddie, shrugged, and said, "Come to think of it, we were walking, weren't we, Ed?"

'With that, they hauled Johnny off in the police car and Eddie had to get an attorney to be in court the next morning to get John out. In the courtroom the next day John was still drunk and handcuffed. When the police pull out the bottle of Scotch as an exhibit, it's half empty, so John bolted out of his seat, yelling, "They drank our booze, goddamn it, Eddie! That was a new bottle! We didn't touch it! Those bastards drank our booze!" and the attorney kept saying, "John, shut up, you're never going to get out of here." But Eddie posted bail and got him out. Later, we had to do a photo layout and I was so mad – you could see how mad I was in those pictures! Eddie told me what [had happened and] kept saying to me: "It was John's fault, honey. John did it!" Johnny would always tell the same story: "It was Ed's fault, Ed made me do it – the devil made me do it." Between the two of those guys, it was always the other guy's fault.'

Eddie shifted gears as easily as anyone I'd ever seen. He didn't put anything down, and music was music if it was good. It didn't matter if it was country, it didn't matter if it was rock'n'roll or jazz. He could play anything and was not dedicated to anything except for music in any form – and that's what I would attribute to the meteoric rise in his capabilities. Today, a lot of it is about how lucky you are and what breaks you get, but that does not contribute to one's ability to play.

Chuck Foreman

Despite his own hectic recording and touring schedule, Eddie continued with his work as a session musician. Playing guitar for Bob Denton, he appeared on most of Bob's singles for Dot Records and contributed to some of Denton's best releases, including *24-Hour Night*, which was recorded at Goldstar in April 1958. Contrary to popular belief, Eddie did not appear on Denton's hit *Playboy* – Joe Maphis provided lead guitar for that particular song – nor did he appear on Denton's *Skinny Minny*.

In the late summer of 1958, Eddie worked on a session for a young singer named Troyce Key, who had recently been signed to Warner Brothers. Lester Sill and Lee Hazlewood produced the session and arranged for Eddie to play guitar. Together with Earl Palmer on drums, Red Callender on bass, Ray Johnson on piano, Howard Roberts on rhythm guitar and a vocal group called The Sharps doing the backing, they recorded three songs, *Drown In My Tears*, *Baby Please Don't Go* and *Watch Your Mouth*.

Troyce Key remembers the session well: 'I met Eddie for the first time at this session. We had three hours. Dig that, *three hours!* We listened to the record *Drown In My Tears* [by Ray Charles] and Eddie said, "I think I got that."

'Eddie asked us to listen, and he sure did have it. I gave him a little rundown on *Baby Please Don't Go* and *Watch Your Mouth*. He just listened to what I had to say and how the songs were supposed to go and said, "Okay."

'You listen to the record and you'll see he did have it. He made up the solo for *Watch Your Mouth* right there in the studio. I thought

Eddie Cochran's guitar playing was the greatest. He was a great dude to work with.'

The beautiful ballad *Drown In My Tears*, a cover of the Ray Charles version, was coupled with the tough blues stomper *Baby Please Don't Go* to make Troyce Key's first single. They both feature excellent guitar playing by Eddie, but on the great rocker *Watch Your Mouth*, Eddie's musicianship stole the show.

In August Jerry Capehart managed to secure a one-off deal for himself with Dot Records and, using the pseudonym Jerry Neal, he leased two songs for release. *I Hate Rabbits* backed with *Scratchin'* seemed to fit in well with the stream of novelty records that were being released throughout 1958. Goldstar's Stan Ross provided strange sound effects while doing his very best to imitate Mel Blanc's Bugs Bunny. 'Nothing ever happened with *I Hate Rabbits*,' Stan recalls. 'We did it as a gag and we had a ball making that thing. Dot Records bought it and thought they had a novelty record, but they never promoted it. Jerry did the talking on the record and I did the sound effects and the silly voices saying, "I hate rabbits". We all know who the guitarist was.'

Capehart did his very best to provide a tuneful vocal, and Eddie can hardly be heard above the noise, but it is a humorous recording and, with the support of Plas Johnson on sax, Earl Palmer on drums, Guybo on bass and Ray Johnson on piano, the backing rocks along at rapid pace.

The B-side, *Scratchin'*, is entirely different. Regarded today as one of Eddie's most effective and menacing instrumentals, this well thought-out rocker possibly featured Eddie playing all the instruments himself, through the technique of overdubbing.

At some point during early to mid-1958, Eddie recorded a track entitled *Cruisin' The Drive-In*. The acetate wasn't discovered until 1993 when Rockstar's Tony Barrett found it at the Cochran family home. This laid-back rocker probably featured The Four Dots on backing vocals and sounds quite awkward in places, so it was probably abandoned as a potential recording experiment without the benefit of a proper run-through or rehearsal. Eddie contributed a rather slow-paced vocal, but managed a good guitar solo.

Eddie and Jerry first met The Four Dots (bass vocalist Warren Crosby with Jewel Akens, Jerry Stone and possibly Eddie Daniels) at the offices of American Music. Jerry soon took them under his wing and used them on many recording sessions before securing the group a contract with Liberty's first subsidiary, Freedom.

Another track discovered by Tony Barrett, again on acetate, featured Eddie singing the Baker Knight composition *One Minute To One*. It is highly probable that Eddie recorded this at some point during the early summer of 1958, maybe prior to his recording of *Summertime Blues*. The arrangement, complete with heavy echo and The Johnny Mann Chorus, makes this rock ballad almost identical to *Sittin' In The Balcony*. Even Eddie's vocals and guitar solo are practically identical. The similarities are startling and Liberty quite possibly considered releasing *One Minute To One* as a single during this period. Prior to *Summertime Blues*, Cochran's chart success had begun and ended with his first release for Liberty, and these were desperate times for Eddie. The thought of going back to material such as *Sittin' In The Balcony* by releasing *One Minute To One* would have been a considerable step backwards in his career, however. Fortunately, shortly after this song was recorded, Eddie and Jerry wrote *Summertime Blues*, and further remakes of *Sittin' In The Balcony* were no longer required.

I guess success is measured by your financial security. *Summertime Blues* was very big. As far as the company was concerned, that was the most important, but as far as I was personally concerned, I liked *Sittin' In The Balcony* because that was Eddie's first record and also it proved that it could be done – to take an unknown, give them a good tune and a good production. Cochran had a great deal to do with the history of Liberty Records, the good part of Liberty.

Si Waronker

In September 1958 Liberty Records launched its first subsidiary label, Freedom. In later years the company formed further subsidiaries to cater for the variety of specific musical styles around. Liberty had a wide range of artists and this diversification into offshoot labels prevented the company being cluttered with too diverse a range of recordings.

Secondary labels also had a very practical marketing purpose. Many distributors and disc jockeys restricted themselves to a limited number of releases from each label, and *Billboard* would also restrain the amount of listings it would credit each company with. Having a subsidiary label therefore allowed Liberty more versatility, and the appropriately named Freedom label was set up by Waronker mainly to release rockabilly music.

'The reason we had Freedom was because at one time we got a little lucky, and we thought that by having a secondary label we could work with the DJs who weren't happy about playing just one label's records. If you had something on Liberty that was great, and you had something on Freedom too, meaning they didn't have to have more than one from the same label. Don't forget there were a lot of independent companies around at the time, where today you don't find the same situation. That's the reason we had the two labels. We started to buy other labels later on, such as Dolton Records, which The Ventures were on. Bob Reisdorff was the guy running it and the amount of hits that came out of Dolton were, at one point, equal to what we had on Liberty.'

Eddie doubled as a session guitarist and as a contributing arranger on a number of releases for Freedom. Recorded at Goldstar, *It's Heaven* and *My Baby (She Loves Me)* were recorded for Jerry Stone with The Four Dots, along with a backing track for *Don't Wake Up The Kids*, which included members of The Blue Caps helping out. With Johnny Meeks playing guitar, along with Cliff Simmons on piano and Clyde Pennington on drums, Eddie played bass guitar as well as providing another guitar overdub. The Four Dots added a vocal at a later date.

In 1965 Jewel Akens, vocalist for The Four Dots, also recorded the hit *The Birds And The Bees* on Era Records, a label initially founded by Waronker's cousin, Herb Newman.

Eddie provided lead guitar on a few of Freedom's releases although none of these recordings made any headway in the charts. In fact, while the later Imperial and Dolton labels produced many hit makers including The Ventures, The Fleetwoods, Jackie De Shannon and even Cher, Liberty's first subsidiary, Freedom, did not enjoy the same success.

One Freedom artist who did eventually prove successful was Johnny Burnette, who, after three unsuccessful releases on Freedom, moved to Liberty and adopted a new pop persona far removed from his rockabilly image of the 1950s, recording the pop ballads *Dreamin'* and *You're Sixteen*.

Although Si had already started to recognise Eddie's ability in the recording studio, he does not claim to have given Cochran or Capehart the responsibility on Freedom that they have been documented as having. At the time of Freedom's launch, the trade press stated that 'all A&R activities for the label will be headed by Jerry Capehart' although any involvement from either Eddie or Jerry, especially Jerry, is denied by Si. 'We allowed Eddie a lot of latitude, as I said before, but Jerry was more of an entrepreneur and he and Eddie were very close. So when they came to me with an idea for something to record I would either say yes or no. Most of the time I would give them the benefit of the doubt. Don't forget, we were hungry for product also. We were small but trying to grow very fast. But giving somebody the latitude to record whatever they wanted? Never.

'At one point Jerry was like Eddie's second arm. They had fights like everybody else does, but I'd say they were quite close in that part of his career. At one point Jerry was in the studio a lot and I got a little tired of that. He was not a musician like Eddie and I would say that the input Eddie had to offer was very helpful, but the input that Jerry had to offer was not as helpful, so I had no time for that kind of stuff.'

At the time of Freedom's inception, as well as Eddie Cochran, Capehart was managing Johnny Burnette, The Four Dots and B-movie actor and would-be rock'n'roll singer John Ashley. Johnny Burnette and The Four Dots both saw releases on Freedom that were produced by Jerry Capehart and featured Eddie on guitar, who undoubtedly assisted in the production as well. It seems possible that, due to the success of *Summertime Blues*, Liberty's renewed faith in Cochran and Capehart meant that the duo had a stronger influence when it came to getting artists signed to Freedom, or at least signed to the label on their recommendation.

'Eddie was friendly with many of the good rock'n'roll artists of the time,' Si explains. 'He was friendly with Buddy Knox, whom I later signed to Liberty, but there were no big artists that were signed to

Freedom except who you now know. We had too many artists on Liberty at one time. Freedom was set up simply to give them a chance.'

In those days we didn't look at these things as history. We did things as it had to be at the time, not because we thought we'd look back at these things thirty or forty years later. So when we cut Eddie Cochran, he was only interested in what he was doing and what his guitar was sounding like.

Stan Ross

After *Summertime Blues* had run its course in the charts, the need for a similar-sounding follow-up became the primary concern for Liberty Records. Eddie and Jerry had been experimenting with a song they had both written, tentatively titled *Let's Get Together*. This song was written using the same formula as *Summertime Blues*, featuring a driving acoustic guitar to propel the song forward and with just the right amount of humour and teenage rebellion in the lyrics. Eddie and Jerry certainly felt that *Let's Get Together* had potential and all the right ingredients to make a perfect choice for Eddie's next single.

On 10 October 1958 Si Waronker booked Eddie an evening recording session at Goldstar Studio and, accompanied by Guybo on bass, Earl Palmer on drums and Ray Johnson on piano, Cochran began to record the backing track for *Let's Get Together*.

Don't Ever Let Me Go, written by Dale Fitzsimmons, had been chosen as a possible B-side. This track had already been recorded at RCA's Studio in Hollywood on 7 July although the Musicians Protective Association contract between Liberty Records and Eddie Cochran for 10 October reads that *Don't Ever Let Me Go* was also recorded with *Let's Get Together*. Signed by Simon Waronker and Eddie Cochran, the document also reads that *Let's Get Together* was originally titled *Come On Everybody*.

After *Let's Get Together* was completed and Eddie's vocals were added to the recording, the finished take still lacked the drive and energy that *Summertime Blues* had conveyed. The problem seemed to be in the title. The line 'Let's get together', which was repeated at the end of each verse, wasn't dynamic enough and was the wrong choice as the title of a rock'n'roll song. The answer came in the opening lyrics 'Well, c'mon everybody and let's get together tonight . . .'

In a moment of inspiration, Eddie and Jerry retitled the song *C'mon Everybody* and a new backing track was recorded, this time with stops at the end of each verse in order to emphasise the song's new title, and a new rock'n'roll masterpiece was created.

The intro, with its menacing bassline played by Guybo on his Fender bass guitar, sets the tone of the song. Earl Palmer's drum roll encourages Eddie's forceful acoustic guitar to drive forth with the melody, and with the added bonus of tambourines to replace the handclaps of *Summertime Blues*, Eddie and Jerry created the ultimate rock'n'roll party record.

In changing the title they gave the song a new lease of life and brought back the dynamics of the previous single. While *Summertime Blues* was a tale of teenage rebellion mixed with a good amount of dry humour, *C'mon Everybody* contained the same ingredients but its overall message was to party away your woes rather than just moan about them.

Let's Get Together survived as a master and was issued on the 1962 Liberty LP *Cherished Memories*. Listening to the track today, it seems to have been played with perhaps a touch more enthusiasm than its later incarnation, whereas *C'mon Everybody* is much slicker and appears to have been meticulously worked out in order to achieve its status as the logical follow up to *Summertime Blues*.

Eddie certainly gives a more passionate vocal performance on *Let's Get Together*, but there is no denying that had the record stayed with its original title, it would certainly have been less memorable.

For full effect, the final master of *C'mon Everybody* was slightly speeded up, a half tone, allowing it to rock that little bit more!

C'mon Everybody backed with *Don't Ever Let Me Go* was released later that month. In early November one critic wrote that 'Eddie Cochran, the man responsible for the year's biggest hit, *Summertime Blues*, could have a huge fall-winter click on this follow-up offering, *C'mon Everybody*. Spirited rocker with Eddie assisting himself with some sensational guitar work. This lad is gonna stay in the big time. Flip offers Cochran on a pretty rock-a-ballad.'

Despite a huge promotional push by Liberty Records, along with Eddie's high-profile tours and television work, *C'mon Everybody* stalled in the charts at number 35 on the Billboard Hot 100. This was not an accurate reflection of the song's popularity, and no one seems to know exactly why it didn't make the Top 10 in the USA. The single was released in the UK in January 1959 and eventually rose to number 6, giving Eddie his biggest hit in Britain to date.

C'mon Everybody was successful enough in America to establish Eddie with a healthy following of fans, maintain his credibility as a rock'n'roll singer, increase the number of his live and television appearances and help Liberty Records rise out of its financial mess.

According to the Musicians Mutual Protective Association contract for 10 October, Eddie received $82.50 for the three-hour session that produced *C'mon Everybody*, while the other musicians were paid $41.25 each.

Goldstar co-owner Stan Ross was still closely involved in engineering these recording sessions: 'Basically there was no one to produce Eddie's records; I think it was a combination effort,' he explains. 'I worked with Eddie and I looked at him and he looked at me and we'd get sounds together. I'd say, "Let me hear something," and he'd play the guitar and I'd put some reverb on it. Then I'd let him hear a little eight-bar playback of what we'd just cut, and I'd say, "What do you think of this?" He'd say, "That sounds good. Could we do it all the way through?" and we would try it. Then Jerry would step in and say "That sounds good, let's leave it that way." It was run by a panel rather than one person.'

Liberty, along with other local independent record labels such as Dot and Challenge, frequently used masters created at Goldstar. Liberty often signed up the artists who cut the demos rather than recording the tracks with their own established artists, and on a number of occasions the demos themselves became big hits. When you look at the classic recordings that were originally created at Goldstar, it seems impossible that some of these were actually demos and equally impossible to term Eddie as a demo artist.

As Stan explains, 'Eddie was never considered a demo artist. He was a star. It happened at a young age; he was at the right place at the right time, during the right evolution of sound. Basically, Elvis

Presley, Eddie Cochran – these are all country-sounding rock'n'roll artists. They're not R&B, they're rock, but basically contemporary country artists. If you like Eddie Cochran, you'll like some of the country artists that came out at that time. You'd like Merle Travis, because Merle Travis and Eddie Cochran could have done the same songs, but Merle Travis was not considered a pop artist, he was considered country. It's a matter of interpretation.'

Most of the time you didn't run around showing others what you were working on. It was kinda uncool to say, 'Hey, listen to what I'm doing.' We jammed stuff from the set when we were backstage waiting to go on. All that was just an exchange of ideas. There was a lot of music backstage on those tours.'

Phil Everly

In a landmark year for Cochran, 1958 saw his recording and touring schedule reach new limits. Touring throughout the United States, reaching cities as far away as New York and Minneapolis and even off the mainland in Hawaii, Eddie was part of the new 'Show of Stars' tour where the nineteen-year-old worked alongside a headliner four years his junior, Frankie Lymon.

Entertainers touring during the 1950s did not have the benefit of personal staff, advance teams and engineers who orchestrate concert tours today – even the roadie didn't exist. Tour organisers may have provided drivers or a limited staff to help set up the equipment, but overall the responsibility lay with the entertainers and musicians themselves.

Life on the road was still very enjoyable, though, and the majority of these stars were still teenagers themselves. Following their lively performances, the young rockers found time to make their own entertainment, as Phil Everly recalls: 'After each show, Cochran, Frankie Lymon, Buddy and the Crickets and Don and I would all be up in the room, which was always full of girls. Eddie would be sitting in the middle of the bed playing his guitar and there would be an assortment of girls sitting around the bed, usually the more attractive ones, too, which was always unfortunate for us. I used to try to sit on the edge just to listen to Eddie play. Frankie Lymon would always jump up and grab the biggest woman there – he did that every time. It would embarrass the rest of us, but Cochran would ignore it. Anyway, one particular night things really got out of hand. There must have been thirty people in this room – I'm talking wall to wall people. There was a knock at the door and it was the manager of the hotel with a policeman, quite deservedly too. Eddie had a bottle of Scotch, which was a road trick that I didn't learn until later, because with a bottle you could do very well on the road if you could actually pour a girl a drink. It was a sure thing for some reason. The manager said, "Everybody out!" And this big giant policeman was with him. Anyway, everybody's filing out of the room and the manager's standing in this narrow hallway next to the door, which if you were walking straight you could just about get down – it wasn't that wide. With the big cop and the hotel manager, who looked like a weasel, we all had to go sideways to squeeze past him. So we were passing this huge policeman's chest! I was next to last leaving the room. Thirty people had already filed past the policeman and he was giving us this look, as we were all teenagers. The last one coming out was Eddie and as we went by, he looked up at the policeman and said, "You wouldn't do this if Eddie Cochran was here!"

'But the buses were a lot of fun. Everybody was on them and there was so much music going on. Four hundred miles of dirty lyrics!

'I remember doing a show up in Buffalo in a blizzard and the only people who made it to the theatre were the entertainers. When we got there, there were about nine people in the audience and we had a hundred and twenty people in the show! I mean a blizzard, snow as tall as a house, no one could get through it, apart from the tour bus – 'cos it had to. Everybody went out into the audience and while we were on Frankie Lymon was selling programmes and most of the audience was made up of acts that weren't on stage at that particular moment.'

On his twentieth birthday, booked by the General Artists Corporation, Eddie joined the GAC Super Attraction Package. Featuring Harold Crommer as MC, the tour included Bobby Darin, Frankie

Avalon, Clyde McPhatter, Jack Scott, The Elegants, The Imperials, Bobby Freeman, The Olympics, Connie Francis, Dion And The Belmonts and Buddy Holly And The Crickets.

At the close of 1958, DJ Alan Freed hosted an eleven-day, all-star show at the Loews State Theatre in New York. Starting on Christmas Day, Johnny Ray was the headliner for the first six days, then The Everly Brothers headlined the final five. Eddie appeared on the bill alongside an impressive list of stars which included Frankie Avalon, Chuck Berry, Bo Diddley, Jackie Wilson, Gino and Gina, Jo-Ann Campbell, Baby Washington, The Cadillacs, The Flamingos, The Nu-Tornados and The Crests.

According to Phil Everly, Eddie was never short of female admirers. 'We were all very moral in the 1950s. There was no such things as groupies – they didn't exist. There was always the local whore, but no one would ever fool with her. But cheap girls in the '50s actually looked it.

'Eddie could pull the prettiest girl without even talking to her. He would sit in the middle of the room and just play. As the parties would dwindle down and everybody was trying to pair up, there was always one that had got near to him and they would stay. I never saw him talk to them. The rest of us were giving the girls our life story and were trying to work out a deal. He just wouldn't talk, he didn't even click his fingers like The Fonz – it would have been uncool to do that. He just didn't do anything.'

Jerry Capehart and Sharon Sheeley accompanied Eddie during his appearances in New York. Although the press were already naming Sharon as Eddie's steady girlfriend, she felt that he didn't take any notice of her endeavours. 'I spent a fortune on a new wardrobe for that trip,' Sharon remembers. 'All new beautiful clothes, and every day I wore a different dress. All the other guys on the show asked me out, but not Eddie. He didn't pay any attention. Then, on New Year's Eve, he had this big party and had his bass player call and ask me to the party for him. He didn't even invite me himself!'

In the late 1980s, Levi jeans picked up the story to use in an advertising campaign. In the sixty-second commercial, Sharon reluctantly attended the party, discarding her new dresses for a pair of jeans and a sweatshirt, which was all that was eventually needed for Eddie finally to sit up and take notice of her. The commercial was a huge success, and ranks along with Levi's previous advertisements featuring

Eddie with his favourite gun,
the Buntline .45

Publicity photograph

PREVIOUS PAGE: Posing
outside LA with his
Gretsch 6120

Eddie with fellow rocker Teddy Randazzo, 1958

Eddie with The Kelly Four; top row, from left to right: Eddie, Jim Stivers,
Mike Henderson; bottom row, from left to right: Dave Shriver, Gene Riggio,
Mike Deasy

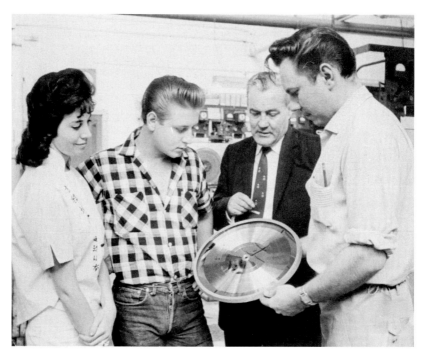

Eddie and Sharon Sheeley visit a pressing plant in LA for a publicity shoot

Relaxing at home

Publicity photograph, 1959

Taking a break at Goldstar Studios, 1959

Rehearsing at Goldstar in 1959, with Mike Deasy,
Mike Henderson and Gene Riggio

In discussion with Jerry Capehart

On stage at the Des
Moines Ballroom,
Minneapolis, 1959

John Rook presents Eddie with a trophy naming him 'The Number-One Male in the Seven-State Area of KOBH'

Eddie takes a bite from his 20lb birthday cake

Eddie rocks! Chadron, Nebraska, 3 October 1959

classic recordings from Marvin Gaye and Sam Cooke. Due to the promotion, *C'mon Everybody*, backed with its original B-side *Don't Ever Let Me Go*, was re-released in 1988, almost thirty years after it was originally recorded, and reached number 14 in the British charts.

In 1958 I was drafted into the army and I went over to Hawaii and even got a special service. Gary went with me as my guitar player, so from '58 to '60 I was gone for two years and that was probably Eddie's best time. The only thing that saved Eddie from being drafted was that he wasn't old enough. If Eddie had lived a bit longer they would have drafted him too – the army didn't care if you had hit records. Bob Denton was in the army with me and he really missed Eddie. When *Summertime Blues* came out I remember Bob and I were drinking beer at the base Scholfield Barracks on Oahu and listening to him on the jukebox and we were so grateful that he had that big hit.

Glen Glenn

Arguably, 1958 was Eddie Cochran's most creative and rewarding year as a solo artist. His first two releases of the year had failed miserably, before *Summertime Blues* and *C'mon Everybody* completely rejuvenated his musical career.

Before the year was over, he had time to go back into the studio to record a song he'd written with a young would-be songwriter named Mario Roccuzzo.

Roccuzzo was working at Wallich's Music City, a huge record store on Sunset and Vine in Hollywood. Eddie used to go there a lot, as did Corey Allen, a young actor who had become famous for playing the character Buzz in *Rebel Without a Cause*. Allen was also acquainted with Jerry Capehart, so in no time at all Eddie and Mario Roccuzzo were introduced. Eddie, Jerry, Corey and Mario went back to Corey's apartment on Sunset Strip and, while knocking back a few beers, Eddie and Mario wrote one of the greatest songs destined never to be a hit for Eddie Cochran – *Nervous Breakdown.*

'Eddie had his big ol' electric guitar with him,' Mario remembers. 'I sat down on the floor with him and I had the first beer of my life, got a real buzz from that, and on a scrap of paper I wrote *Nervous Breakdown.* I kept feeding the lines to Eddie. He'd say, "Okay, give me another line," and that's how I wrote it. I'd hand the lines to him and he'd sing 'em. Then he called me at Music City one day and said, "What are you doing in your lunch break?" I wasn't doing anything, so he said, "Come on down to Goldstar."

'I went down there and he was recording *Nervous Breakdown.* I was thrilled. This was the first song I'd ever written and here it was being recorded by Eddie Cochran – who I thought was an absolutely tremendous talent. A real gentleman was what he was. He was unique, he was talented and he had his own sound, which was very, very good.'

Nervous Breakdown is a powerhouse of a rocker. A song that has been covered countless times over the years by a huge cross section of artists, *Nervous Breakdown*, like *Summertime Blues* and *C'mon Everybody*, will always remain a Cochran original.

The song fits perfectly alongside the hard-edged rock'n'roll Eddie had created with his last two singles and it is hard to imagine the reasoning behind the decision not to release the song after *C'mon Everybody* had run its course. It was the logical follow-up, but was not released until late 1961, on the British EP *Cherished Memories Of Eddie Cochran.* With its driving bass and forceful acoustic guitars, the song carried on the Cochran tradition of powerful rock'n'roll and great lyrics that featured the same degree of teenage angst and humour that his previous singles possessed. *Nervous Breakdown* is a masterpiece.

Towards the end of the year, Eddie continued with his session work for the Freedom and Crest labels, working with his close friend Bob Denton on his Crest single *Thinkin' About You* backed with *Pretty Little Devil.* Eddie worked with Jerry Capehart's doo-wop group The Four Dots, who, during one session at Goldstar on 11 December, recorded *Fontella, Once More, Bread Fred, Hide And Seek* and *If I Were Dying.*

Even on tour in New York at the end of the year, Eddie managed to find time to play guitar for Al Lee Perkins on a demo recording of a song entitled *One Sweet Tomorrow.*

As 1958 drew to a close, Eddie Cochran was at last established as one of America's top rock'n'roll artists. His fame was spreading outside the United States, especially in the UK after *C'mon Everybody* hit the Top 10. It seemed that there would be no stopping Eddie Cochran as a chart force, but 1959 again proved to be an uncertain year for his career.

Eddie came over to the house and kicked on the door. When I opened it, there stood Eddie with both arms full of beer, and we celebrated his success. I told him I was going to Nashville to see if I could do the same, so he wished me good luck and we hugged. That was the last time I saw him.

Hank Cochran

Eddie opened the New Year recording new material for his role in the movie *Johnny Melody*. Produced by Alan Freed, Eddie – along with many of his co-stars – was booked for his appearance in the film while he was performing in Freed's All-Star show during the Christmas period.

After a few days' rest, Eddie returned to Goldstar studios on 17 January to record a session which included the Cochran and Capehart compositions *Teenage Heaven*, *I Remember* and *My Way*, along with *Rock'n'Roll Blues*.

Just as the previous year had started with a change in musical direction, with the tough-sounding *Jeannie, Jeannie, Jeannie*, 1959 opened in a similar fashion with *Teenage Heaven*. This laid-back rocker with tough vocals and a great saxophone solo was a clever rewrite of the country classic *Home On The Range*. Capehart and Cochran had taken the melody and rewritten the lyrics using their usual wit and understanding of teenage rock'n'roll fans to create a mini-masterpiece of teenage rebellion.

By now Eddie and Jerry had found their niche within rock'n'roll songwriting. *Summertime Blues* had set a standard, both rhythmically and lyrically, which was easily repeated with their follow-up single *C'mon Everybody*. *Teenage Heaven* stayed true to this tradition, with lyrics that described every teenager's desire to stay up all night, spend less time at school and have their own private telephone.

Although the two previous singles were based around a clever use of the standard three-chord progression and driven by acoustic guitar, *Teenage Heaven* marked a departure from that style. The song had a fuller, more produced feel to it, aided mainly by the addition of Plas Johnson on saxophone, whose presence is felt even more on the track *My Way*. This is a powerhouse of a song, and lyrically one of the most sexist rock'n'roll songs ever written. 'I've always gotta have my way!' Eddie claims, as he tells the object of his desire to toe the line. Plas Johnson joins in with another cracking solo, trading licks with Eddie's lead guitar, and Earl Palmer features prominently on the drums.

I Remember is the complete opposite of this. Eddie had already recorded more than his fair share of ballads during his spell with Liberty, but none was quite so beautifully played, produced and written as this. A dramatic song that featured lead guitar work played by Eddie on the Martin acoustic guitar, and sung with tremendous feeling and passion, this song is now widely regarded by fans and critics as Eddie's most convincing ballad performance. According to most of his friends and associates, he never saw himself as a great vocalist but it was to his credit that he worked hard to try and improve this aspect of his performance.

The fourth song recorded during the session, *Rock'n'Roll Blues*, is a laid-back pop song rather than the rocker that the title implies. It features acoustic guitar work from Eddie which involved overdubbing the guitar to a slower version of the song, which, when played back at its correct speed, almost sounds like a harpsichord.

From this session, *Teenage Heaven* backed with *I Remember* was released in January 1959. The single was enthusiastically reviewed in the trade papers, which stated that 'Eddie Cochran, who scored heavily with *Summertime Blues* and *C'mon Everybody*, should make it three in a row with *Teenage Heaven*. The chanter is at his R&R best as he contemplates all the pleasures found in a teenage paradise.'

Another wrote: 'Cochran should coast to a high position on the charts with this strong side. It's a smart new adaptation of *Home On The Range*, with clever lyrics, done in a rockabilly fashion.'

One reviewer in early March was less impressed: 'This bumptious rebellion will capture the crowd under age twenty, when both life and melody are viewed simply, and beat and rhythm are a lot more important than grace or subtlety. The flip, *I Remember*, is a rainbow of melodic colour with fine musicianship and could gather sales speed as easily as the top side.'

For Eddie's ninth solo release, the sales results proved disappointing as *Teenage Heaven* entered the charts for just one week and only just managed to scrape into the Billboard Hot 100 at number 99.

Teenage Heaven and *I Remember* were also the two songs Eddie performed for the movie *Johnny Melody*, which was released in January 1959, under its new title *Go, Johnny, Go!*.

Starring Alan Freed, Jimmy Clanton and Sandy Stewart, the film follows the orphaned Johnny Melody in his quest to become a singing star. The story opens in the Loews State Theatre featuring Alan Freed's All-Star show, where Eddie performed at the close of 1958, and he appears as a special guest alongside artists including Chuck Berry, Ritchie Valens, Jackie Wilson, Harvey And The Moonglows, The Cadillacs, The Flamingos and Jo-Ann Campbell.

Although *Teenage Heaven* remained in the movie, his performance of *I Remember* was cut from the final production, a decision which probably influenced Liberty to push *Teenage Heaven* as the A-side.

On early promo copies of the single, *I Remember* was credited 'As featured in the forthcoming movie *Johnny Melody*'. This credit seems to indicate that this track was originally destined as the A-side and the movie executives' decision to favour the hard-rocking *Teenage Heaven* did not fall in line with Liberty's initial plans.

Go, Johnny, Go! is a typical 1950s rock'n'roll B-movie with a wafer-thin script that does just enough to keep the audience's attention between the rock'n'roll artists performing their one-song cameos. As a marketing tool, *Go, Johnny, Go!* gave these artists the opportunity to promote their latest release in the hope that the teenage fans watching would flock to the record shops to buy it. Where Eddie Cochran and *Teenage Heaven* were concerned, unfortunately, that scenario did not happen.

Go, Johnny, Go! features some excellent performances from Chuck Berry, who proves throughout the film that he had the potential to be a fine actor. His performances of *Little Queenie* and *Memphis, Tennessee* provide some of the film's rare highlights.

Jackie Wilson looks cool and dances well throughout *You Better Know It*, The Cadillacs perform *Jaywalker* and *Please Mr Johnson*, while Jo-Ann Campbell sings *Can I Go Out?*.

For his part, Eddie is introduced by Alan Freed and launches into *Teenage Heaven* while nonchalantly pacing the stage. The ecstatic audience provide the screams on cue and, during the saxophone solo, it is bizarre to watch Eddie remove his guitar and dance with it across the stage. It all adds interest and he certainly comes across as extremely confident. It is perhaps this confidence – after all, this was his third movie appearance – that disguises what is otherwise a pretty mundane performance. Only Eddie's facial expressions show he is in complete control of the situation. He was never a particularly animated performer with an act full of gyrations and wild movements. As a singer and lead guitarist, Eddie had to work on his stage persona to compensate for his lack of movement. He developed a method of performing that involved a great deal of eye contact with the audience, very often picking out individuals and singing the song to them. He used his guitar as a prop while singing, rocking it back and forth, and during solos he would sometimes drop to one knee. He used a lot of shoulder movement and would hunch over slightly while pacing the stage holding the guitar in front of him.

Eddie was a seasoned performer; his early days of playing fêtes and local fairs, together with the hardships of the road working with The Cochran Brothers, meant that he built up a considerable amount of stage experience and could work an audience with ease. According to Joe B. Maudlin, bassist with Buddy Holly And The Crickets, 'On stage Eddie was great. When he was singing he did what he kind of did in *The Girl Can't Help It*. When he would take a solo he'd step away from the mic and he'd work the crowd with his guitar. He was just a phenomenal artist.' Eddie certainly wasn't Elvis or Little Richard, but he developed his own unique but highly effective stage act that contributed to his image as the complete rocker.

Ritchie Valens also made an appearance in *Go, Johnny, Go!*, rocking through the track *Ooh, My Head*, complete with a Gretsch 6120 – obviously Eddie's influence had rubbed off on him. The two originally forged a great friendship after appearing together on the 'Show Of Stars' tour in 1958, as well as appearing together on the 1959 'Cavalcade Of Stars' package, and the pair often socialised away from the music business.

Eddie also became good friends with Duane Eddy. The two of them and Ritchie Valens shared a passion for Mexican food, which wasn't always easy to find when they were on tour.

'I first met Eddie when he played a gig over in Phoenix,' Duane remembers. 'He was the headliner and he was just a fantastic guitar player and a great singer too. I didn't see him again until I had my first hit record when I was in New York in the fall of '58. We were all working in different rock'n'roll shows around there, and Eddie and I and Ritchie Valens used to hunt for Mexican restaurants in New York City and hang out together. All three of us came from California and we loved Mexican food. We looked in vain for Mexican restaurants. Eddie called one day and said, "You've gotta meet me for lunch because I've found a place." So we went out and met him, and it didn't look that appetising. "Well, it looks different by day," he said, but it looked so bad we decided to give the whole thing a miss. We never did get our Mexican meal.'

It changed Eddie when Buddy died. We both heard it on the radio and he was devastated, absolutely devastated. He looked at music and everybody differently from that moment on.

Sharon Sheeley

On 3 February 1959 rock'n'roll fans around the world were stunned by the tragic news that the young singers Buddy Holly, Ritchie Valens and The Big Bopper had been killed in a plane crash in America's Midwest.

From Lubbuck, Texas, twenty-two-year-old Buddy Holly was considered one of the brightest new stars in rock'n'roll. Along with his band, The Crickets, he had already enjoyed eight hit singles including such classics as *That'll Be The Day*, *Peggy Sue*, *It's So Easy*, *Lonesome Tears* and *Heartbeat*. Seventeen-year-old Ritchie Valens hit the rock'n'roll scene in 1958 with the self-penned classic *Come On Let's*

Go, which was followed by the double A-side *Donna* and the million-selling *La Bamba*. Former DJ Jiles Perry Richardson aka The Big Bopper was on the tour promoting his hit *Chantilly Lace*, the third most played song of 1958. At the time of his death, his wife Adrian was pregnant with their second child.

All three were appearing on the Winter Dance Party tour, and were suffering from the effects of the cold weather conditions. The tour bus was cramped and had no heating and, eager to reach his next destination in some form of comfort, Holly chartered a four-seater plane to take himself, Waylon Jennings and Tommy Allsup to their next destination at Moorhead. By a twist of fate The Big Bopper took Waylon Jennings' seat, as he was suffering from the flu and needed to visit a doctor. Ritchie won his seat from Tommy Allsup at the flip of a coin.

The extreme weather conditions caused the plane to crash shortly after take-off and all three singers, along with their twenty-one-year-old pilot Roger Peterson, were killed. The wreckage was discovered in a cornfield the following morning, and the news horrified rock'n'roll fans around the world.

On 5 February, just two days after the accident, Eddie recorded *Three Stars* at Goldstar Studios. The song was written as a tribute to the three dead singers by eighteen-year-old Tommy Donaldson, a DJ working for the San Bernardino radio station KFXM. In an interview Tommy Donaldson gave to Buddy Holly fan Steve Vitek, he states that after he played the song to Dale Fitzsimmons and Sylvester Cross at American Music, they asked him if he would allow Eddie to record the song.

'I was on the air at KFXM when the news came across the wire that the singers had been killed in a plane crash,' Tommy recalls. 'I read it over the air and so many people called up, kids crying, girls crying, that it really upset everybody. It made such an impression on me that, when I got off the air at about three or four o'clock, I wrote the song in the car. The next day, I had the day off so I called American Music to see if they'd be interested.

'I put *Three Stars* on tape and Mr Fitzsimmons listened to it and came back with another man whose name was Sylvester Cross. They listened to it again, then went out into the hall and started whispering among themselves. I thought, "Lord, they're gonna steal my song!" but actually they were thinking of having Eddie Cochran cut it.

'About fifteen minutes later Eddie listened to the song and said he'd cut it. So that night, the night after the plane crash, Eddie recorded *Three Stars* at Goldstar Studios. It was a Friday night. Liberty said they'd wait until Monday to decide whether to release it.'

For Eddie, recording the song was a distressing experience. He had been close to both Buddy Holly and Ritchie Valens and found it difficult to record the song, as Tommy explains: 'After three takes Eddie ran out and started crying. It meant that he couldn't sing the song, but that was so touching for him. The reason Liberty decided not to release it was that they felt they couldn't get a cut that was really saleable.'

'It's very difficult to think about what's going on in someone's head,' Stan Ross adds. '*Three Stars* was a very difficult thing, but you're out to sell records, too, y'know, but it was a tough thing to work on.'

American Music decided that Tommy Donaldson should record his own version with Carol Kay, which was released on Crest Records. Using the pseudonym Tommy Dee, and despite another strong cover by Ruby Wright, the Crest single became the label's first national hit, rising to number 11 on the Billboard Hot 100.

Eddie's version did not see the light of day in America until 1972, when it was included on the United Artists double LP *Legendary Masters Series No.4*. In the UK, however, *Three Stars* was released as a single in 1966 coupled with a re-release of *Somethin' Else*.

Eddie spent the early part of 1959 working in the studio. The Freedom label provided both him and Jerry with the opportunity to work with artists such as Johnny Burnette, Jerry Stone And The Four Dots, Jay Johnston and Barry Martin, and along with his work with other artists who recorded for the small labels throughout Holly-wood, Eddie cut down on his hectic touring schedule and involved himself in as many projects as possible.

Eddie had a very definite presence. He had that good
combination of recording and musical sense, stage
presence and a sense of writing. He was one of the
best guitar players I ever knew.

Dick D'Agostin

Throughout the latter part of 1958, Eddie began to use Dick
D'Agostin And The Swingers as an occasional back-up band for his
club dates in LA and on occasional short tours.

The Swingers had already carved out a solid reputation as a back-
up band working with rock'n'roll artists who visited the Los Angeles
area, and they were also enjoying local fame in their own right
through the singles they were releasing on Dot Records.

The band were formed in the mid-1950s by Dick, a multi-
instrumentalist adept at playing piano, guitar and bass, along with his
brother and rhythm guitarist Larry D'Agostin. Drummer Gene
Riggio and lead guitarist Dave Oster were the first musicians brought
in by the brothers, saxophonist Paul Kaufman and bassist Wayne
Messick being added in 1956 to bolster the line-up.

The group made a couple of singles for the small Accent label
before signing with Dot Records in 1958 where one of their songs,
Nancy Lynne, achieved Top 40 status in the LA charts.

By the summer of 1958 Eddie had tentatively looked into adopting
a group of musicians to use as a road band after becoming disillusioned with the tour musicians provided by his promoters. The
only trusted musician he could take with him was Guybo. Occasionally, on local club dates, Jerry Capehart, or whoever was available,
would sit in on drums and this unsatisfactory situation, along with the
usually inept but well-meaning musicians provided, helped make
Eddie's mind up to form a permanent road band. With the success of
Summertime Blues and *C'mon Everybody*, he could demand a higher fee
for personal appearances, making affording a band less of a problem.

During late 1958, Eddie handpicked a group to take on a short tour
of Canada. Guybo was on bass, Gene Riggio was on loan from The
Swingers, house pianist Jim Stivers came from The Whip, a club
Eddie frequented in Long Beach, and Jimmy Seals was added on saxophone to complete the line-up.

The tour went well and Eddie's decision to form a permanent backing band seemed validated. Besides, Gene Vincent had The Blue Caps and Buddy had The Crickets, so it seemed only right that Eddie should be accompanied by his own personal musicians.

On flyers advertising Eddie's performances throughout 1958 and '59, the group's name changed on a regular basis. Eddie Cochran And His Orchestra was a popular choice in early 1959 and The Swingsters also made an appearance (although that could be a misspelling of The Swingers). Eventually The Hollywood Swingers was chosen for the band and it was used throughout the summer of 1959 and onwards.

Just as the group's name changed frequently, the line-up did so too, and wasn't settled until the late summer. Guybo decided to quit the road after marrying his long-term sweetheart Marilyn. He continued to remain Eddie's first choice in the recording studio, and would occasionally help out on television appearances, but he had grown tired of life on the road and wanted to settle down. 'Connie had the opportunity to go on tour,' his wife Marilyn explains, 'but we were recently married so he didn't know what he wanted to do. He was disillusioned with the management and he decided not to go. I'm glad he decided that.' Along with Dick D'Agostin And The Swingers, Guybo continued to work with Eddie throughout early 1959 until a replacement could be found.

In an interview with noted Cochran researcher Tony Freer, Dick D'Agostin reminisced about his time spent with Eddie: 'I've got to say that the guy I worked with most, and liked best, was Eddie Cochran. I first met him when we were signed to Liberty Records after our time on Dot Records. We became stablemates and toured.

'Although Dick D'Agostin And The Swingers worked with just about everyone, Eddie was the most fun to work with. I liked his intensity but he always had a good time. There was always something going on – some joke brewing!'

During this period, a tour of the Midwest was arranged and Eddie turned to Jim Stivers and asked if he could work on tour as his bass player. Dick D'Agostin had already taken up the piano-playing duties and along with the other members of the Swingers (Gene Riggio on drums, Paul Kaufman on sax and Larry D'Agostin on rhythm) all that was needed was a replacement for Guybo. Jim Stivers had never touched a guitar in his life but decided to ignore that minor detail and go on the tour.

The first stop was Montana and the band travelled together in Eddie's 1958 Ford stationwagon, with a U-Haul trailer at the back to transport all the instruments and equipment. The stationwagon was reportedly bought by Liberty Records from the royalties claimed for *Summertime Blues*, although Si Waronker denies this, so it seems likely that Eddie bought the car himself, with his parents' help on the initial payments.

During the journey, Jim Stivers' conscience got the better of him and he decided to confess his inability to play the guitar to Eddie and the band. According to Jim, Eddie found the situation highly amusing, and even funnier when Jim added that he hadn't even brought a bass along with him. They decided to stop their journey and purchase one and Eddie spent the rest of the trip teaching Jim the rudiments of the instrument.

Shortly before his death in 1992, Jim Stivers recalled the first night of that tour: 'For our first performance that night, Eddie took a piece of white tape and stuck it on the back of the neck of the bass guitar. He marked each fret and where all the chords were at. Most of Eddie's songs were in A or E. I really wasn't doing very well and my fingers were bleeding because they were not used to the strings. When we all got off the stage, the local DJ said to Eddie, "Hey, the band sound great, but what's wrong with the bass player?" Eddie said, "Don't worry, he's a jazz musician!"

'After that, Eddie told me he wanted me back on piano because Dick D'Agostin could play bass, and that was that!'

Shortly after this tour, Dick D'Agostin was drafted into the services, so Eddie asked Jim to find him a new road band. Mike Henderson was brought in on tenor sax, along with his friend Mike Deasy, who played good lead guitar and also baritone sax. Finally, Don Meyer became the bassist, and the ever-present Gene Riggio retained his role as drummer. By the summer of 1959 the band was complete, rehearsals were undertaken and another tour of the Mid-west commenced, although Don Meyer left shortly after the tour and Jim bought in Dave Shriver to replace him.

The Hollywood Swingers were at last complete and remained with Eddie not only on his tours and television appearances, but also on many of his studio sessions from the late summer of 1959 onwards.

We'd sit and play acoustic guitars. We'd swap licks and chords and I learned a lot from watching Eddie play. We used to go to Johnny Burnette's and hang out, everyone would just get out acoustic guitars and we'd play all night. It wasn't competitive. It wasn't that we were trying to play faster or better than him, but everybody knew that Cochran was the best player.

The fun never left what he did. He may have been intense but he had a joy in music that he didn't have in anything else.

Mike Deasy

Once Dave Shriver joined the band, the line-up for The Hollywood Swingers didn't change again – although the group's name altered one last time, to The Kelly Four. This didn't happen until later in the year, as right up to October 1959 the band were still appearing with Eddie as Jim Stivers And The Hollywood Swingers.

The reason behind choosing The Kelly Four as the group's new name centres around an instrumental single that Eddie and Jerry Capehart recorded during the late summer of 1959, which was leased to Silver Records, another label owned by Sylvester Cross.

Silver Records operated from the American Music headquarters and may have been set up to provide Eddie and Jerry with an outlet for the various recording projects they were working on. The success of *Summertime Blues*, *C'mon Everybody* and later Cochran singles helped raise Eddie and Jerry's standing with the LA music fraternity. As they were both under contract to American Music, who saw a remarkable improvement in fortunes after publishing *Summertime Blues*, Cross may have decided to allow the pair a certain amount of control over the releases on his new label.

Guybo backed with *Strollin' Guitar* was issued on Silver 1001 in late 1959; Eddie's desire to make an instrumental record had been long standing. It was obvious that Liberty Records had no interest in releasing an instrumental from him – they believed that Eddie's fans were not particularly interested in his guitar playing and a record in this style would only confuse their attempts to establish him as a successful singer.

Cross, on the other hand, was more sympathetic to Eddie's desire to be seen as a more versatile musician, particularly as Cochran and Capehart were under contract to American Music and he would be guaranteed the copyright on anything he allowed them to release on Silver or Crest.

Of course, as a Liberty artist, anything released on these labels could not be credited to Eddie, so a fictitious name was created for the purpose of the single. Apparently The Kelly Four was chosen as an indication of Eddie's Irish ancestry, but whatever the reasoning behind the name, it was added as the credit for the record.

Some of Eddie's later singles on Liberty Records were published by their own in-house company, Metric Publishing. This seems to indicate that any contract Eddie had initially signed with Cross and American Music was not long term and may have expired by mid-1958. Eddie remained loyal to Sylvester Cross, however, and they continued to work together on various projects throughout his recording career.

Guybo, with a title chosen as a tribute to Eddie's long-standing friend and sideman, started life in April, but Eddie decided to return to the song on 25 August and record it in a satisfactory master. It is possible that he played all of the guitar parts and the bass himself through overdubbing, and that after the track was finished a drum overdub was added. This may have been more as an afterthought rather than through any real planning, as the drum seems out of place and Eddie had to spend time getting the track to run smoothly with the drum intro. The song is often referred to as *Drum City* because of the final overdub, and although this was considered as a title at one stage, loyalty to his friend won out and the name *Guybo* remained.

The menacing *Strollin' Guitar*, recorded the day after *Guybo* on the 26th, is again built up with layers of guitar and bass overdubs. These were all produced by Eddie, and the two songs made a very impressive instrumental release. A great deal of thought and effort went into the recording of both songs, and in no way can the record be viewed as a throwaway single for either Eddie or Jerry Capehart.

One review for this on 12 December read: '*Guybo* – exciting drum-beat is a solid gimmick, and guitars also do their share in producing this worthy combo date. Could happen strong. *Strollin' Guitar* – A nice-sounding, no-hurry pace on this end. Guitars get the important work.'

The next release after *Guybo* and *Strollin' Guitar* on Silver Records was a single credited to The Voices Of Allah, which turned out to be John Ashley and The Four Dots featuring Eddie on lead guitar. *Seriously In Love* was written by Johnny Burnette as a fairly slow piece of late-'50s doo-wop and was actually recorded the previous year, on 5 September 1958.

The song was one of four recorded at Goldstar Studio between 5 and 18 September that year. The other recordings were *It's Heaven* and *My Baby She Loves Me*, which were released as a single on the Freedom label, credited to Jerry Stone With The Four Dots. Then, the final song, *Take My Hand I'm Lonely* remained unissued until Rockstar Records released it on the *Hollywood Sessions* LP in early 1986.

Jerry Capehart also teamed up Jewel Akens and Eddie Daniels. With Cochran assisting on their musical arrangements, playing guitar and supplying bass vocals, a further two songs were released on Silver Records – *Opportunity* backed with *Doin' The Hully Gully*. These tracks were released in early 1960 and received lukewarm reviews, one stating that the A-side 'might move' and that the B-side was an 'infectious rock novelty'.

Interestingly, *Opportunity* was originally coupled with *Strollin' Guitar* for some reason and given the catalogue number Silver 1004. The single was re-pressed with *Doin' The Hully Gully* replacing *Strollin' Guitar*, but still retained the same catalogue number, making both records real collector's items.

A second single by The Kelly Four, this time featuring Henderson, Deasy, Riggio, Stivers and Shriver, was released by Silver in May 1960. *Annie Has A Party* backed with *So Fine, Be Mine* may have been recorded towards the end of 1959 with Eddie at the helm as the producer.

Rock'n'roll was not violent. It's very angry and violent now and I don't care much for where they've taken our music. The rock'n'roll concerts we did were in skating rinks and auditoriums and people came there to have fun. It was a whole different attitude.

Mike Deasy

According to Jim Stivers, the change of name for the band proved extremely fortunate for the owners of The Whip, the club where the guys would return to play a residency whenever Eddie was not on tour. Apparently their name, Jim Stivers And The Hollywood Swingers, would not fit on the advertising marquee above the club, and was always the cause of friction between Jim and the club owners. Eddie's decision to rename his backing band The Kelly Four meant that Jim and the boys now had a name that fitted perfectly on the marquee, immediately solving the problem.

Dave Shriver, bass player for the group, explains how he came to be a member of The Kelly Four, and recalls his experiences on the road with Eddie Cochran: 'Jim Stivers had seen me playing with a group called The Russi Brothers, who were a lounge group. He was running around looking for me when he found me playing in Long Beach with Gene Connor. He said that he had been looking for me for two weeks and we would be working with a guy named Eddie Cochran. Eddie Cochran was only a rumble then, but he said we were going to make records and go on the road, so I said, "Great, I'm into it." Jim Stivers made a deal with Gene Connor to get him another bass player, so Gene let me off.

'We went out once as The Hollywood Swingers, then we became The Kelly Four. That was Mike, Mike, Gene and Jimmy and myself. We toured all the way back to Michigan and Canada – the whole thing, Washington, Oregon, Idaho. We really did a lot in Canada. I think the farthest south we went was Texas. We played a big rock'n'roll show in Dallas during Thanksgiving with Snuff Garrett who was a DJ at the time. Just Gene and I went down to that. Actually we played with Trini Lopez at Jack Ruby's club. We weren't booked to gig at Jack Ruby's, we just went and sat in. We were playing a big concert down there, back when The Four Seasons were still The Royal Teens.

'When I wasn't on the road with Eddie, I did a residency down at The Whip. Eddie would come in and play maybe once or twice a week. He was doing his Hollywood stuff – going places, being seen.'

As far as his own promotion was concerned, Eddie was more interested in music than in enjoying the media attention his position as a pop idol imposed upon him. He often didn't turn up for his many appointments, choosing instead to concentrate on making music and helping other musicians.

According to Sharon Sheeley, Eddie 'did everything not to be a star. He didn't go to parties, he didn't do magazine layouts, he didn't hang out with the other rock stars. They all hung out with him, but he wanted to be taken seriously as a musician. I remember a reporter in England asked Eddie how it felt to be a star and he said, "Well, I don't know, I've never been up there. It's a long way to go." That's how he felt. He was so modest he took it all as a joke.'

Dick D'Agostin also recalled a story that highlights Eddie's lack of interest in self promotion: 'He made an appointment with one of the local radio stations to do an interview. Later, he told me he didn't want to go through with it. I tried to talk him out of missing it, as he had made the commitment. Eddie said that if I felt so strongly about it, I ought to go in his place – which I did! The disc jockey did the interview thinking that I was Eddie. Having been friendly with Eddie, I did know quite a lot about his life and career and was able to respond accordingly. Following the interview and during the show later that evening, the disc jockey arrived with two girls and was obviously telling them how he'd met Eddie Cochran earlier in the day. Just at that time, I got on stage to announce: "And now, the pride of Liberty Records – Eddie Cochran!" and of course the DJ suddenly realised that it wasn't the same person he'd interviewed! He just stood there with his mouth wide open and those two girls on his arm!'

Although they knew his feet remained firmly on the ground, Eddie's associates also believe that he enjoyed his fame. Dave Shriver remembers that life on the road, although innocent by today's standards, was often eventful: 'There were never any drugs, never ever. We hardly ever had any hard liquor – we just drank beer. Stories have been told about Eddie and Gene trashing hotel rooms, but we never trashed anything ever. The toughest thing that ever happened when I was with Cochran was that Mike and Mike stole some pillows from a motel in Nebraska – that's the extent of it. It was just wine, women and song. We used to have girls who followed us called the Okie Chicks – we met them in Oklahoma and they travelled all over with us in Oklahoma and then we would play other places and they'd show up too. They were like our first groupies. There was about six of them. They were really nice girls. No demands. In some places, the people were so jealous of you because the girls would just flock towards us, so people resented it.

'We were heckled by the small-town big guys, but I never saw

Eddie get into any trouble. He didn't have to – if anything happened, we were there. He used to take his gun on tour with him and he would do a fast-draw trick to see if you could clap your hands before he put a gun between them.

'Gene was the inside packer, and I was the outside packer, then Mike and Mike would bring all the stuff out. Apparently some guy came out threatening to beat Eddie up once, but Eddie pulled the gun on him, saying, "If I was you I'd back off" or "Turn around and get out of here if you can." But it was no big face off.'

Guitarist Mike Deasy also remembers his experiences with Eddie and The Kelly Four: 'In the last couple of years of high school I had a band called Mike Deasy And His Big Guitar. We backed different people and worked weekend concerts with people like The Everly Brothers and Ritchie Valens. The band at various times had everyone in it from Sandy Nelson to Jim Horn and Mike Henderson, Mike Vermay and Steve Douglas, and we were all in high school at the time. We also did occasional recordings in people's garages.

'We went on the road with The Coasters in the summer of 1959. Then, through Jimmy Stivers, I got into the Cochran tours. Guybo had been playing bass with Eddie; I don't know the circumstances in which Guybo left, but Stivers was originally hired into Eddie's band as a bass player. When he came off this first tour, he hired me and Mike Henderson and The Kelly Four guys, then Stivers played piano and Dave Shriver played bass, I played guitar and sometimes I played baritone sax. Gene Riggio came over from the previous road band.

'We did most of our touring in cars that were always going as fast as the car would go. We got to everywhere we were supposed to be by the hair on our chinny-chin-chins! There was one tour in North Dakota where it rained so hard that the mud got really thick, and the roads were not that good anyway. By the time we got there, the concert was almost over but we went in there covered in mud. Eddie was covered in mud, but he got out his guitar and played for as long as the people wanted to hear him. He really liked his audiences and he played there, mud and all, and we went back later and gave them another concert for free. He was very cool about stuff like that.

'There wasn't really a lot of time – it wasn't as if we could go fishing or golfing when we were on the road. We were driving hundreds of miles, then we'd do a concert, go to sleep, get up and drive hundreds of miles again the next day. There wasn't any down time. One of the things Eddie would do was shoot rabbits out the car window – that was quite a trick at a hundred miles an hour.

'Stivers was in charge of our entertainment. He was older than the rest of us and quite a hustler, so he would run things. Some of the guys were married and some weren't, so the parties were not for everyone. Eddie liked the ladies, but he wasn't stupid about it. As far as I could see, Eddie and Sharon were very serious. He was pretty straight with her as far as I knew.

'Jim and I got along fine, but if he was in charge of the money, we knew that by the end of the week someone wasn't going to get paid. He always had some story and even took out taxes every week that were supposed to go the government and he never sent them in – so he was entertainment within himself.'

I saw an album cover hanging in my local record store when I was growing up. That black-and-white picture of Eddie on the cover with his hair slicked back and a Gretsch just spoke to me. I didn't know who he was, or if he was any good, but I had to buy that record.

Side one, track one was *Somethin' Else* and it just blew my socks off! You have to remember, when I bought this record in 1969, the type of music being played then was psychedelia, yet this cut right through all that. It was the hardest-rockin' song that I still think I have ever heard. And hard rock doesn't just need your guitar turned up to eleven; it's the attitude.

Brian Setzer

Along with members of The Kelly Four, who were frequently being used on recording sessions, Eddie completed an impressive amount of material throughout 1959, although many of these recordings were not released until after his death.

On 23 April at United Recorders in Hollywood, he recorded *Weekend* and *Think Of Me*. *Weekend* had been written with Eddie in mind by Bill and Doree Post, a husband and wife team who also made their own recordings for Crest Records. They were contracted to American Music and recorded eight singles from 1958 until 1961, all of which flopped, but found success when Connie Stevens took a song of theirs entitled *Sixteen Reasons* and made it a Top 10 hit on both sides of the Atlantic.

Eddie took *Weekend* and turned it into a true rocker. Again, the acoustic guitar took centre stage and provided the main drive and energy, then hand-claps were added along with a female chorus. The finished product became a Cochran masterpiece.

It is hard to understand why *Weekend* was never released as a single during Eddie's lifetime, as it had all the qualities of his previous successes. The humour was present, including Eddie's Kingfish impression (which he had used to great effect on *Summertime Blues*) and the music was certainly based heavily around his trademark bass riffs and powerful acoustic chords. The song was eventually released in June 1961 in the UK and rose to the number 15 position, enjoying a long stay in the charts and becoming one of Eddie's best-loved rockers.

Also completed at United Recorders during the same period was *Think Of Me*, a syrupy ballad that did not suit Eddie at all. The female backing chorus, although irritating but not overpowering on *Weekend*, were completely over the top on this track and Eddie's vocals were strained during the chorus. All in all, this recording deserved to stay buried, but it eventually escaped onto the B-side of *Never*, a UK release in 1962.

During the summer of 1959 Eddie also appeared as a session musician for a variety of artists. On the Freedom label he played guitar on Jay Johnson's *Walk The Dog* and for Barry Martin's *The Willies* and *Minnie The Moocher*. On the Coral label he supplied vocals and guitar for Baker Knight on the track *Just Relax*.

In June Eddie also recorded an early demo version of *Three Steps To Heaven*, a song that would later become a huge hit. Written by him and his brother Bob Cochran, Eddie supplied lead vocals and guitar for this recording along with Guybo and probably Gene Riggio on drums, but this version remained unreleased until 1980 when it was included on the United Artists 20th Anniversary box set, two decades after the singer's death.

The main difference between the original demo and the later commercial version is in the lyric. In the demo Eddie starts the song with the line 'The formula for heaven is very simple . . .' whereas the later recording opens with the familiar 'Now there are three steps to heaven . . .' It was just the matter of swapping two verses around.

The music and the arrangement remained the same, but the demo retains a certain haunting quality, probably due to the heavy reverb on Eddie's vocals and the overall sparseness of the backing.

Eddie's tenth single for Liberty Records, recorded at Goldstar Studios on 23 June 1959 and released the following month, would prove to be as enduring a rock'n'roll classic as *Summertime Blues* and *C'mon Everybody*: *Somethin' Else* backed with *Boll Weevil Song* would also prove to be one of Eddie's most powerful rockers. After The Sex Pistols took the song back into the UK charts in the late 1970s, it is easy to understand why Eddie became regarded by many as 'the Grandfather of Punk'. The driving bass and crashing drums, tough vocals and superb lyric that was another wry commentary on teenage woe and hardship (this time telling the tale of not having the right car to attract the object of his desire) meant that the song was maybe too tough for 1959.

Overall, *Somethin' Else* did receive good reviews, especially in *Billboard*, where it was given special mention as the magazine's 'pick of the week': 'Cochran could bounce back into the charts with this strong effort,' the review claimed. '*Somethin' Else* is a moving rocker that is given a rhythmic chant. *Boll Weevil* is a rockabilly adaptation of the traditional folk tune.'

Sharon Sheeley and Bob Cochran both wrote *Somethin' Else*, although Jerry Capehart later insisted that he and Eddie also contributed both to the lyric and the musical arrangement during the recording session.

Eddie and Jerry were credited as the writers for *Boll Weevil Song*, although the song was regarded as a traditional folk tune. It was probably inspired by the Fats Domino version, although Pat Boone also recorded a song entitled *Rock Bo Weevil* which appeared around the same period.

Eddie's *Boll Weevil Song* stayed true to its roots until the last verse, which included the line, 'If anybody should ask you who it was that sang this song, say a guitar picker from Oklahoma City with a pair of blue jeans on' – a comment that not only reinforced the myth that

Eddie was an original Okie, but one that gave the song a personal touch, adding to the recording's charm.

Somethin' Else was performed on *Dick Clark's American Bandstand*. Eddie had already made appearances on the show to promote *Jeannie, Jeannie, Jeannie* and *Summertime Blues*, as well as his classic performance of *C'mon Everybody* on 24 November 1958. His final appearance on *Bandstand* was on 10 October 1959, when he performed *Sittin' In The Balcony*. As with all his other appearances on the show, he mimed to his recordings.

Despite the promotion and promising reviews, *Somethin' Else* stalled in the Billboard Hot 100 at number 58. In the UK, by contrast, it reached number 22, a sure sign of Eddie's increasing popularity across the Atlantic.

We all loved to jam. If there was a place open at three in the morning we would go and play, whoever was there. Whether it was Bo Ramble or B.B. King, it was cool. There we were, a bunch of skinny kids, and they didn't care. Sometimes we would sit there and not do anything until they eventually did something we could play, but I learned more about playing the guitar by sitting in with those people than I ever did at school. It was a great time for music.

Mike Deasy

As already mentioned, on 25 August Eddie booked a session at Goldstar to complete work on the instrumental *Guybo*. Throughout the course of the day, with the help of The Kelly Four, he also completed two of the most outstanding blues instrumentals recorded by a white rock'n'roll artist during that era. *Eddie's Blues* (originally entitled *Blues For The Boss*) was based around a typical three-chord blues progression by pianist Jim Stivers and *Chicken Shot Blues* proved beyond doubt that Eddie could play any style of music that he wished.

Jim Stivers and Mike Deasy were both great blues fans, and maybe it was their influence that encouraged Eddie to experiment more. However, as B.B. King later told BBC Radio DJ Andy Kershaw, 'The only white artist that could play the music with any skill and feeling was Eddie Cochran.' King added that he and Eddie used to jam on a regular basis with fellow blues legend Lowell Fulson, writer of *Reconsider Baby*, on Fulson's front porch in LA. This was confirmed when Irish rockabilly artist Seannie Foy met Fulson during a gig in Dublin in the early 1980s, where Fulson recalled his jamming sessions with both Cochran and King. He also added that he respected and admired Eddie's grasp of blues guitar playing, and spoke of the singer with great fondness.

Eddie's Blues and the similar-sounding *Chicken Shot Blues* feature Mike Deasy on rhythm guitar, superb drumming from Gene Riggio, tough piano from Jim Stivers and great bass playing from Dave Shriver. The Kelly Four had proved to be excellent musicians on the road and Eddie's confidence in them rightly extended into the recording studio.

On these two instrumentals Eddie's guitar playing is superb. He pulls out all the stops to create one blistering solo after another, incorporating lavish amounts of banjo-style rolling of the strings, heavy use of the Bigsby tremolo and some of the fastest single-string runs to emanate from a rock'n'roll guitarist. He may have been fast with the gun on a quick draw, but if these two songs had been released during his lifetime, he may have easily earned the title of 'the fastest hands of the West'!

Eddie's Blues was released in the UK as the B-side to a reissue of *Three Steps To Heaven* in 1967, although it had previously appeared on the album *My Way* in late 1964. It remained unissued in the United States until 1972 when it was included on the double album *The Legendary Masters*.

The blues boom of the mid-1960s helped regenerate the careers of many of the music's originators. Artists such as John Lee Hooker, Sonny Boy Williamson and B.B. King gained a new generation of fans throughout England clamouring to see their shows and buy their new releases. White British blues bands such as The Yardbirds and The Rolling Stones also enjoyed huge successes by forsaking the influence of 1950s rock'n'roll and staying true to the originators of the music.

When Eddie toured the UK in 1960, he cultivated an interest in the music by performing songs such as Little Willie John's classic *Fever* and Sleepy John Estes's *Milkcow Blues*. While Elvis Presley turned *Milkcow Blues* into a furious rockabilly track, Eddie preferred to keep the song slow and mean, growling out the lyrics, and incorporating another stunning guitar solo.

Certainly, many blues artists regarded Cochran as one of the best rock'n'roll performers to experiment with the music. In one of his last interviews, Jimi Hendrix paid honour to Cochran, stating that when he died, he wanted Eddie's music to be played at his funeral. His wish was granted when he died shortly afterwards from a drug overdose.

The session of 25 August produced *Guybo*, *Eddie's Blues*, *Chicken Shot Blues* (unissued until 1982 when it was included on the Rockstar Records LP *Words And Music*) and *Milkcow Blues* as well as three songs recorded with singer and songwriter Darry Weaver, *Lovin' I'm Wastin'*, *Iddy Bitty Betty* and *Bad Baby Doll*. This last is an awful piece of pop music, complete with Weaver's flat and ponderous vocals. *Iddy Bitty Betty* fairs better and is a fine rocker complete with great guitar work from Eddie. *Lovin' I'm Wastin'* returns to the pop approach, but is far superior and probably features Eddie on bass guitar.

Darry Weaver was probably an acquaintance of Jerry Capehart's, but it is unclear in what capacity Cochran and Capehart were trying to help by allowing him time at the end of the day's session. It is possible that American Music had a share in the songwriting, or that Capehart felt he could get the songs released on Crest or Silver.

We are fortunate enough to have been afforded the luxury of hearing the many out-takes from this session. On *Bad Baby Doll*, Eddie tells the band that his guitar is out of tune and Gene Riggio yells, 'Well, tune up!' And, as Jim Stivers mentions that his foot pedal is slipping, Dave Shriver joins in by playing an out-of-tune bass run. It is clear that the band had done little or no rehearsing of the songs, and Jerry Capehart becomes increasingly annoyed with the various blown introductions. His mood is not lightened when he tells Eddie to count the song in properly, and Eddie shouts, 'One, Two, One!' at the top of his voice, causing the band to break into laughter and mess up another intro.

On other out-takes, after a messy introduction to *Milkcow Blues*, Eddie yells, 'Oh, you guys know that. Jesus Christ!' Then after completing the first take, which is loose but which contains a fantastic solo along with Eddie's best blues vocal committed to tape, the band prepare for the second take and Eddie asks Stan Ross for plenty of piano. A decision is made to change the key from A to C for the start of the next take and Eddie clearly struggles during the first few bars and exclaims, 'It's probably too high,' before Capehart calls for a halt to the proceedings soon into the take. A master was achieved, even though it contained a shorter guitar solo, on Eddie's choice rather than editing it out, and the final result was issued on the Liberty LP *Never To Be Forgotten* in 1962.

Chicken Shot Blues, although similar to *Eddie's Blues*, does contain some unique touches. Stops are incorporated into the song to allow Eddie to demonstrate his favourite blues licks, and the out-takes, which were also featured on the 1992 Rockstar CD *LA Sessions*, show the band in good humour during one of the two false starts.

The following day, 26 August, Eddie returned to Goldstar to record *Strollin' Guitar*. After this song was completed, Eddie and the band knocked out another blues instrumental, simply entitled *Instrumental Blues*, followed by ten takes of both the Hal Winn song *Little Angel* and the Cochran and Capehart oldie *My Love To Remember*.

A great admirer of Ray Charles, Eddie returned to Goldstar towards the end of the month to record Charles's classic *Hallelujah I Love Her So*. The song had already been covered by MGM artist Conway Twitty, who kept his recording fairly close to the original, but Eddie decided to approach the song from a completely different angle. As the best part of late August had been spent recording some serious blues material, Eddie and the band stayed in that vein to record a laidback bluesy version of the song, featuring a strong saxophone accompaniment from Mike Henderson and Mike Deasy. Jim Stivers adds some extra touches on the piano, while Gene Riggio and Dave Shriver drive the rhythm with drums and bass respectively.

Again, Eddie sounded completely at home with this style, and the effortless vocal phrasing and devastating guitar solo – one of Eddie's finest on his own singles – made for an exciting interpretation of the song. The whole thing was recorded live in 12 attempts, with the final take chosen as the master.

According to Jim Stivers, *Hallelujah I Love Her So* was part of The Kelly Four's set whenever they opened for Eddie on his live shows. Eddie liked their version so much he offered Jim a brand new suit in return for recording it. Whatever the truth may be, *Hallelujah I Love Her So* became Eddie's eleventh single release, in October 1959.

In 1959 Liberty employed Snuff Garrett as the label's first A&R man, who soon worked his way up through the company to produce Johnny Burnette's first Liberty single *Settin' The Woods On Fire*. Snuff eventually became the main reason for Liberty's second revival in fortunes in the early part of 1960 when he produced hit after hit for both Johnny Burnette and Bobby Vee.

Garrett's vision for rock'n'roll was to add big orchestral arrangements in order to create commercial recordings, and it was hoped that this same would work with Eddie's material. The masters for *Little Angel* and *Hallelujah I Love Her So* were then taken to Liberty Custom Recorders for further overdubs. On 21 October, without Eddie's knowledge, Garrett supervised the overdubbing of lush orchestral violins on *Hallelujah I Love Her So* and the adding of a gospel backing group to *Little Angel* two days later. By all accounts Eddie was horrified with the end results and complained bitterly to Garrett and Liberty executives.

In early November the single picked up some promising reviews: 'Eddie Cochran, who recently completed a solid chart run with his *Somethin' Else* slice, should head right back to hitsville with his newest Liberty effort. It's a sensational thumping-rock-string of the great Ray Charles-penned *Hallelujah I Love Her So*. Watch it zoom. On the under end, the chorus and ork ably assist Eddie as he emotionally knocks out a hip-swinging rock-a-ballad romancer entitled *Little Angel*. Also bears watching.'

Another wrote: 'Cochran belts *Hallelujah*, the great Ray Charles tune, over a gospelish arrangement that includes strings. It's a standout side and a likely winner. *Little Angel* is also in the spiritual side, and it's accorded a smart warble.'

Unfortunately, the single failed to chart in the US. Although Snuff Garrett's creations were later successful with other artists on the label, the teenage record buyers were not ready for a white rock'n'roller recording blues songs with heavy (and rather overbearing) violin overdubs. In the UK, however, the single made two appearances in the charts, managing to reach number 22.

I don't think any of us at the time, including Eddie, thought that we had made any major mark. Rock'n'roll was still in its infancy, we didn't know if it was going to last until next Tuesday. The so-called intelligent ones out there were telling us it wasn't going to last, so how did we know that we were going to be the originators of it?

John Rook

Eddie frequently visited Biff's Restaurant, a burger joint close to Goldstar Studio. Its manager, Maurice McCall, was an aspiring song-writer. Maurice often took the opportunity to impose his work on the young singer, which Eddie reluctantly recorded sometime during 1959.

Unfortunately, Eddie became ill during the recording session and only two songs, *Jelly Bean* and *Don't Bye Bye Baby Me*, were completed. Both were powerful rockers that remained undiscovered until the early 1980s, when Tony Barrett located them.

Present at the session were Earl Palmer on drums, The Johnny Mann Singers, Guybo on bass and possibly Ray Johnson on piano. Although Eddie was unwell, he did manage to spend a considerable amount of time on both songs, and various out-takes from these recordings can be found on a selection of albums released by Rockstar Records.

Eddie attempted to record both songs live, but eventually used a backing track for *Jelly Bean* as he initially struggled with the melody and found the lyric confusing. Listening to the out-takes, Eddie exclaims, 'Man! These words!' before launching into another take. Both *Jelly Bean* and *Don't Bye Bye Baby Me* are not particularly well-written songs, but Eddie and the band turn in strong performances, especially the guitar solo on the former and a fine gravelly voice on the latter.

It is not known if Eddie contemplated using these songs for his own purposes, as they may have been recorded as demos for McCall. However, the time was taken to add a train sound overdub to the finished master of *Don't Bye Bye Baby Me*, which indicates that Eddie, or more likely Jerry Capehart, felt the song had potential. As it turned out, the backing tracks to both songs ended up being released on the Hollywood-based Era label, but without Eddie's vocals and credited to a band called The Tigers. A doo-wop vocal group was added, which may even indicate an involvement by The Four Dots, in order to salvage a master from the session.

The two songs are difficult to place chronologically. For many years it has been assumed, from information passed onto Rockstar Records by Maurice McCall, that both were recorded during the latter stages of 1959. However, it may transpire that the session was not specifically arranged to record these tracks but that they were added to the end of a session featuring other material or even recorded at an earlier point in the year.

Eddie Cochran can never be forgotten because he created a sound and an image that to me will always be rock'n'roll, that's the look and that was the sound and the rest of us have messed around with it.

Cliff Richard

Although not released during his lifetime, Eddie's own instrumental recordings – *The Scream, Fourth Man Theme, Hammy Blues, Have An Apple Dearie* and *Jam Sand-Witch* – complete his Goldstar recording sessions for 1959.

The Scream was so named after vocal overdubs were added to Eddie's basic backing track in the early 1960s. The track was eventually released by United Artists in 1971 on *The Legendary Eddie Cochran* album.

Hammy Blues is another solo effort from Eddie and may have been considered for release on Silver Records. It shares many similarities with both *Guybo* and *Strollin' Guitar* as the bass guitar prominently drives the song with other guitar overdubs providing the melody. Drums do not feature at all in this recording.

Have An Apple Dearie and *Jam Sand-Witch* were recorded in

October and, as both titles seem to have a Halloween flavour to them, it is possible that they were intended for release on some small independent label for novelty value alone. *Have An Apple Dearie* features The Kelly Four complete with wailing sax solos and incredible drumming from Gene Riggio. Goldstar Studio boss Stan Ross provided all the weird vocal gimmicks and creaking-door effects.

Jam Sand-Witch is a highly underrated piece of Cochran magic. This mid-paced funky rocker, with an acoustic guitar providing all the lead and rhythm, first made its appearance on vinyl on the 1964 UK album *My Way*.

Fourth Man Theme featured Eddie playing all the guitar parts on his Martin acoustic. The track is an obvious take-off of the Anton Kara record *Third Man Theme*. A final guitar overdub was added and the track retitled *Song Of New Orleans* and released on Crest Records in 1961. The Crest release was not credited to Eddie, nor was he given a co-writer's credit. Instead, full artist and songwriting credits were given to Jerry Capehart.

Following these recording sessions, Eddie was back on the road with The Kelly Four. Appearing in venues throughout the Midwest, one misinformed press reporter wrote that Eddie was 'back from London where he appeared in the London Palladium with The Ted Heath Orchestra'. The article also stated that the singer was planning to embark on a new phase in his career as a nightclub entertainer, claiming that: 'He is preparing his songs and arrangements, but the highlight of the act will be a Gene Kelly-type dance. He also plays the drums, trumpet and piano in the act.'

On 3 October Eddie celebrated his twenty-first birthday on the road. Booked by the radio station KOBH for an appearance in Chadron, Nebraska, Eddie was presented with an enormous birthday cake and a trophy naming the singer 'The Number One Male in the Seven-State Area of KOBH'.

Eddie was headstrong. He would do what he wanted
to do, whether Capehart liked it or not. I guess Jerry
was a pretty talented person as far as writing songs
was concerned, but, for me, as a manager he blew it.

Bob Denton

As 1959 drew to a close, the Cochran family had made a new start,
moving from Bell Gardens to a home in Buena Park, an affluent
suburb within Orange County. Eddie still lived with his parents,
Frank and Alice Cochran, along with his eldest sister Gloria, her
husband Red and son Ed Julson.

'I was still young when Eddie was around,' Ed recalls, 'but whenever he was home, he and I used to play together a bit. We would play
army, or cowboys and indians. He and his friends were constantly
teasing me and playing little pranks on me. I had a sandbox in the
back garden in our house at Bell Gardens and Eddie would shoot me
with a water pistol through the screen.

'We all lived in the same house on Priory Street in Bell Gardens.
All the family lived really close to each other. Pat and Hank lived in
an apartment behind us, Bill lived in Lakewood and I think Bob lived
someplace in Bell Gardens. Then in October or November '59 we
moved into our new house in Buena Park.

'To me Frank was always kind and generous. He loved his family
and all of his grandkids so he and I got on very well. My mom ran
Eddie's fan club from home – she spent an awful lot of time on it,
sending out newsletters and starting up new clubs.'

'After Eddie got started, he and Dad were trying to save enough
money so that they could move out to Buena Park,' Hank Hickey
explains. 'Red and Gloria were buying a place out there which Red
bought on a GI loan, so they asked Dad and Mother to come out here
and live with them for a while.'

As far as Eddie's career was concerned, 1959 had appeared so
promising. After the successes of *Summertime Blues* and *C'mon Everybody* the previous year, then starting the next with an appearance in
another major motion picture, it seems as though Eddie was ready to
take his place as one of the most successful rockers of the era. All the
faith Si Waronker had placed in Eddie was finally paying off and it

briefly looked as if Cochran's career might finally explode into the lofty reaches of superstardom. It wasn't to be. Of Eddie's three single releases of 1959, only one, *Somethin' Else*, had made any headway in the charts, and that was only as far as number 58.

Things were looking up, though: from a creative point of view, of course, his work with Freedom and Silver Records proved that his talent was untainted by his lack of commercial success. And Eddie finally had a permanent backing band and his personal appearances throughout the country were proving popular. When he was not on the road, he could rely on his studio work to provide a regular income, so the necessity of appearing on large package tours, such as the 'Show Of Stars', began to diminish. He was still appearing on national television, most notably *American Bandstand*, where he made three appearances during 1959.

Eddie had also lost two good friends in Ritchie Valens and Buddy Holly after their tragic demise in the plane crash in Iowa. Over the years, it has been suggested that Eddie was also booked for that tour but had pulled out at the last minute. According to myth, he convinced Buddy Holly to take the 'Winter Dance Party' tour, and after Holly's death, Eddie remained racked with guilt for the rest of his own short life. No amount of digging reveals any proof to substantiate these stories but it is clear that Eddie did not become a recluse after the deaths of Holly and Valens. He certainly didn't reduce his workload throughout the year and he continued with one-nighters around the country. These mini tours were arranged to suit Eddie, in preference to the strict package tours, which usually involved weeks of gruelling nightly performances across the length and breadth of the country, all the acts travelling together on a cramped tour bus. Cochran's successes from the latter half of 1958 allowed him to go on the road as and when he wanted, travelling in the relative comfort of his stationwagon, with the added bonus of his own highly skilled backing band to accompany him.

As the decade reached its conclusion, cracks were starting to show in Eddie's partnership with Jerry Capehart. 'Let's put it this way,' Si Waronker says, 'I don't understand his part in the picture as far as Eddie Cochran is concerned at all, and I certainly didn't allow him much leeway. I don't understand where the rumours came from that he was going to run Freedom. I have no idea how that happened.

'Eddie came to me a few times and started to complain about his songwriting, that Capehart was putting his name on it. So I said, "Well, Eddie, look, that's one of the things that I don't dare mix into. If Capehart is your manager, or your agent, however you wanna put it, then whatever happens personally I don't think I can get involved in. As an artist who is under contract to the label, I'll do anything I can to help you. Now, if you come to me and tell me that you wrote this tune by yourself – fine, we'll give you credit for it. But if both you and Capehart come to me and say, 'We wrote this tune,' then I have to put it on the label as such."

'Anyway, he complained to me in several instances that Capehart did put his name on the tunes that were recorded. Jerry didn't help him at all. In fact, if Cochran had had a first-class manager he would have gone a lot further, quicker. I don't think Capehart was a hindrance particularly, but I don't think he helped him either.'

Bob Denton agrees: 'If Eddie didn't have Capehart as a manager, he would have been a lot bigger than he was. Jerry held him down, big time, I know he did. I don't understand it, I really don't. He did the same thing with Glen Campbell and Glen didn't do doodly until he got rid of Capehart. I don't think he knew enough about the music business to be handling Eddie. I never could quite figure out why Eddie kept Capehart around, except that he was under contract to him. I'm sure he would have got rid of him eventually. There were times when we had some very serious conversations about Jerry Capehart, real serious talks. He wasn't happy with Capehart, that's why I couldn't understand why he kept hanging with him. But Capehart was a pretty good songwriter too, he could write some songs.'

Certainly, Capehart's managerial relationship with Eddie was rapidly deteriorating over the course of the year. Jerry was not involved with Eddie's plans to tour the UK in the New Year, nor was he present at his next recording session at Goldstar – the producer's role for that was already taken by Snuffy Garrett with Si Waronker on hand to supervise.

It is quite possible Eddie felt that Jerry Capehart was not devoting enough time to his career. He was upset at the lack of money coming his way from his recording royalties and may have felt that his financial and business affairs were being mishandled. Capehart had spent a large part of 1958 and '59 managing The Four Dots, John Ashley, Johnny Burnette – for a brief period only – and Sharon Sheeley, as well as his regular behind-the-scenes dealings with an

Publicity photograph, 1959

Celebrating his twenty-first birthday with a lady friend,
while the Kelly Four look on, 3 October 1959

Interesting headwear! Maybe taking a leaf from Frank Sinatra's book

Eddie and Gene

Billy Fury, Eddie and Joe Brown, 1960

Eddie's official welcome to England, 11 January 1960. Vince Eager, Gene and Eddie are surrounded by female admirers

Vince Eager, Eddie and Gene smile for the camera, 11 January 1960

Gene Vincent, Eddie, Larry Parnes and British rocker
Terry Dene with two unknown females

Eddie on stage at Wembley for the NME Poll-Winners' concert

OPPOSITE PAGE: Running through *Twenty Flight Rock*
for Jack Good's *Boy Meets Girl*

Eddie with Gypsy Rose Lee,
backstage at the Liverpool Empire

Publicity photograph – a Cochran
family favourite

A mass of flowers surrounds the young singer's grave
following his burial, April 1960

assortment of tiny local record labels. It is more than likely that the pair had simply outgrown one another and, without blaming each other, Capehart and Cochran probably decided that their partnership had reached its conclusion.

In those early days we were still dealing with parents who preferred Stan Kenton and big-band shows and suddenly people like Eddie and Elvis and Jerry Lee Lewis were coming out and I think they were probably just a little too much too soon.

Cliff Richard

In 1959 the British television show *Oh Boy!* was required viewing for every teenager. The show was produced by Jack Good, a former actor who had been inspired by rock'n'roll. Jack's first television show was broadcast in February 1957. *The 6.5 Special* was aptly named as it filled the television slot directly after 6 p.m., one which had previously remained blank to allow parents to put their children to bed.

Jack had originally intended *The 6.5 Special* to be purely a showcase for rock'n'roll music but the BBC, believing that rock'n'roll was little more than a fad, disagreed with him, preferring a more family-oriented show.

His new television venture *Oh Boy!* began airing in September 1958, broadcast live from the Empire Theatre in Hackney every Saturday night. The show featured the young British rock'n'roll talent of the time, including one eighteen-year-old Cliff Richard. 'Jack was a raving rocker,' Cliff explains. 'I mean he was a rock'n'roll fanatic. He liked other forms of music but he liked the rawness and the way that we as artists, who were new to the scene, were pliable – we could do whatever he wanted. Basically *Oh Boy!* was a group of British musicians performing the hits that came from America. In other words, we'd say, "Look, we can't get Elvis but here's Vince Taylor to sing . . ." and he'd sing the new Elvis hit and I would sing a

Conway Twitty hit, or something like that. That was it – it was a very basic sort of show, a very down to earth type of show.'

Rather than continue using British artists to mimic the rock'n'roll coming from America, Jack began to look for ways to bring over American artists. In September 1959 he began to produce the *Boy Meets Girls* television show. Using the variety agents Fosters, negotiations were opened with the American promoter Norm Riley, who could guarantee appearances from artists such as Eddie Cochran, Gene Vincent and Ronnie Hawkins.

Gene Vincent first arrived at Heathrow airport on 5 December 1959. At EMI's expense, fans were driven to the airport to greet their idol before Gene was whisked away to an appointment on the BBC radio show *Saturday Club*, hosted by Brian Matthew.

Gene was booked for an appearance on *The Marty Wilde Club*, then for three appearances on *Boy Meets Girls* where he was billed as Elvis's greatest rival. His appearance on British soil was a huge success, before he moved further into Europe on to France and Germany.

By the end of 1959, however, Gene's popularity in the United States was already starting to diminish. He was almost free of commitments in the New Year, so it was announced that he would return to the UK to tour in the Larry Parnes production The Gene Vincent Show.

Larry Parnes managed a variety of contemporary British acts including Marty Wilde, Tommy Steele, Billy Fury, Joe Brown, Vince Eager and Johnny Gentle. He regularly organised a variety of package tours for these artists throughout the United Kingdom and was one of the leading rock'n'roll promoters of the era.

The Gene Vincent Show opened on 6 January 1960 in Maidstone and ran until the 17th, but Larry Parnes had already made an announcement that delighted rock'n'roll fans throughout the UK: Gene was to headline a second tour at the end of the month where he would be joined by Eddie Cochran.

It seems that the English were able to recognise talent even more than we were able to over here in America. I was going to record him over there, I was going to go to London with him and I was talking about that with the people in my company. We knew he was so big over there, it would be just as easy to record there as it was over here. So we were planning on it, but unfortunately it never came to pass.

Si Waronker

On 8 January 1960, before Eddie could leave for England, he was booked for one final session at Goldstar. Although Eddie worked throughout 1959 with The Kelly Four, Guybo and members of Buddy Holly's backing band The Crickets (Jerry Allison on drums and Sonny Curtis on guitar) accompanied him on this session. Snuff Garrett took over the producer's role for this, his first and only session with Eddie, and it was his decision to use Sonny and Jerry, who were the only musicians involved in this session.

The Crickets had only just moved out to the West Coast and Sonny recalls their beginnings in Lubbock, Texas: 'We were just Elvis clones, we hadn't figured out any particular style. I was emulating Scotty Moore, but I was really a Chet Atkins fan. When Elvis came out it blew our minds. I remember the very first night I saw him. He wore red pants and an orange jacket and white buckskin shoes. It was something. He was a good-looking dude and of course all the girls were going nuts. We were younger than he was, so he turned our heads around and the next day we started picking out Elvis stuff.

'We moved out to California on New Year's Day in 1960 and we went out there and did a little hanging out with Snuff Garrett. Snuff had moved from Lubbock down to Wichita Falls and The Crickets made it big while he was down there, so they were pretty fast friends. I hadn't met Snuffy before then.

'After we moved to LA we rented an apartment up in the Hollywood Hills. Snuff and Eddie were going to do some recordings, so my main exposure to Eddie was through being involved with those recordings. Eddie was extremely nice, a real pleasant person, even unlike he was on stage – because he came out kinda cocky on stage. I understand that he could burn people down, but in the little time I spent with him he was incredibly nice to me.

'Of course he was a big star to me at the time. I really had a lot of respect for him, he was a really good guitar player and a great singer. I loved *Summertime Blues, C'mon Everybody* and *Twenty Flight Rock*.'

As his mother and sister Gloria packed his luggage for his British tour, Eddie recorded the timeless *Three Steps To Heaven* along with *Cut Across Shorty* and *Cherished Memories*. Si Waronker was in attendance during this session. He had definite views on how the recordings should be undertaken, but as Sonny Curtis explains, the session didn't seem to work out exactly as Si planned: 'We cut *Three Steps To Heaven, Cut Across Shorty* and *Cherished Memories* down at Goldstar. I was playing the electric guitar and Cochran was playing a Martin, I think. It might have been a D18 as I recall. I was playing drums and Guybo was on bass. What a good bass player Guybo was.

'Our previous exposure to recording studios was just in Nashville, where you all stood in the room and formed a circle and they put a mic up and we went for it. But that time they were putting baffles up and we couldn't see each other. We had some timing problems and I'll never forget Si Waronker – he was already a great musician in his own right with his film work – got out in the middle of the room with his metronome and was trying to direct us. We could all see him, but we couldn't see each other and it just went from bad to worse. We solved the problem because finally Eddie said, "Hold it, this is not going to work, we're not going to make this." He was pretty much the director of the session, more so than Snuff Garrett was. Si either went home or went into the other room, and we started practising and got the song together. We could pick the songs, it was just a matter of learning to feel them, you know. It was a good, fun session, but Eddie was really under the gun for time because his plane was leaving for London at midnight. So we recorded those three songs and then he had to get ready to go to the airport.'

With the help of Jerry Allison and Sonny Curtis, this recording of *Three Steps To Heaven* ended up far more polished than the original demo. Eddie changed around the verses but basically kept the song faithful to his original recording. Again, it is driven by acoustic guitar, but good use of the backing singers – most notably The Johnny Mann Singers – added to the overall performance. The end result was a perfect example of late-'50s pop-rock and rightly deserves its status as one of the era's best-known songs.

Cut Across Shorty was a welcome return to Eddie's country roots but had a tough enough edge to be regarded as rock'n'roll. It has been suggested by Rockstar's Tony Barrett that the version of *Cut Across Shorty* that ended up as the B-side to *Three Steps To Heaven* had been recorded months earlier, as the version that emerged from the final session at Goldstar was markedly different to the single release. It was done at a much more laidback pace and this gave the song a more pronounced country feel. The B-side to *Three Steps To Heaven*, in contrast, was speeded up half a tone, just as Eddie had done with his recordings of *C'mon Everybody* and *Boll Weevil Song* in order to give them a little more drive and energy. However, on aural evidence, the two versions are different enough to suggest they were recorded at separate sessions.

Cherished Memories, written by Sharon Sheeley, is a fantastic, up-beat slice of doo-wop rock'n'roll. Jerry Allison's military-style drumming is to the fore, as are the backing vocals which give the song its doo-wop influence. Eddie sings with enormous gusto, although at times his vocals sound fairly tongue-in-cheek, as if he is having too much fun with the song. A good guitar solo adds to the impression that all the musicians involved were having a great time recording this particular track.

Three Steps To Heaven backed with *Cut Across Shorty* was released in the United States in March 1960. Despite favourable reviews, it failed to chart, although it is interesting to note that *Cut Across Shorty* was initially pushed as the A-side – particularly in America.

One review read: '*Cut Across Shorty* – A good, happy, swingin', country-rhythm side, and Cochran hands it a solid reading. Side has also been cut by Carl Smith, but this can garner plenty of the action. *Three Steps To Heaven* – An interesting rocking beat side that has a lot of spirit. Side has a fine guitar accompaniment in the folkish style.'

Another review almost failed to mention *Three Steps To Heaven*: 'Cochran's reading of the C&W tune *Cut Across Shorty* (cut by Carl Smith on Columbia) can go places in the pop field. Story of a race between two fellas to decide which one wins the gal's hand is conveyed in strong rapid-fire beat fashion. Coupler is a contagious medium-beat date.'

The single managed to get to number 108 in the charts before disappearing entirely. In the UK, it was released in May and eventually rose to number 1.

Cherished Memories was issued as a single in the UK in 1961. It was coupled with *Weekend* and rose to number 15 in the charts. It was also the title of a Liberty album which was released in the UK in late 1962 featuring a collection of songs recorded by Eddie and stockpiled in the Liberty vaults. When heard together on this album, the strength of Cochran's recorded material throughout his career is more than evident. Songs such as *Nervous Breakdown*, *Let's Get Together*, *Never*, *Rock'n'Roll Blues*, *Pink Peg Slacks* and *Sweetie Pie* together with the title track *Cherished Memories* created a powerful album release that intensified Eddie's fan base in the UK.

Another track that appeared on the album, *I've Waited So Long*, appears to have been another experiment by Liberty, or perhaps even Eddie, at attempting to crossover into more of a 'lounge-music' style. He was very impressed with artists such as Bobby Darin, and after seeing him perfrom in Las Vegas, Eddie perhaps felt that he too could branch out into this genre. The song was recorded at Liberty Custom Recorders on 1 October 1958. Some 22 takes of *I've Waited So Long* were recorded, and quite a serious attempt was made to give the song a decent production, and indeed the finished master does sound very convincing. A good vocal by Eddie, crooning away in a very good Dean Martin fashion, helped by an unknown organist and accordian player, give this gentle, almost jazz-influenced track an exceptionally authentic performance from all involved.

Seven days later, Eddie returned to Goldstar to record *Let's Get Together*, which of course later evolved into the classic *C'mon Everybody*, and this alone is probably responsible for Liberty and Eddie's decision not to pursue the idea of releasing *I've Waited So Long* as a single. However, with today's interest in 1950s lounge music, this particular recording by Eddie certainly deserves a closer listen.

Step Three . . .

When I heard he was going to England, I thought,
'Oh, God! He's going where?' We didn't put much on
to it. But when he got there, he would call and tell his
mom what was happening, and she would pass the
news on to me. I said, 'My God! Isn't that sensational,'
because they were going crazy for him. Later, when
you meet The Beatles and The Rolling Stones and they
tell you that they copied their act from Eddie's, you
think, 'Well! He didn't bother to tell us he was going
to do that!' We were really flabbergasted by what went
on there.

John Rook

By January 1960 London Records – Liberty's UK distributor – had
released six Cochran singles in Britain with varying degrees of
success. *Twenty Flight Rock* was released in April 1957 in preference to
Sittin' In The Balcony, which became Eddie's second British single.
Neither charted. *Summertime Blues*, however, reached number 18.
This was followed by *C'mon Everybody* which reached number 6, but
Teenage Heaven, the next release, failed to make any headway. With
the impending release of *Hallelujah I Love Her So*, which got to
number 22, Eddie's popularity continued to grow steadily and, as he
flew into London's Heathrow airport on 10 January 1960, he was
greeted enthusiastically by his fans.

Decca Records welcomed him on 11 January with an official reception at the company's offices on London's Albert Embankment. Then,
in accordance with Jack Good's schedule, Eddie began rehearsals for
his first two appearances on *Boy Meets Girls*. He hadn't been able to
bring any musicians with him from the United States (although
coincidentally many other musicians and entertainers he had toured
with frequently such as Duane Eddy, Bobby Darin, The Crickets and
The Everly Brothers were also due to tour Britain during the same
period). Ideally, The Kelly Four would have accompanied Eddie:
'Right up to the end I thought I was going,' Dave Shriver recalls. 'But
they said they couldn't work out the musicians' exchange.'

Joining him for the *Boy Meets Girls* shows were guitarists Joe
Brown, Eric Ford and Brian Daley. Red Price accompanied him on

saxophone and Alan Weighall provided electric bass while Bill Stark played the upright bass. The Vernons Girls, resident singers from Jack Good's original *Oh Boy!*, provided the backing vocals and the musicians were completed with Andy White and Don Storer on drums.

Eddie's first appearance on *Boy Meets Girls* took place on 16 January. He proceeded to growl his way through a bluesy *Hallelujah I Love Her So*, complete with a fantastic guitar solo, before immediately launching into *C'mon Everybody* and *Somethin' Else* almost as a medley, and ending with *Twenty Flight Rock*. (His second appearance, on the eve of his UK tour, featured *Money Honey* and *Have I Told You Lately That I Love You*, both popularised by Elvis Presley, followed by a reprise of *Hallelujah I Love Her So*.) All these songs were performed with tremendous power and enthusiasm, and were greeted with wild applause from the studio audience and a healthy amount of screams from the female contingency.

Following this impressive start to his UK television début, Marty Wilde interviewed Eddie. The singer immediately asked Marty to thank the musicians for doing such a great job. When Eddie was questioned about his fascination with guns, he simply replied, 'Well, I like guns, don't you?' He quickly justified the comment by explaining, in an exaggerated accent, 'Well, I was raised in Minnesota and it's a kinda hunter's paradise there.'

Although the interview was brief, Eddie's warm and friendly personality shone through. His humour was evident, as usual, and his confidence was tempered so he certainly didn't appear egotistical. Wilde closed the interview by asking Eddie to perform *Twenty Flight Rock*, describing it as a rock'n'roll classic as early as 1960.

Complete with an upright slap bass, this performance was probably the highlight of Eddie's first appearance on *Boy Meets Girls*. Even The Vernons Girls chirped away happily in the background during the chorus. Eddie performed the song in the same style as the re-recorded version that eventually made its way onto a Liberty single in late 1957. (When the single was released in the UK, in April 1957, British record buyers were treated to the original version that was performed in *The Girl Can't Help It*.) This television performance of *Twenty Flight Rock* was a fine rocking performance by Eddie and the band, especially bass player Bill Stark, who managed to recreate Guybo's original bass patterns accurately.

On his second appearance on the show, Eddie opened with a gutsy version of *Money Honey*, a Cochran favourite, complete with a fine guitar solo, that had been a part of his stage act for the best part of a year. *Have I Told You Lately That I Love You* immediately followed, and gave Eddie the chance to show off his deep, sensuous bass vocals, encouraging a few girls in the audience to sob uncontrollably.

To round off the appearance, Eddie gave another healthy plug to his latest UK single release by performing *Hallelujah I Love Her So*. A string section was later added to this track and to *Have I Told You Lately That I Love You* by the Halle Orchestra prior to the transmission of the *Boy Meets Girls* shows.

Those guys were raised on those blues. Eddie used to do *Hallelujah I Love Her So* and I loved the way he played that. When I was on the road with him, we used to sit around for hours and hours just with the guitars. Gene Vincent used to drink so much and we used to stay up all night with him to make sure he was okay. Twice he'd been to hospital and we were worried he was going to hurt himself.

Joe Brown

Rehearsals for the impending UK tour took place in the heart of London's West End at Max Rivers' Club in Gerrard Street. Larry Parnes had arranged with Marty Wilde for Eddie to use Marty's backing band, The Wildcats. The group comprised some of the UK's finest young rock'n'roll musicians, with Big Jim Sullivan on lead guitar, Brian Bennett on drums, Tony Belcher on rhythm guitar and Brian Locking on bass.

Big Jim Sullivan recalls the group's first meeting with Eddie: 'Eddie saw us the night before, playing with Marty, and it was decided that we should back him. Originally we were going to back Gene Vincent – that's what we were told – but when it came down to it Eddie had some chart material.

'It was quite incredible, really. I was doing all the finger-style stuff, Chet Atkins, Scotty Moore, that sort of thing. The first thing Eddie did was sit down and play the Chet Atkins version of *Birth Of The Blues*, which knocked us out completely. There was nobody else in this country who could play all that stuff, and to hear someone play it so good was great.'

Brian Bennett has similar memories: 'I believe Larry Parnes and Marty Wilde came down to the rehearsals at one stage. Marty was going into the West End to do *Bye Bye Birdie*, which was a musical. Eddie was extremely helpful in showing me different drum patterns to suit his songs. He had this big orange Gretsch and I remember that the most important thing about the discussions, apart from my point of view of getting the drum patterns right, was that Jim Sullivan couldn't bend the strings as he wanted to. Of course, I'm no guitarist, but Eddie had strings that weren't as thick-gauged as the ones we were using. In fact, he had thin strings on the low notes which enabled him to get these amazing bends, which he taught to Jim and Joe Brown.'

Joe Brown was discovered by Larry Parnes while playing guitar for Clay Nicholls And The Blue Flames at a holiday camp. He clearly remembers the influence Eddie had on his guitar playing: 'Eddie was the first American guitarist we met,' he explains. 'If James Burton had come over, or if Vincent had brought Cliff Gallup with him it may have been different. Eddie had that Gretsch with him with a Gibson pickup – and I was a Gibson man myself – but you couldn't even get them over here.

'In those days we copied everything we heard from the Americans. Sure, you could listen to a song and tell what the notes were, but until you saw how it was done and the positions they were playing, it didn't make any sense because it just sounded wrong. Eddie was the only American guitar player that could sit down and show us, and we learned a lot from him.

'We never had gauges on strings either, we just had guitar strings. We didn't have light gauge, or medium gauge, or any gauge. Then all of a sudden Eddie explained it to us. In those days we didn't know what was happening, but now it's common knowledge. We were just trying to find someone who could actually play. Eddie was a good rock'n'roll guitarist, and the first guy that actually took the time to sit and show us.'

The remarkable combination of Eddie Cochran and Gene Vincent on stage together marked the first pure rock'n'roll show ever to tour the UK. Bill Haley, Buddy Holly, Jerry Lee Lewis, Frankie Lymon and Charlie Gracie had all toured the British Isles previously, but each one appeared as the only rock'n'roll artist on a bill that consisted mainly of variety acts.

By 1960, rock'n'roll was starting to suffer a decline in popularity. America was already experiencing the changing tastes of the record-buying public and popular artists on both sides of the Atlantic were starting to change their style accordingly.

The arrival of these two influential rockers from the United States revitalised the British rock'n'roll scene. Here was Eddie Cochran, the blond Elvis, a cool-looking, talented guitarist and pop idol, accompanied by Gene Vincent, the true rocker. Adding this tour to their appearances on British television and radio, the impact Eddie Cochran and Gene Vincent made on every budding singer and musician in Britain is immeasurable. Eddie's own innovative style influenced George Harrison, Paul McCartney, Pete Townshend, Jeff Beck, Joe Brown and Marc Bolan, to name but a few, adding to the continued influence that rock'n'roll would have on musicians for decades to come.

Cliff Richard, although himself on tour at the time of Eddie Cochran's arrival, remembers the influence of American rock'n'roll: 'When we first started off, we recorded rock'n'roll songs like *Move It*, and then you'll see a slow decline until *Living Doll* – which was a song we didn't want to record, but had to because we'd completed a film and it was in the small print in the contract. Of course the public bought it by the million so we suddenly thought, "Crumbs, they actually prefer this kind of soft country stuff." It wasn't what I wanted to do, it's just that the public didn't want rock'n'roll – they weren't used to it, but people are far heavier now. I was fairly ambitious, as were my band The Shadows, and we just thought, "Well, we'll do our rock'n'roll stuff on the B-side." Some of our best records were the B-sides.

'You won't find any of us who weren't influenced by what was going on at that time, and there's no doubt that the sound of Eddie Cochran's records has been emulated on other people's recordings. Even if you don't even know what you're doing, I always think that you can be influenced without plagiarising. You don't have to go around stealing other people's ideas, but somewhere on your records you'll find a sound on your voice that's like a slap-back echo that he and Elvis used to use. Somehow or other, you'll find that the records that affected you affect how you make your own records. I'm not suggesting that if you listen to a Cliff Richard record I'll sound like Elvis or Eddie Cochran, but somewhere along the line there'll either be a drum sound, or a vocal sound, or a guitar sound that takes you back to that.

'Those who started in those days will always be part of the revolution; that cannot change, and that's the one thing I grasp on to. Most pundits looking into music think that rock'n'roll started with The Beatles. Well, it didn't. It started in the States and that's never going to change. The history books will show that people like myself were introduced to it by the American artists. I mean, it's an American art form, let's face it, but it no longer belongs to them, that's the amazing thing.'

Eddie Cochran looked to me like a blond version of Elvis Presley. He soon endeared himself to the audience because when he came on stage he said, 'It's great to be here in Hipswich,' and flicked his hips to the side as he said it. I have never heard anyone refer to Ipswich as Hipswich before or since.

Pat Wallis, Ipswich

Pat Wallis was one of many anxious teenagers who crowded into the Gaumont Theatre in Ipswich on 24 January to witness Eddie's first appearance in the Larry Parnes production *A Fast-Moving Beat Show*.

'Eddie's set lasted maybe half an hour, if that,' Jim Sullivan remembers. 'In those days there were no hour-long sets. When you consider how many people had to get on and off stage – you got Gene Vincent and Eddie Cochran, then you'd probably have Billy Fury,

Duffy Power, Vince Eager, Dickie Pride, all the Parnes mob and some of them would only do a quarter of an hour. A two-hour show! How many people could you get on?

'We probably did six or seven songs at the very most with Eddie. They'd be *What'd I Say*, *C'mon Everybody*, *Summertime Blues*, *Milkcow Blues*, *Hallelujah I Love Her So*, *Sweet Little Sixteen*, *Twenty Flight Rock*, that sort of thing.'

Although looking like the boy next door compared to Vincent, Eddie's remarkable guitar-playing skills immediately made an impression on his British audience. Wendy Rose, who attended the show on a trip organised by her local youth club, remembers the evening well: 'A group of us, twenty-nine teenagers in all, went to the Ipswich Gaumont to see Eddie perform in a production which also included Gene Vincent and Vince Eager With The Silent Three. Mulleys coaches departed from the Angel Hill in Bury and I think the tickets were twelve shillings and sixpence.

'We could all identify with Eddie. He could have been the boy from our street. He didn't dress too outrageously and had tremendous charisma to accompany his good looks. We admired the rebellious streak that came across in some of his songs – quite harmless compared to today – but most of all he played the guitar with such individuality, the beat is still as fresh today as it was forty years ago.'

Musical accompaniment for Gene Vincent was provided by Colin Green And The Beat Boys, featuring a sixteen-year-old Clive Powell on piano. Christened Georgie Fame by Larry Parnes, the teenager, later to record the hit single *Yeh Yeh* in 1965, was given his own spot in the production performing *High School Confidential*. Appearing on the bill as 'the new singing pianist', Georgie also shared the role with Lance Fortune.

The leading British performer appearing on the tour was the nineteen-year-old Liverpool-born Ronald Wycherley, better known as Billy Fury. A regular performer on *Oh Boy!*, *Boy Meets Girls* and on Jack Good's later venture *Wham!*, Billy Fury went on to record the hugely successful *Halfway To Paradise* along with *I'll Never Find Another You*, *Jealousy*, *A Thousand Stars* and the sensational *Sound Of Fury* album.

The compère for the show was Billy Raymond. Billed as the star of HMV Records, Raymond had made several appearances on television's *6.5 Special* and *Cool For Cats*. He started his career in show-business at the age of twelve when he was described as 'Scotland's Wonder Boy Soprano' on BBC's *Children's Hour*. After moving to London the twenty-year-old was offered TV appearances on BBC's *The Night And The Music* series before landing a recording contract with HMV.

Joe Brown, star of *Boy Meets Girls*, also appeared on the bill, and the support acts included Peter Wynne, Dean Webb and The Tony Sheridan Trio. Billed as 'The New Golden Voice' and recently signed to the Parlophone label, Peter Wynne was the nephew of Covent Garden's principal tenor, Furness Wynne-Williams. Dean Webb, a former dishwasher in Soho's Two I's club, was currently enjoying success on *Oh Boy!* and was said to be one of the most promising newcomers of 1960. Tony Sheridan started by singing in coffee bars around London and found fame when he was spotted by Jack Good and signed as a regular on *Oh Boy!*.

As former road manager for Marty Wilde, Hal Carter was now chaperone to the young Billy Fury and was assigned the task of taking care of Parnes' American guests as well: 'I started working for Larry Parnes after I helped get Marty Wilde into a theatre in Liverpool in 1958,' Hal explains. 'They couldn't get him in as all the kids were in the way, so by hook or by crook I actually got him into the theatre. Larry Parnes was impressed, so he offered me a job and I did a six-day tour with Marty, The Dallas Boys and Johnny Gentle around major cities. When we got back, Marty spoke to Larry Parnes and told him, "I've got to have that guy travelling with me and I want him with my tour," so I was with Marty for about a year.

'When Marty got married in 1959, Larry Parnes transferred me to Billy Fury and then I was with Bill for five years. When Eddie came over in 1960, I met Norm Riley and he said, "What do you do?" I said, "I look after Billy Fury," so he gave me twenty pounds extra a week – which was twice what Parnes was paying me – to look after Eddie and Gene.

'As tour manager, my job involved getting them into the theatre, getting them out, making sure they had something to eat, booking hotels and arranging the transport from one city to another. Ed and I got on extremely well, so I spent a lot of time with him. I didn't have to look after Joe Brown, because Joe always travelled on his own as he had his own car. Once he'd done his show he'd take off, as he had all kinds of friends all over the place and he'd go shooting and things like that. In fact, he carried his shotguns in the boot of his car.

'In those days we travelled everywhere by train. Sometimes we would use a coach for one-nighters, but we would usually do a week in each venue so it was pointless taking a coach because it would sit there all day not doing anything. Once we'd booked into the hotel we'd use taxis to get around.'

While Gene Vincent was singing he was heckled by someone in the audience. He stopped singing immediately and said, 'I don't know what it is that makes you tick, but I sure hope it's a bomb!' He got huge applause for that.

Victor Azzopardi, Southampton

Wearing a red shirt and a silver waistcoat, Eddie Cochran stepped out on stage to conquer his next teenage audience on Sunday, 31 January, at the Guildhall Theatre in Southampton. Tickets for the matinee performance at 3 p.m. were priced at six shillings and sixpence (roughly 32p today), while teenagers with a greater freedom could catch an evening show at 8.15 p.m. for eight shillings and sixpence.

'I remember going to the afternoon show and thought it was amazing,' Gloria Snellgrove recalls. 'Eddie was brilliant. Both Eddie and Gene were in good voice and the whole hall was really rocking. After the show I went backstage and managed to get Eddie's and Gene's autographs, both of which I still have.

'When I left, some chap offered me a spare ticket for the evening show. I snapped it up, even at eight shillings and sixpence, and went back in the evening to enjoy it all again.'

Another local fan, Diane Beckett, was also lucky enough to meet the American rock'n'roll stars after the concert: 'Eddie looked great that night and after the show I had the great privilege of going back-stage to meet him and Gene. Eddie was tanned, blond and gorgeous and very polite with those of us lucky enough to be there. Gene

Vincent didn't say much but looked very handsome in his black leathers. Seeing Eddie and Gene that night was like a dream come true – being American and the next best thing to my idol Elvis. Although it was forty years ago, I can remember it as if it was yesterday. As it happened, unknown to me then, my future husband was also in the audience.'

In photographs taken in early 1960, Eddie looks striking. Although in later shots the tiredness from Parnes' long schedule started to show in his face, his tanned skin, dark sultry eyes and brilliant blond quiff made him every inch the American rock'n'roll star. Unlike many of his contemporaries, he allowed his fans to actually meet their idol, increasing his popularity to the extent that many fans are still devoted today.

'I still have my programme,' Pauline Amey recalls. 'The Tony Sheridan Group, Eddie Cochran, Vince Eager, Billy Raymond and Gene Vincent all appeared. The Viscounts were also listed to appear, but having crossed through their names, I think that they didn't perform that evening. After the concert, I went backstage and met Eddie, Gene and Vince who all autographed my programme.'

It has often been stated that, later in the tour, Larry Parnes considered raising Eddie's status to headliner due to his growing popularity over Gene. Such drastic changes to the billing, although discussed, were never made, as Hal Carter explains: 'The truth of the matter is that Ed was going down a storm and so was Vincent – everybody was, they were all going down well. At this point, Billy [Fury] didn't have a hit record. He had a couple of things that he'd written himself that were small hits but he didn't have *Halfway To Paradise* at this point, but he was the English lead and Joe was the second lead, then Vincent was the American lead and Eddie was the second lead.

'They'd actually worked together before, but when Vincent was booked to do the tour he was the headliner. He'd been booked and all the dates had been arranged. Then Parnes got cold feet and started to worry that they wouldn't do the business with just Vincent, who was only known for *Be Bop A Lula*, and it was Norm Riley that said to him, "Why don't you bring Eddie Cochran? It won't cost you much. He's toured with Vincent before and it was quite successful and he knows him, so it should work." He wasn't very expensive – I think Ed was on two hundred pounds a week.

'Once we got on the road, it was obvious that Ed was the teenage idol, the sex symbol. Vincent was more for the lads. The girls didn't like him because he had very strange eyes, but they were all in lust with Eddie. At one point, because it was going so well, Larry suggested that it would be better for the show if Ed was to close, but Ed said, "No. If you change the running order it would destroy Vincent." And it would have done – he would have been a wreck and caused so much trouble, and then he would have blamed Ed and there would have been all kinds of reprisals. So it never happened.'

'Eddie had a great presence on stage,' Jim Sullivan adds. 'He had a great presence all the time but even more on stage. He was the Fonz of the rock stable, if you like. He was a good-looking guy. He always had his hair done, and he always looked the same off stage as he did on. He used to wear make-up all the time – you'd never see Eddie without his make-up on. Dark glasses, leather trousers, that was his image. Just like the Fonz, doing his quiff in front of the mirror with a bit of grease. His whole presence must have intimidated Gene Vincent. Whereas Gene was a star on the way down, Eddie was a star – in this country – on the way up.

'There was always a big thing about who was going to top the bill, but it used to be an alternative thing. One would do it one night, the other the next, and so on.'

I remember Eddie had a sore throat. In fact he apologised for sounding 'a bit like Fabian' because of it. You no doubt know Fabian was temporarily a big star and heartthrob in the US, but he didn't raise a stir here.

Terry Taylor, Southampton

Throughout 1959, Fabian, or Fabiano Forte Bonaparte, did raise a stir in the United States and could easily be described as the first manufactured teen idol. Spotted by producer Bob Marcucci for his looks rather than his singing ability, Fabian's hits included *Turn Me Loose*, *Tiger* and *Hound Dog Man*, the title track for his screen début in November 1959 when he co-starred alongside Stuart Whitman in the movie of the same name. In 1960, although his record sales were diminishing, Fabian's on-screen appeal increased when he worked alongside Bing Crosby in the film *High Time* and with John Wayne in *North Of Alaska*, beginning a successful movie career that flourished throughout the next three decades.

As Fabian's movie career quickly dominated his record sales, another Bob Marcucci discovery, Frankie Avalon, had already taken over his place in the charts. Signed to a solo career while performing with Bobby Rydell in the group Rocco And The Saints, Frankie enjoyed a huge chart success with *Venus*, and by January 1960 his second million-seller, *Why*, had already taken a firm hold on the US number 1 slot.

At the close of the 1950s, rock'n'roll had taken a step backwards. Easy-listening tunes were made popular in the early 1950s by artists such as Frank Sinatra and Dean Martin, before the arrival of artists such as Elvis Presley knocked that kind of music from the chart. Towards the end of the decade, however, artists such as Fabian, Frankie Avalon, Bobby Rydell, Bobby Darin and Pat Boone brought easy-listening music back in a new, younger form, winning over their female audience with ballads rather than the rebellious performances that the decade is traditionally remembered for today.

As his army discharge grew closer, music critics around the globe were beginning to speculate about Elvis Presley's future as a rock'n'roll singer. Once the epitome of teenage rebellion, the twenty-five-year-old singer had recently been promoted to sergeant. Had the army tamed Elvis Presley?

Thanks to the enterprising Colonel Tom Parker, Elvis's manager, a stream of singles recorded prior to the singer being drafted into the service, such as *Hard-Headed Woman*, *I Got Stung*, *I Need Your Love Tonight* and *A Big Hunk Of Love* kept Presley at the top of the charts throughout his two-year absence, along with the album releases *A Date With Elvis* and the movie soundtrack *King Creole*. When he was discharged from the army, his first recording sessions produced a selection of blues tracks and ballads such as *Soldier Boy* and *Fame And Fortune*, certainly a move away from rock'n'roll. Then, in April, Elvis recorded *It's Now Or Never* and *Are You Lonesome Tonight*, a change in direction that marked the start of one of the most successful recording periods of his career.

The ever-changing nature of popular music was certainly evident in 1960. Tracks riding high in the British charts throughout January and February included Adam Faith's *What Do You Want*, *Oh Carol* by Neil Sedaka, Cliff Richard's *Travelling Light* and *Voice in The Wilderness*, while Tommy Steele scored a hit with the novelty *Little White Bull*. Anthony Newley covered the single *Why*, which was also a huge hit in the United States, alongside Paul Anka's *It's Time To Cry*. February's big hit in the United States was *Teen Angel* by Mark Dinning, followed closely by Jim Reeves's *He'll Have To Go*, Percy Faith's instrumental *Theme From A Summer Place* and Bobby Darin's *Somewhere Across The Sea*.

Ironically, when Elvis Presley's soundtrack album *King Creole* was released during his absence, it only got as far as number 2 in the United States charts, kept back from the top spot by Frank Sinatra's *Only The Lonely* album. It was more evidence that the balladeers, once under enormous threat from rock'n'roll, were regaining their place in the charts.

Although Simon Waronker always looked upon Eddie as Liberty's first rock'n'roll singer, he continued to promote Eddie as an all-round entertainer. With hindsight it was a wise move. However, Eddie's British single releases such as *Twenty Flight Rock*, *Summertime Blues*, *C'mon Everybody* and *Somethin' Else* put the record-buying public in no doubt that this was a rock'n'roll singer they were listening to.

Whether rock'n'roll's popularity was diminishing or not, Eddie's appearances alongside the notorious rocker Gene Vincent assured British teenagers of the day that rock'n'roll would always remain the music of their era.

Eddie's guitar went everywhere with him. He didn't leave it lying around. I think he loved that guitar, that's for sure. It was always clean and never grubby or dirty.

Big Jim Sullivan

On 16 and 23 February Eddie and Gene returned to London to pre-record two shows for the BBC radio programme *Saturday Club*, hosted by Brian Matthew. These were recorded at the Piccadilly Studios in the West End, and The Wildcats provided the backing.

For Eddie's first performance, which was broadcast on 5 March, he performed the Ray Charles classic *What'd I Say*, the song he had been using to open his act throughout the tour, along with *Milkcow Blues*, *Hallelujah I Love Her So* and *C'mon Everybody*.

For the second show, which was broadcast a week later on 12 March, he performed *Somethin' Else*, *Hallelujah I Love Her So* and *Twenty Flight Rock* as well as joining Gene Vincent to play lead guitar on Gene's latest UK single, *My Heart*.

In a brief interview with Brian Matthew, Eddie talked about his ability to play bass, drums and piano as well as guitar. His main ambition, he told Brian Matthew, was simply 'to be successful'.

Eddie also stated that the tour would end on 17 April, after which he would return home for ten days, before returning to the UK to undertake a further ten weeks of touring.

Eddie's performance on *Saturday Club* lacked some of the drive and energy that was so evident throughout his *Boy Meets Girls* appearances, and his voice sounded tired on many of the songs. He had been in England for just over a month and the strain was beginning to show. But, however tired Eddie may have been, it didn't stop him wanting to jam with Gene during the recording of the show, as the host Brian Matthew revealed to fellow broadcaster and author Spencer Leigh: 'We did a session at which they both appeared and we recorded Gene Vincent first. As he was leaving the studio, Eddie Cochran got on the tiny stage. He was the more laconic of the two and he shouted to the back of the room where Gene was limping out, "Hey, Vincent, you ain't going nowhere. I got your crutches. You're going to jam with me."

'Gene went back and did indeed jam with him for ten or fifteen minutes, which was great, and Vincent then left the studio. The engineer came out of the control room onto the balcony overlooking the theatre and said, "Was I supposed to have recorded that?" I was amazed because I thought he would have gone "Wow!" and recorded it.'

Spencer Leigh also spoke to Brian Bennett about the *Saturday Club* shows. 'Eddie used to cringe at Broadcasting House because there was only one microphone for the drum kit, and a couple for the guitars. His vocal mic was suspended from a large hook, which he thought was very funny. The songs were almost cut live. We'd play one title and Brian Matthew would say, "That was Eddie Cochran singing *What Did I Say*," and we'd go into another number. We'd do six numbers for *Saturday Club* and the band would pick up ten shillings and sixpence and then leave.'

The time was so right for Eddie's music. We had been listening to people like Tony Bennett and Frankie Laine which, although good at the time, didn't satisfy our taste. In hindsight, I guess we were looking for something more exciting.

James Clark, Dundee

Throughout February 1960 the Larry Parnes Fast Moving Beat Show jumped around the British Isles from the Glasgow Empire to the Granada Woolwich, then back up to the Midlands to the DeMontfort Hall in Leicester, where, on 18 February, sixteen-year-old Barry Robinson saw Eddie perform: 'After going to the local Wigston cinema that afternoon to see *The Inn Of The Sixth Happiness* along with my mate Johnno, I went down to the DeMontfort Hall to see Eddie Cochran and Gene Vincent. The tickets for the front stalls were five shillings each, and I remember being somewhat disappointed that the hall only seemed to have about one and a half thousand people in there. I had bought all Eddie's singles and I was really looking forward to seeing him. He didn't let me down, he was absolutely brilliant. I was only sixteen – good title for a song – but can still recall the show pretty well, although it escapes me as to who closed the show. I think it was Gene but couldn't swear to it. This was the first pure American rock'n'roll show to tour the UK. Up until then we'd only seen the British rockers like Marty Wilde and the other Larry Parnes packages. Five weeks or so later, another

American show came to the De Mont, which I also went to see. It was ten shillings and sixpence for Bobby Darin, Duane Eddy, Clyde McPhatter and Emile Ford, so it was an exciting time for us rock'n'roll fans.'

The excitement generated by the appearance of these wild American rock'n'roll stars in traditional British theatres reached its peak the following Saturday evening when Eddie and Gene appeared at Dundee's Caird Hall. Bill MacGregor, a local, remembers it: 'Eddie Cochran came on next to last to a great welcome. Although he gave a gutsy performance – jumping around, swivelling his guitar and sounding as good as he did on his records – I remember feeling a bit disappointed because he looked a bit clean-cut. He was a little heavier than I thought he would be and he wore a checked lumberjack shirt that made him look like a country-and-western singer – not the slim, mean-looking Elvis lookalike who sang *Twenty Flight Rock* in *The Girl Can't Help It*.

'Gene Vincent clearly did not disappoint. The lights came up on the lean, mean-looking guy with greasy black hair, completely attired in a black leather suit and gloves. Gene milked the audience and the crowds went absolutely wild.

'For only his third or fourth song, he sang *Be Bop A Lula* and the crowd went berserk. Suddenly three or four guys I knew by sight, who attended a popular jukebox café in Dundee, managed to get on stage, and, with their arms around Gene Vincent, were singing along with him. Not to be hijacked in the publicity stakes, Eddie Cochran joined in and soon everyone wanted to be at the front where absolute bedlam broke out. Bouncers were throwing people from the stage, girls were screaming, fights were breaking out and inevitably the police arrived in force. Before they could clear the hall, rows of seats had collapsed and the police and the public were injured. I particularly remember that a ceramic bust of Sir James Caird, who originally presented the hall to the people of Dundee, was smashed to the ground.'

'I was at the back, I knew nothing!' Hal Carter laughs. 'Sure, these things happen. We would get out anyway we could, through the fanlight, even through the roof, to get away from the crowd. It was horrendous. They would put big holes in the car! Half the time we couldn't get a taxi to come and get us. They would say, "We're not coming out there, you must be joking." So we had to use all kinds of favours to get friends to pick us up.

'As soon as Vincent finished we would go dashing out into the car. Or maybe while Vincent was on, I'd take Ed and Bill round to the hotel and drop them off, then as soon as Vincent finished we could get straight out to the car and go. Otherwise they would pull you to pieces.'

Local newspapers were keen to report on the mayhem caused by the touring rock'n'roll show. Since the arrival of Bill Haley on British soil in 1956, the media have believed that rock'n'roll accelerated teenage violence, but in the words of James Clark, who also attended the Dundee show, the evening's events were quite innocent in nature: 'I didn't think for one minute that these stars that I listened to on the radio would ever appear in my home town. The whole city was buzzing. We eventually got tickets, a good seat, and then Eddie appeared, red guitar swinging, and the place was jumping. Gene Vincent was the big star at the time but Eddie stole the show – he was brilliant.

'Eddie sang his songs and we went wild, then he made way for Gene Vincent. In our excitement we invaded the stage, as we wanted to be close to our heroes. I ended up in the wings and found Eddie hiding there with his guitar clutched between his knees with a startled expression on his face. I said, "How's it going, Eddie?" He replied, "Crazy, man, but I don't like the fighting."

'There was no fighting – just youthful exuberance. It was good to have our music on our stage in our town.'

Teenage excitement was a minor consideration for road manager Hal Carter. Eddie's and Gene's antics off stage often left Hal with a lot of explaining to do: 'We were in Scotland and we arrived at the hotel and Gene said he was going to have a bath. Ed said, "Are we going out, Boody?" – he called me that because when I first met him I said, "Pleased to meet you, buddy," and as I had quite a Scouse accent it sounded like "boody". So he said, "Okay, me and Boody are going for a walk," and Gene got in the bath, but mischievous Ed took Gene's leg iron and hid it up on top of the wardrobe and off we went shopping for about two hours.

'When we got back to the hotel the manager was yelling, "You've got to get him out of here, I'm not having him in here!" and I said "What's the problem?" and he said, "It's the American, he's crazy, he's threatening to sue the hotel for a million dollars, he reckons somebody in the hotel has stolen his leg." So we got up into the room and tried to pacify Gene, but for the next two days he hated everybody.

'Vincent was horrible at times. If something went wrong he would blame Ed. They were always play-fighting but Vincent was vicious. He actually elbowed Eddie in the eye once – that's when Eddie had to wear dark glasses on stage, which caused murder. He would play with them on, and occasionally peer over them and look at the audience and they would all scream, but he couldn't see through them.'

Eddie had the whole package. He was a songwriter, he was a guitar player – boy, was he one of the first guitar players – and he had a great natural voice that just rocked, and he was good-looking, but he was cool-looking too. He put the whole package together and that's probably what shouted across the room to me when I was a kid. He had the whole package and changed my life.

Brian Setzer

Eddie and Gene made their two final television appearances on *Boy Meets Girls* in late February. For the first, broadcast on 20 February, Eddie kicked off his performance with short versions of *Hallelujah I Love Her So* and *Twenty Flight Rock* before launching into a tremendous *Summertime Blues*. He ended his stint with a breathtaking version of *Milkcow Blues* that contained a guitar solo that was far superior to his studio version recorded back in August 1959. Eddie also joined Gene to play guitar on his two songs, *My Heart* and *Dance In The Street*, before the grand finale where Eddie and Gene were joined by Marty Wilde, Billy Fury and Joe Brown for a rousing rendition of the old blues standard *My Babe*.

His final *Boy Meets Girls* appearance on 27 February featured Eddie performing the Bobby Darin-influenced *I Don't Like You No More*. This song was written by one of Eddie's old touring buddies, Teddy

Randazzo, an artist in his own right who appeared in *The Girl Can't Help It* as the lead singer of The Chuckles. He also took the lead role in the Alan Freed film *Mr Rock'n'Roll*. *I Don't Like You No More* was a swinging big-band-style song and seemed a strange choice for Eddie, but he sang it with energy and enthusiasm, appearing at ease with this radical departure from rock'n'roll.

After completing the number, it was straight back to rock'n'roll with a powerful version of Chuck Berry's *Sweet Little Sixteen*. The show ended with a wonderful duet between Gene and Eddie as they furiously ad-libbed to the Big Bopper composition *White Lightning*. They had undoubtedly heard George Jones's version of the song back home in the United States. Played out at the end of the show as the credits were rolling, the audience's reaction to the song was manic and, during the guitar solo, the screams became almost deafening.

On 21 February, following an exhausting schedule, Eddie travelled to London for his performance on the *New Musical Express* Poll-Winners' Party at the Empire Pool in Wembley. The Wildcats' drummer Brian Bennett remembers the show well: 'There was a red rope where the conductor used to stand and it was still up there, and in all the famous pictures of the band with Gene and Eddie you can see that red rope. Both of them wanted the drums right up their back-sides because there were no fold-back speakers in those days, so they stood right in front of me. The only reason [the sound from] my kit carried, as my drums weren't mic'd at all, was because it all went through their vocal mics. That's the only reason you could hear it at the back of the hall.'

Also faced with a tough touring schedule, British pop singer Cliff Richard had flown in to London for the same event, briefly leaving a tour of the United States where he was appearing in Irvin Feld's 1960 'Show Of Stars' tour. After his appearance at the Poll-Winners' Party, Cliff still had to perform at the London Palladium that evening before returning to the United States the following day, but he made a special effort, despite being jet-lagged, to greet the American star. 'I met Eddie only once,' Cliff remembers. 'It was backstage at Wembley Arena. He'd been on tour and was very tired. But I'm glad I met him and shook his hand. I never got to meet Elvis. We never saw anything on the stage, we just knew that they were all there and we wanted to say hi.'

The next day, 22 February, Eddie, backed by The Millermen, made an appearance on the radio show *Parade Of Pop*. Only his version of *C'mon Everybody* has surfaced, although it is possible that he recorded more than one song for the show.

Then the great moment was upon us. Silence fell over the whole theatre, the lights went down, the curtain came up and there before our eyes was the one and only Eddie Cochran.

Twenty Flight Rock came booming out and we went wild. There was the man. Not on record, not on radio or a jukebox, but here with us singing the hits we knew.

It was great, it was loud, and it was rock'n'roll. Before we went into the theatre that night we were told 'no dancing'. No chance! Rock'n'roll is not, and never was, listening music!

Chris Fergus, Leeds

The tour continued throughout the rest of the month with dates at the Cardiff Gaumont, the Manchester Hippodrome and the Leeds Empire, where, as Hal Carter explains, the management of the Grand Hotel were less than impressed with the visiting celebrities: 'Bill and I were staying with some friends – a Mrs Green, with whom we would stay every time we were in the area. She knew we were there for a week and she'd go mad if we didn't stay with her, so we'd do that and I would communicate with the hotel.

'I checked Eddie and Gene in and everything and said, "I'll see you tomorrow." The next morning I arrived to take them to a TV or radio interview and when I got to the hotel the manager was screaming, "Get them out of here, I don't want them in my hotel, I want them out now!" He was furious so I went to find out what had happened. It turned out that they had invited all the chambermaids in the hotel to their room. It seems there were around sixteen young ladies and just the two of them, so they were in paradise. The housekeeper had heard all the noise and banged on the door and they all went scurrying into corners and cupboards. Anyway, she went in and found about eight or nine of the girls and ordered them all out. She thought they were all gone, but there were still about six of them left. One had hidden in the wardrobe, one was under the bed, one was in the bath and had pulled the shower curtain across and so on, so they carried on partying again and the housekeeper came back and found all the others. Finally, the manager was told and they had to leave.

'Well, there was a convention going on and I couldn't find them anywhere to stay. Eventually, with a bit of luck, I found a little boarding house out of town and I told the lady who ran it that they were very nice Americans – country boys. We went up to see this room and, I have to tell you, it was tiny. There were two beds in there and you had to close the door to get into bed, and there was a little basin in the corner and you had to sit on the bed to get washed. I didn't tell them this, I just told them it was a lovely family-run hotel, a country hotel where they could get to know the locals.

'I pulled up to the house and said, "Right, look, I've got to get back to the theatre. I'll send a car for you." I got their luggage out and put it on the step and said, "The lady will sort you out, the porter will do that. I've got to go," and I drove off. I made sure that I kept out of their way – I sent a cab for them, when usually I would go to get them. It's funny they never said anything until about Wednesday, then it was: "Hey, what's this goddamn hotel you put us in! I keep banging my head on the door." They also had to go down the corridor for a shower when they were used to *en-suites* – Americans had them in the 1950s – but they stayed there and were quite good about it and the woman had no problems. In fact, they were as good as gold in that pokey room, but it was all their own fault.'

That very week, Eddie's and Gene's performances on stage were just as memorable, as Michael Lynch, a local, recalls: 'I saw Gene Vincent, Eddie Cochran, Joe Brown and Billy Fury at the Leeds Empire when I was fifteen. Eddie closed the first half of the show performing all his repertoire. He wore a silver-coloured waistcoat and a red shirt, and got a tremendous reception from the females in the audience.

'Fury appeared in a blue drape jacket, and at one time finished up almost lying on the stage with the microphone stand. I remember there was a group of girls hanging out of the gallery and one nearly fell out!

'I paid two shillings and ninepence to see the show, which is roughly fourteen pence in decimal currency. It must have been the bargain of the century!'

During a break in the tour, Eddie and Gene visited Blackpool, where they both entered Gypsy Rose Lee's booth on the seafront to have their palms read. Several stories emerged later in the newspapers that Eddie had a premonition of impending doom and his visit to the palm-reader upset him enormously when she saw danger in his immediate future.

Jack Good wrote an article in which he told of Eddie waking up from a nightmare while staying in Manchester, where he screamed over and over again that he was going to die. In an interview with Spencer Leigh in the late 1980s, however, Good stated that he 'never saw Eddie with a sense of doom. If he thought he was going to die he never would have recorded *Three Steps To Heaven*.'

Jim Sullivan agrees: 'You walk around Blackpool and what do you see? A palm-reader. Well, I can't remember anyone ever saying or predicting that Eddie was going to die. I'm sure that if that had happened, it would have got out. I think those stories are just fables put on to add to the legend.'

In an interview with Jim Newcombe, when questioned on the premonitions, Georgie Fame wasn't so sure: 'Eddie was a bit worried about it. He went to see a doctor and all sorts.'

Indeed, these stories have certainly added intrigue to the final weeks of Eddie's life, but it has also been mentioned by people close to him in the UK that he was prone to bouts of depression, probably caused by homesickness or his continuing conflicts with Jerry Capehart.

Eddie also suffered from periods of insomnia, and his occasional seeking solace in a bottle of bourbon probably didn't help his state of mind. He may well have been battling certain demons in his personal life, but he rarely allowed it to interfere with his music. Very few people saw this side of Eddie's personality, making it difficult to prove whether he had any morbid premonitions during his stay in the United Kingdom.

The shows these guys gave were fantastic. It was
wonderful to see so many of our favourites on one bill.
I remember one girl shouted, 'Eddie, I love you!' and,
to gales of laughter, in his deep American drawl, he
replied, 'I love ya too, baby.'

Mrs J. James, Birmingham

On 7 March 1960, almost two months after his arrival in Britain,
Eddie opened at the Birmingham Hippodrome. Further week-long
engagements continued as the tour performed at the Liverpool and
Newcastle Empire theatres, then back again to the Manchester
Hippodrome. Every seat would be filled for the weekend dates but, as
some fans remembered, during the week the entertainers sometimes
played to almost empty concert halls. Compared to today's touring
standards, it seems to be a waste of finances and the performers'
energy to play the same venue all week but, as Hal Carter explains,
this was far from unusual at the time: 'I remember once Dickie Pride
said to the audience, "If you all stay till the end, I'll get a cab to take
you home," because there were six people in the audience. But it was
always packed on Friday, Saturday and Sunday. We were still in
variety then, and sometimes we would do two shows a night. We
would do one-nighters but it was cheaper to book the artist and the
theatre for the week. It didn't matter because you only really paid for
the Friday, Saturday and Sunday and the other days were thrown in as
a token. So, whatever you got in then was a bonus. Also, the artists
were on a week's salary, so it didn't really matter how many you got in
because the artist was still paid the same.'

Whether the tour played to a full house or a few people, diehard
rock'n'roll fans greeted the show with unbounded enthusiasm, and the
era is always remembered with affection, as Leighton Wardell, who
saw the show in Birmingham, recalls: 'I went to the concert in the
company of a girl from night-school – Bernice Evans. This was our
only date and Bernice was rather up-market, in as much as she had a
nice name, spoke well, and her parents did not possess a television.

'Eddie Cochran was "somethin' else". The girls were screaming
and us guys were looking shy, clapping our hands. At one point he
came over to the right-hand side of the stage towards the girls, and

said in his best American accent: "You'd better be careful, girls, or I'll come down and kiss you in a minute," and they all went crazy. I used that line at parties for years and it always provoked the right response. Good to be young, eh!'

Annie Harris, who also saw the show in Birmingham, shares the same great memories: 'My friend Jean and I were both very excited to be seeing two big American stars, along with our own Joe Brown and Billy Fury. We had, as usual, spent hours getting ready to go out. In those days it took time to put lots of rollers in our hair, then the two cancan underskirts under our dresses and four-and-a-half-inch stiletto heel shoes with winklepicker toes.

'The atmosphere was wonderful as usual, and Jean and I went to all the shows. It was a wonderful time to be a teenager and it remains with you all your life. We all felt very special to have been there at such a great time. After the show we waited at the stagedoor to see all of them come out. Our stars were accessible to us then.'

Finally, one simple recollection comes from an entry made in the diary of Mr G. Page some forty years ago:

> 9/3/60 Wednesday
> Ember day
> John and I went out at 7.30 for the Hippodrome. The show started at 8.30 and finished about 10.30. Eddie Cochran, Gene Vincent, Billy Fury and Joe Brown were on. Gene Vincent was supposed to be the star but I think Eddie Cochran was the most popular. The show was noisy and great. The only trouble was the screaming women. Arrived home about 11.15.

We were all very young back then. We weren't aware of what was going on around us, we didn't understand the psychology of it all. We observed though innocent eyes.

Big Jim Sullivan

Eddie was used to touring. He had travelled extensively during his beginnings with The Cochran Brothers and, once his career with Liberty developed, his touring schedule became unrelenting. After three months in England, though, he began to grow tired and homesick. California couldn't be any further away from the cold British winter and Eddie found relief in the fact that he was sharing the tour with a fellow American, Gene Vincent, as they inevitably became more dependent on one another to relieve the homesickness.

'I never saw Eddie and Gene fight – they were very close,' Joe Brown remembers. 'Gene was totally lost without Eddie and Eddie used to look after him. Gene was a big drinker because he was in a lot of pain with his leg. Eddie wasn't a big drinker – I mean, he drank, all right, but not like Gene. Gene was what you could call a steady drinker – so steady he couldn't even move!'

During the last few weeks of the tour, it was reported that Eddie had begun to drink heavily to relieve his depression. Photographs reveal his bloodshot eyes and bloated appearance, but friends close to him during the time strongly deny that this was the case. It is naïve to think that the twenty-one-year-old never touched alcohol, but to believe he had descended into alcoholism during this period is equally misguided.

As Hal Carter recalls, the tour did take its toll on the entertainers, but he remembers the period, and their antics, with affection: 'Although Ed was only twenty-one, he was seventeen going on thirty-five. He was a kid at heart but very mature too. He was a lot of fun to be with – though if he did anything to upset you he would be mortified. He didn't want anybody to be hurt, he wouldn't stop apologising. Of course, Bill was very young and naïve; Ed had been to quite a few places in the world, whereas Bill was lucky to have visited half a dozen places in the country.

'Ed and Vincent would finish the show and then have a drink. They were used to going to bed late and getting up late. By the time they'd had a shower and something to eat, it was time to go to the theatre. Bill and I would always be out in the day – we would go to movies.

'One time we went up to Manchester, and Ed got Bill drunk on the train from Euston. Bill agreed to have one drink but Eddie would distract him and kept filling up his glass. Ed tried to convince him that the white stones on the track were snow, and when we got to Manchester Bill was so drunk he dropped down between the coaches and said, "See, I told you they were stones."

'They were staying at the Piccadilly and we were staying some-where else. Eddie asked us back for a drink, and then, at about two o'clock in the morning, Eddie wanted a comic. So I said, "All right, I'll take Bill out and look," but he said, "No, you leave him here," because he knew that if I took Bill, I'd be gone and I wouldn't come back.

'So I went downstairs and picked up a handful of magazines and I took them back up and said, "Right, there's the books. Let's go, Bill," and I dragged him out before Eddie had the chance to look at the magazines.

'The next morning the management were talking about throwing them out again. I didn't notice, but while I was out, Vincent, Ed and Bill got all the shoes that people had left outside their rooms for polishing. They'd opened the fire extinguisher box in the wall and had filled this full of shoes. Also, in those days you had these big heavy leather screens across the door on each floor to stop the draught, and so they had put more shoes all along the top of these screens. Of course, in those days every third pair were brogues. It was murder! None of the guests knew which were their shoes. They were thrown out of there as well. They would also knock on doors in the night and ask: "Would you like tea or coffee with your breakfast in the morning? Brown toast or white toast?" But it wasn't vicious, it was just mischievous.

'Ed was like a big brother to Vincent, although Gene was older and had been around a lot longer than him. They stuck together because this was in the days of the great English countryside, bacon butties, fish and chips, sausage and mash. There was no junk food then – no hamburgers or milkshakes – that they had been used to in America.

'Ed was so homesick and desperate to get back. He missed his family and especially his mum. He would talk to his mum for hours on the phone and these were on their hotel bills, so I had to clear them up. They hated the food and they hated the weather.'

Big Jim Sullivan and Brian Bennett have their own accounts of how Eddie coped with the gruelling tour schedule: 'Eddie and Gene spent a lot of time together,' Brian recalls. 'Gene was a very bad influence on Eddie. He was quite a hardnut, and I think he used to put quite a few Jack Daniels down Eddie's gob and get him into all sorts of mischief.

'In those days you had first-, second- and third-class carriages on British Rail. We were in third while Eddie and Gene were in first. We'd meet halfway in the buffet car and we'd get sent back, but Eddie would say, "Come and sit with us," so we'd sit and talk. It was a case of the singer being the star, while we were the scumbags behind him.

'We would talk quite a lot backstage in the dressing-rooms, because we did two shows a night, 6.15 p.m. and 8.15 p.m., so we'd hang out backstage and tell stories. Eddie was a very warm American. In the late 1950s, if someone came over from America, it was magic to us. Trying to get room service after nine o'clock in a hotel in England meant a ham or cheese sandwich! There was nowhere for artists to go when they were on tour. We thought, because he was American, that he was gonna be "big time" and have a big ego, but he was great. Just a down-home American. Vincent was a different bloke altogether. He was hard, but if you were good at your job, you were all right and Gene was okay with you. But they weren't "big time"; they taught us a lot and were very gracious to us.'

Big Jim Sullivan vividly remembers the personal problems Eddie and Gene encountered on tour: 'They both seemed like very lost human beings,' he explains. 'I don't think that Eddie wanted to be over here for one minute, and I don't think Gene gave a shit. He had a vicious streak in him, ol' Gene. There was a couple of times when he got his knife out on the tour coach threatening to stab someone.

'They both drank heavily. At one stage Eddie was getting through a bottle of bourbon a day, if not two. At one point in the tour, he ended up with these great big blotches in his eyes caused by alcohol. Another time we had to prop him up at the Liverpool Empire where the mic stand came up through a flap in the stage. We had to put his guitar over the mic as it came up so he wouldn't fall over!

'Almost from the start, something said that he didn't want to be here, touring round a strange country with a hillbilly like Gene – although they were supposedly good friends. I think they were good friends for the tour, but I'm not sure if they were good friends beforehand. All we knew was that there was this American guy who was very talented, brought up in the cradle of rock'n'roll and country music, and here he was in a different country, in the bowels of rock'n'roll with somebody who was basically a biker like Gene Vincent. He was caught up in a web. It's hard enough touring around your own country, let alone somewhere foreign where you don't want to be.

'What I remember of Eddie was that he was quiet and actually quite introverted. That's the impression I got. I can't ever remember any happy-go-lucky signs. He always seemed to be Eddie Cochran – the star. The man underneath it, whoever that was, was kept on a pretty tight leash.

'I should imagine that there were some pretty wild parties, but that would have been more between him and Gene, because Gene was his only link to the States and he really missed home.

'The guy was rather a nice human being, a sensitive guy, and I can understand his feelings, but I didn't understand them at the time. Now I look back at Eddie and I feel quite sorry for him. I think, "Poor bugger." What we should have done was go to his room and say "Hi, Ed. How are you? You all right?" which we did, but then sit down and have a real good chat with him.'

For Larry Parnes, the tour was now proving successful and he added new dates to it, keeping Eddie and Gene in England until July. Eddie already had a recording session planned back in California, so a ten-day break beginning on 17 April allowed him to fly home to honour that commitment before returning to the tour on 27 April.

On 4 April, Sharon Sheeley flew into the UK to meet up with Eddie. She confirms that he was homesick and longing for his brief return home. 'Eddie hated England,' she says. 'When he first got there, he loved it. I mean, the fans were receptive and he got to do his own kind of music, but after months of the cold and the hard tour, he was so tired. He was burnt out. He just wanted to get home.'

There wasn't a lot of difference between the American and British audiences, but the tours were a lot of fun. People dressed in suits in those days. They were young people, they looked like suits when they were sitting down but they were Teddy Boy suits. In those days a sixteen- or seventeen-year-old kid would wear a suit if they were going to a party.

Phil Everly

After signing a ten-year, million-dollar recording contract with Warner Bros, The Everly Brothers left the United States to embark on their first UK tour, backed by The Crickets. Lead guitarist Sonny Curtis immediately made contact with Eddie, whom he hadn't seen since 8 January when Cochran completed his final recording session at Liberty Records. 'It was my first time in England,' Sonny recalls. 'We arrived in London really early in the morning. The Everlys were staying at the Savoy Hotel and The Crickets were staying down the street in the Cumberland Hotel. At the time I thought the Everlys were really staying uptown, but the Cumberland is really uptown these days. A rocker like me couldn't afford to stay there now!

'I was only twenty-two at the time and Joe B and J.I. were even younger than I was. It's really funny to remember what my perspective was back then. These days, the first thing I would want to do after a flight like that would be to go to bed, but we said, "Golly, man, Eddie Cochran's down there in Jermaine Street." So we called him and Eddie said, "Come on over." By the time we got over there to his place it was just about daylight. Sharon was asleep, but Eddie and Gene Vincent had just been roaring all night, I don't know if they'd had a couple of days off or what. I was still pretty green, I was straight out of Texas, but they were walking around with Jack Daniels and we all had a sip of it. Five o'clock in the morning and we just broke into the Jack Daniels and had a big party!

'I've got an old friend whom I met that first morning in England. He was twelve years old at the time and his name was Tony O'Sullivan. He came over to the Cumberland – this was after I'd been to Eddie Cochran's – and rang my phone and said, "Sir, can I have your autograph?" So he came up and I gave him my autograph and I had my guitar with me, so I picked a little for him and told him that we'd just been over to Eddie Cochran's. I'm sure Eddie didn't appreciate it much, but Tony said, "Man, I'd sure love to have Eddie Cochran's autograph." So I gave him the address and that little Tony O'Sullivan went over there and knocked on the door. Eddie and Gene were probably still in the throes of their Jack Daniels, but they treated him like royalty, gave him their autograph and made him a hero at school.'

Following the UK success of singles such as *Yep!*, *Forty Miles Of Bad Road* and *Some Kinda Earthquake* the previous year, Duane Eddy also arrived in England to tour with Bobby Darin, Clyde McPhatter and Emile Ford.

'I was coming out the hotel and I ran into Eddie and Sharon,' Duane remembers. 'We went up to his room and he said, "By the way, I've written a song for you," so I brought my guitar over and he showed the song to me. It was quite complicated, but very beautiful. It was so complicated that he didn't have time to teach it to me. He said he would have to cut a demo when he got home. The song was called *Rain*. It wasn't something I could learn that quickly as there were some chords that he'd made up and some strange passing chords that meant that I couldn't learn it immediately, and it would have taken a few attempts to memorise.

'Of course after the story appeared in print, people came forward and said they had the demo. I can't remember the song exactly, but I can remember certain parts of it and I was also watching him play it, and that's something that always sticks in my mind – watching him do these chord changes. People say they have heard some old tapes of Eddie's where they claim that he is playing *Rain*, but they're nothing like it. Maybe he just liked that title and gave it to two different songs.

'We sat up most of the night and Sharon gave up, so Lee Hazlewood and I went back to our room. I was in bed for about twenty minutes when I heard this horrible racket – Eddie had borrowed the vacuum cleaner from the maid. I looked down at the foot of the bed and there he stood. He shut off the vacuum cleaner and said, "Let's go to breakfast."

'I said, "What time is it?"

'"It's five-thirty," he replied. "Come on, I want to have breakfast."

'Well, I looked over and Lee was sitting up in his bed with his hair sticking up in all directions. "I'll go," he said. "I'll go to breakfast with you. Just give me a few minutes," and he slowly got up.

'"You should have seen him jump!" Eddie laughed. "He jumped up and was in his robe in one smooth motion – ready to fight!"

'He was just having fun. That was just like him and that's how I remember Eddie Cochran. Later, I got to the restaurant downstairs and that's when we all said our goodbyes to each other.'

He was an icon, a teacher. He showed us how they played rock'n'roll in America. We had our ideas over here, as the British always have done, hence the big upsurge in the 1960s of British styles, but those styles got their foundations from people like Eddie Cochran, Gene Vincent, Carl Perkins and Chuck Berry.

Big Jim Sullivan

As the tour reached its conclusion, both Brian Bennett and Jim Sullivan noticed a drastic change in Eddie's personality. 'He changed from how he was at the beginning of the tour to how he was at the end,' Brian claims. 'He was very homesick, there was no question about that. I guess he had a good family life because his mum used to write and he used to talk about her. She actually wrote to me after it all finished, saying thank you for looking after the lad – that sort of thing.

'When he first came over, he was very precise about how he wanted things to sound. He would say, "This is what I want," and he'd sit at my drums, or just tap me on the shoulder and say, "This is what the bass drum does." It was difficult to do those rhythms in *Sweet Little Sixteen* and *Twenty Flight Rock* the way he did it. We hadn't played like that before. The rock'n'roll records we did listen to were like Bill Haley and some Presley tunes that were very simple – four in the bass, one and three in the bass drum maybe – but then Eddie came and it was all "syncopated rhythms" as we used to call it. It was difficult and it was different, so it was a challenge. I would turn around and say, "I can't do that, it's impossible," and he'd say, "Well, hang on, have a look at this," and then he'd play the bloody thing!

'He was foremost concerned with getting his act and the band the way he wanted them to sound. There was a great rapport with Jim Sullivan because he was a great guitarist. But towards the end of the tour, and after a few late nights with Gene and being homesick, he just let it slip towards the end. He got very melancholy, just being away from home.'

'I think we all got on pretty well with Eddie,' Jim Sullivan continues. 'I think he respected us because we were all budding musicians, but we were as close as he allowed us to be. I don't care what anybody says, Eddie didn't let anybody get that close to him. All right, we'd go and sit with him in the dressing-room and sometimes we might go up to the hotel room, but he kept himself to himself.

'You try to keep things in perspective, because it can be blown out of proportion. I remember him teaching me *Birth Of The Blues*. He also sat down with Colin Green and taught it to him, so he gave a bit in that respect.

'All I know is that I owe a lot to Eddie Cochran, because he was one of the first people with whom I had direct contact who really knew how to play. Of course, it's all part of British rock history because he showed Brian Bennett those drum patterns that probably changed the course of British rock drumming. Brian, at the time, was probably the best drummer about, so Eddie was a big influence on us kids, especially The Wildcats.

'I remember Brian learning that beat that Eddie taught him, the one that used to be in everything then. He was one of the great legends of the rock industry, with his particular style and his songs. And to think the man made most of them by himself. The guy had great talent.'

When the curtain came up, there stood Eddie with his back to the audience. He was wearing a leather jacket with the collar turned up, playing his guitar.

Everyone was yelling, 'Turn around!' When he did he was wearing dark glasses so we all yelled even louder, 'Take them off!'

He pretended to take them off several times, then eventually he took off the glasses and there stood Eddie Cochran. It was fantastic, and I've been a fan ever since. Going to Bristol, everyone on the coach was talking about Gene Vincent, but going home we were all talking about Eddie.

Brian Urch, Bristol

A Fast-Moving Beat Show opened at the Bristol Hippodrome on Monday, 11 April, for a week-long engagement. Checking into the Royal Hotel in the city to begin their extended tour, Eddie and Gene were now accompanied by Pat Thompkins as tour manager. Hal Carter, as he explains, already had a prior commitment for the week: 'When we did Manchester, Jack Good had come up with this show called *Wham!*, which was a TV show that he'd devised for solo acts using one big band. So, because I worked for Parnes, I had to stay in Manchester with Bill and Joe as well, so I got Pat Thompkins to come in and take them on the week in Bristol while I stayed in Manchester.'

With Billy Fury and Joe Brown away, the British acts billed to appear alongside Eddie and Gene included Dean Webb, The Tony Sheridan Trio, Georgie Fame, Billy Raymond and Peter Wynne. With only six days to go before Eddie could return to the United States, not surprisingly his enthusiasm for the performances was lacking. But for British fans, the excitement of seeing these American stars perform never decreased over the months, as local David Venn remembers: 'I attended the Thursday-night performance along with a party from my local youth club, and was completely knocked out by Eddie and Gene. The sight of two genuine American rock'n'roll stars in the flesh was an unbelievable thrill. I was so impressed by the show that on the Saturday afternoon I rode to Bristol on my old 250cc BSA motorcycle and managed to get a ticket for the first performance that evening. Eddie was electrifying, performing all his well-known songs along with such numbers as Ray Charles's *What'd I Say* – the first time I had ever heard that song. The backing group of British musicians was rather poor and Gene's act suffered a little from this, but Eddie, being able to play his guitar so brilliantly, was not so affected.'

'We didn't do the last night in Bristol,' Jim Sullivan explains. 'It was unexpected, because I'd arranged to come back with Eddie and Gene, if they had room, as I lived in Hounslow at the time, which was on the way back to London Airport. One of the big stars fell ill at the London Palladium and Marty Wilde was called in to do *Sunday Night At The Palladium*. Of course, he wanted us to do it with him and nicked us off the tour.'

Brian Bennett adds: 'All the dates were put in the diary for the next tour. He was going back for a little while and then we were going to meet up and rehearse for another tour.'

Eddie was delighted when Pat Thompkins finally presented the flight tickets for his return home. It was Saturday, 16 April, and Eddie was booked to fly from Heathrow at one o'clock the following day. Larry Parnes had arranged dates for Gene in Paris until Eddie got back and the pair could continue the tour on 27 April.

For the final show, British pop star Johnny Gentle took the place of Dean Webb, who had fallen ill. Johnny had driven to the theatre, while the rest of the performers were travelling by coach, and Eddie was keen to catch a lift back to London with him. As his car was already full, Johnny was unable to help, and as the local train service did not run so late at night, Eddie called for a taxi.

Joined by Pat Thompkins, Gene Vincent and Sharon Sheeley, the Ford Consul taxi left for London as the last group of fans made their way home with memories of that final performance.

'A party of us booked to see the concert on the Wednesday,' Peter Burrows remembers. 'Gene was the recognised star and finished the second half of the concert while Eddie, being the up-and-coming star, wound up the first half. We were all totally enthralled by Eddie's guitar playing, and had heard nothing like it in the UK before. His mean, sultry look and gravelly voice brought a tremendous response from the audience, so much so that we booked tickets to repeat the experience on the Saturday, which on paperboy's money was a big decision. By this time, the stagecraft and sheer quality of Eddie had been recognised, and he was topping the bill and closing the show and Gene was winding up the first half.

'We all went home and I played the one or two records that I had and retired to bed, only to report for my paper round on the Sunday to hear the rumour that there had been a car crash down the road in Chippenham involving Eddie. Later the official news came through on Radio Luxembourg that he had died. I'm sure you can imagine our feelings. We had seen him only the night before.'

For the whole journey I just sat there waiting . . . waiting for that car to crash. It was a very strange feeling. The minute the car door shut, it felt like I was shutting a tomb. The driver was speeding and Eddie kept telling him to slow down. I remember seeing the trees zipping by because we were going too fast, and thinking there's nothing I can do to stop this and that's the last thought I had. I don't remember the accident.

Sharon Sheeley

George Martin, driver of the Ford Consul, explained that the car had been used for a wedding during the day. Brushing the confetti aside, Eddie, Sharon and Gene climbed into the back seat while tour manager Pat Thompkins took the front passenger seat. Sources state that Eddie already knew George Martin and remember seeing him hanging around backstage with Eddie and Gene in their dressing-room enjoying a bottle of beer.

The cream-coloured Consul left the Royal Hotel around 11 p.m. Although the flight from Heathrow wasn't until the following afternoon, as Hal Carter explains, Eddie was determined to make the journey that evening: 'Ed had rung me about coming back into town to their flat in Piccadilly. I said, "What for? There's no point, you've got to pass the airport, Ed. You might as well leave a bit later and go straight to the airport. You've got all your gear – you don't need anything." But he said, "I have to go back, I've got some things to do and I've got gifts and things to pick up." I told him to go in the morning but he was adamant, and he got Pat to book a taxi-driver.'

In 1960, before the M4 motorway to London was constructed, George Martin had to take the old A4, driving down through Bath and across to Chippenham to reach it. 'The driver took a shortcut as the A4 in those days was terrible,' Hal remembers, after hearing the account first-hand from Pat Thompkins. 'You come out from under the viaduct and come across a bridge right in front of you. On your right is the A4, and then the bridge, and on your left is the A4 to London. Well, he saw the A4 and turned right, going back the wrong way. When he saw the milestone, he realised he was going the wrong way and hit the brakes.'

Reports from the accident state that as George Martin drove out from under the viaduct he misjudged the curve in the road that followed. Other reports from the accident stated that it was a blown tyre that caused the crash. Another theory is that George Martin lost his way after reaching Chippenham town centre. Thompkins suggested they double back to get their bearings, and as the car sped out of town towards the viaduct, Martin lost control driving downhill onto the bend and the car spun backwards into a concrete lamp-post. By all accounts, the gently curving road that inclines towards Chippenham today was a narrow, hazardous and notorious black spot in 1960. To make matters worse, the road had recently been re-gravelled, making driving conditions even more difficult.

'Eddie was sitting in the safest place you could be,' Sharon says. 'He was in the middle on the back seat so he had a body on either side protecting him. The road manager testified and Gene Vincent testified that when the car went out of control, which I remember none of, Eddie leaned over and he shielded me with his body and pulled me over his lap. He totally covered me, so he was exposed, so he really died saving my life.'

As the Consul hit a concrete lamp-post, the force caused Eddie to fly upwards against the roof of the car. The impact, against the rear left-hand wing of the car, forced the door open, propelling Eddie through it and onto the road.

Facing into the centre of the road, the Consul came to an abrupt halt. Petrol trickled from the damaged tank as the car came to rest partly on the road and partly on a grass verge. The front of the vehicle was hardly damaged – George Martin and Pat Thompkins walked away from the wreckage without any injury. Gene Vincent, seated on the right-hand side of the car, fractured his collarbone.

A local farmer, Dick Jennings, and his wife Phyllis on their way home were the first to come across the accident. Mr Jennings was immediately concerned with Eddie and Sharon. 'The driver was just standing around in a daze,' he told author Rob Finnis. 'Eddie Cochran and the girl, and this Gene Vincent, were all lying closely together about ten yards over on the verge. A lady [from the house] opposite came out in her nightdress and then went back in and phoned for an ambulance. The girl was kicking up a devil of a noise, crying out, "Eddie! Eddie!" and we did our best to calm her down. We told her that the ambulance was coming and to lie still. Gene Vincent was very quiet. He said nothing. We only found out who they were later. At the time they were just people to us.'

The noise of the accident brought local residents out to the scene of the crash. 'I was just getting into bed when I heard a whistling noise outside,' David Chivers told a reporter from the *Wiltshire Times*. 'This was followed by a series of bumps and smashes and my first reaction was that it was a plane crashing. I went outside and saw the wrecked car in the road, several people lying about and a large guitar and scattered photographs, which had come from the open boot, in the road. I telephoned for an ambulance from the kiosk nearby.'

Dick Jennings went over to help Eddie, who had been thrown with considerable force from the vehicle. As his wife Phyllis explained to Rob Finnis, it was obvious that the singer was seriously injured. 'My husband went over to Eddie Cochran and he was making funny noises in his throat and foaming slightly at the mouth. Blood was coming out of his mouth and also his ears, so my husband rolled up his coat and put it under Eddie Cochran's head and turned his head on one side to stop him choking, and we put his arms out straight on each side to help his breathing. There wasn't much we could do.'

An ambulance was immediately dispatched from Chippenham, although the Jennings were convinced that it was already too late for Eddie. 'Just before the ambulance came the street lights all went out.' Phyllis said. 'They were due to switch off at midnight and this was about 12.15. So when the ambulance arrived to take them away, it was quite dark. It was a bit symbolic after what had happened.'

At 1 a.m. house physician Donald Pilton awaited the arrival of the Consul's passengers in the casualty department of St Martin's Hospital in Bath. Eddie was unconscious, and on examination showed signs of severe brain damage. His pupils were fixed and dilated, his reflexes were weak and he did not respond to painful stimuli. Suffering from serious head and chest injuries, he was given artificial respiration, but his condition deteriorated rapidly over the next few hours. Despite the efforts of the St Martin's medical team, Eddie died at 4.10 p.m. on Sunday, 17 April.

A couple of days after I saw Eddie, we were on the coach and Bobby Darin said, 'I need to talk to you.' So we went to the back of the coach and Bobby told me about Eddie and Sharon. I thought they were probably okay if they got to the hospital, so we stayed on the coach. It was an all-day drive to where we were playing and when we arrived we were met by the press who told us that Eddie had died.

Duane Eddy

Norm Riley immediately rang Hal Carter with the news of the accident, then later with confirmation that Eddie had died. 'I was too upset to go to the hospital,' Hal says, 'so Norm went over there and I stayed in the hotel and took all the calls. When Norm came back he told me about everything that had happened so I went over to see Sharon. Gene was okay. He'd been asleep at the time of the accident.'

When Sharon arrived at St Martin's Hospital her condition was just as critical as Eddie's. As well as sustaining leg and head injuries, she also suffered serious damage to her neck, back and pelvis and had to endure a lengthy recovery process on top of having to cope with Eddie's death.

On hearing news of the accident, Phil Everly took the first available opportunity to reach the hospital. 'We were only about an hour away from where they were,' he recalls. 'So I took the tour bus and the driver drove me over to the hospital to see Eddie and Sharon. When I came through the door I ran into Gene Vincent. Sharon was in the ward. I hadn't met him before. I wanted to say goodbye to Eddie. Jerry Allison was there, but he didn't want to go. It's not that he didn't want to, it was hard for him. That was such a shocking night, the whole thing was so surreal.'

The news was equally shocking for Eddie's fellow musicians on the Larry Parnes tour. Colin Green passed the crash site just after the accident and didn't find out until the following day that his colleagues were involved, while Johnny Gentle, who was unable to offer Eddie a lift, politely asked a officer on the scene if he could take some of the petrol from the damaged vehicle, as he was unable to fill his own car up so late at night. Johnny had no idea his friends were involved.

Vince Eager, who became good friends with Eddie during his stay in Britain, was due to fly to America as Eddie's guest, but didn't hear about the accident until he arrived at the airport to check in. 'He was a great artist and a real hard worker,' he told a reporter from the *New Musical Express*. 'He had faith in me as an artist and helped me in every possible way with my act. I'm telling you, Eddie was the greatest. I will miss him – believe me, I will.'

Billy Fury also added to the tribute: 'Eddie was one of the most dynamic performers I have ever seen on stage,' he told the reporter. 'This has upset me more than I can tell you.'

Monday, 18 April, and news of the accident broke internationally. 'Rock Star Dies In Crash' read the British newspapers, while the *Los Angeles Times* carried the headline 'LA Singer Eddie Cochran Dies In English Taxi Crash'.

British newspapers covered the story for days, but in the United States, despite the initial headlines, the story generated only a few column inches.

'The unfortunate end for Eddie was something I never forgot,' Si Waronker says. 'I was at home in bed when the phone rang and woke me up. It broke my heart to hear the news. Then I got a phone call from a disc jockey here in Los Angeles who wanted me to comment on the radio. In those days, rock music was just beginning, so these things didn't really make the headlines. It wasn't as important to people as it is today.'

It wasn't real. It was so strange. Over the years many of my friends have passed on, some young, some tragically, and I guess you never get used to it. But my first major shock, when somebody that close dies, just took the wind out of me. To this day I do not listen to Eddie's records. I have tapes and things from England and I've set them aside, thinking I just don't want to right now. If I hear him come on the radio on the oldie's stations I'll listen to that, but when I listen to things like *Dark Lonely Street*, I remember when he

recorded that and to hear him singing is just too
painful, and I don't want to do it. I have pictures of
Eddie and me which I look at now and then and
realise that we just didn't have a clue.

John Rook

A post-mortem examination was completed the following Tuesday
morning at 10 a.m. Abrasions on the left-hand side of Eddie's chest
and on his lower legs were present, while bruising was identified
around his forehead, left eye, upper lip and under his chin, evidence
of the head injuries he had sustained.

Although Eddie did not have a fractured skull, he suffered severe
haemorrhaging and there was an accumulation of fluid and bruising
within the brain tissue. Haemorrhages were also present in the tissues
surrounding his larynx, thyroid and left lung, while fluid had
accumulated throughout both lungs.

Observing the examination were Inspector James Thompson and
Constable Ronald McIntyre of the Wiltshire Constabulary. Also at
the scene of the crash, PC McIntyre submitted a full report on the
accident, writing that he arrived just after 12.07 a.m. on Sunday to
see the cream Ford Consul saloon, registration RBO869, facing
obliquely towards the crown of the road and in the direction of
Chippenham. There were skid marks on the road extending for fifty
yards and traces of cream paint from the car were found on the lamp-
post. The statement also revealed that the injured were taken to
Chippenham Cottage Hospital first, before being transferred to St
Martin's in Bath.

'The deceased,' he wrote, 'is a United States citizen and was by
profession a well-known "Rock and Roll" singer. His personal
manager is Mr Riley of room 212, Stafford Court Hotel, Mayfair,
London. Mr Riley may be called upon to give evidence of identifica-
tion.'

In accordance with section 8 of the Road Traffic Act, 1956, George
Martin was charged with causing death by dangerous driving. The
court hearing took place at the Bristol Assizes on 24 June 1960, where
he was convicted of driving the Ford Consul at excessive speed. Fined
fifty pounds, Martin was also disqualified from driving for fifteen

years and a prison sentence of six months was ordered in the event that Martin failed to pay the amount imposed.

Patrick Thompkins gave evidence in court, but the other passengers, Sharon Sheeley and Gene Vincent, were unable to attend the hearing.

I heard the news of Eddie's death on the radio. It was early in the day and I jumped up out of bed. It was like being hit between the eyes with a baseball bat.

'This can't be,' I thought. 'No, not Eddie.'

It didn't really sink in until I was down there at Forest Lawn for his funeral. It was a small, select group and a bright day, but I was numb. I couldn't even drive.

Later, on occasion, I used to pick a different freeway to come home when I was in Orange County. I would drive out past Forest Lawn and look over to the right of the passenger window of the car and talk to Eddie.

'Well, I'm still doing it,' I would say. 'And I wish to God you were too.'

Chuck Foreman

Gene Vincent flew home to Los Angeles on 20 April. 'I still can't believe it's true,' he told a reporter from the *New Musical Express*. 'You see, it seems so strange now. Eddie and I were rarely apart. I keep wanting to call out for him.'

It was Gene's intention to fly home with Eddie, but after discharging himself from St Martin's Hospital he had to fly alone, while Eddie's body was flown home the following day.

The Cochran family were devastated by their loss. When she saw her son's body, Alice Cochran was barely able to believe that this was her youngest child. He had been on tour so frequently during the last few years of his life that finally Alice came to terms with his death by believing that Eddie was simply away working.

Eddie Cochran was buried at 10 a.m. on Monday, 25 April, at the Forest Lawn Cemetery in Cypress, near to his home in Buena Park. The service was conducted by Reverend C. Sumner Reynolds and was attended by his family and friends.

Bill and Bob Cochran, who first introduced their youngest brother to the instrument that ultimately became his passion, laid a wreath of red and white carnations in the shape of a guitar.

Engraved with a border of ivy and a picture of Eddie holding his Gretsch guitar, his gravestone has a moving inscription added by the Cochran family:

> If mere words can console us for the loss of our beloved
> Eddie then our love for him was a false love.
>
> Heavenly music filled the air
> That very tragic day.
> Something seemed to be missing tho'
> So I heard the creator say:
> 'We need a master guitarist and singer.
> I know of but one alone.
> His name is Eddie Cochran
> I think I'll call him home.
> I know the folks on earth won't mind
> For they will understand
> That the Lord loves perfection
> Now we'll have a perfect band.'
>
> So as we go through life; now we know:
> That perfection is our goal
> And we strive for this
> So when we are called
> We'll feel free to go.

Postscript

Many of Eddie's friends and associates have commented over the years that he found rock'n'roll incredibly easy to perform on the guitar. This tends to give the impression that Eddie had a rather snobbish attitude to the music – a view commonly found with jazz guitarists, who were often employed for rock'n'roll sessions in the 1950s, and made no secret of their disdain for this form of music. Many jazz guitarists perceived rock'n'roll to be far below the standard required for jazz, which they regarded as a much more cerebral form of music.

As Chuck Foreman testified, Eddie could play jazz to a very high standard as well as classical, country and blues, but he realised that rock'n'roll's main ingredient was its simplicity. Indeed, its primary appeal to budding musicians was that only three or four chords were needed for most songs. This meant that anyone could write and perform their own material or strum along to their favourite record, provided they had natural rhythm and the ability to learn three chords.

The beauty of rock'n'roll was that you did not necessarily have to possess a great deal of musical talent in order to become a successful artist, giving hope to every teenager from Memphis to London with starry-eyed dreams of success.

For every Elvis Presley, Carl Perkins or Gene Vincent – artists who did possess huge talent and who, consequently, have stood the test of time – there were a hundred one-hit wonders who were influenced to perform rock'n'roll because of its simplicity, propelled only by the youthful exuberance that enabled them to get up on stage and perform.

It was mainly teenagers who were buying rock'n'roll records. They were not interested in hearing clever chord progressions and deep, meaningful lyrics. They wanted to hear the music played with energy and aggression, and these catchy tunes with nursery-rhyme lyrics were viewed simply as fun to dance to and sing along with.

As the guitar became a more prominent instrument in rock'n'roll, almost taking centre stage along with the singer, so the standard of playing began to increase. In fact, some of the early originators would elevate the lead guitar work in rock'n'roll songs into a highly complex art. Drawing on their influences from jazz, country and blues, guitarists such as Cliff Gallup (an original member of Gene Vincent's Blue Caps) and top Nashville session player Grady Martin (who provided the stunning lead breaks on many early Johnny Burnette, Brenda Lee and Johnny Carroll recordings, as well as countless classic rockabilly records) along with Elvis Presley's first guitarist Scotty Moore and James Burton's work with artists such as Bob Luman, Dale Hawkins and Ricky Nelson, together with Eddie Cochran, set a standard of playing that would go on to influence generations of rock guitarists.

Eddie Cochran would later be forever associated with a handful of deceptively simple three-chord acoustic guitar-led songs such as *C'mon Everybody*, *Summertime Blues* and *Three Steps To Heaven*. In helping to create and champion this heavy, rhythmic style of rock'n'roll, he placed emphasis on the beat and lyrical content of his songs rather than impressing the listener with his skilful musicianship. In doing so, he restricted his guitar playing, undermining his role as one of the most influential rock'n'roll guitarists of his time. As he was pushed into the role of a rock'n'roll idol and star of film and television, his Gretsch guitar was relegated to the role of a highly decorative prop that he occasionally brought to life if a guitar solo was necessary. Then, and only then, a short, understated solo was deemed sufficient.

For many years following his death, Cochran's guitar skills were unrecognised and he rarely received the credit he deserved. It has only been in the last twenty years or so that Cochran researchers have unearthed details of his earlier career as a session guitarist, making these recordings available on various collector's labels.

Although Cochran perfectly understood the concept of rock'n'roll, creating his own niche by carefully and meticulously crafting his songs to suit his teenage audience, it is important to separate his rock-star status from his dual role as a session guitarist. Throughout his lifetime, Eddie continued to work with small labels in and around Hollywood. Regardless of how successful his own records became, Eddie still found time to work with other artists and quickly gained a reputation as a down-to-earth, likeable person, as well as a highly skilled, forward-thinking and innovative guitarist.

It appears from the countless testimonies gathered in this book from Eddie's friends, family and fellow musicians that his main motivation came from a natural desire to learn and progress as a musician. His enthusiasm in being involved with the exciting young world of rock'n'roll would also be a contributing factor, and Eddie realised that he was part of a musical change that had a profound effect on the youth of the 1950s. He also predicted rock'n'roll's development, stating in interviews that the music would continue to change and survive, and he had the musical ability to move with the times in order to maintain his celebrity status.

It is almost certain that he would have travelled down the same musical path as his fellow Liberty artists, Johnny Burnette and Bobby Vee. Most of the great pioneers of 1950s rock'n'roll gave up on the music after it became clear to them that their audiences had moved on to other forms of music. Eventually, they too had to follow this trend if they wanted to continue selling records and enjoy a career in the music business.

However, as Si Waronker explained earlier, he never saw Eddie as just a rock'n'roll artist. He wanted the artists on his label to sustain a long career in music and encouraged Eddie to make music that was as diverse as possible. Eddie reinvented his career and image whenever it became clear that it was not working, hence his transition from Liberty's mould as a cross between Pat Boone and Elvis Presley, with songs such as *Sittin' In The Balcony*, *One Kiss* and *Drive-In Show*, to his innovative period of *Summertime Blues*, *C'mon Everybody* and *Somethin' Else*, through to his last recordings of material such as *Three Steps To Heaven* and *Cherished Memories* with their radical image change to that of a rock balladeer. All this was done within the space of three and a half years, and had Eddie lived it is fair to assume that he would have remained a musical chameleon in order to maintain his pop-star status.

His role as a session guitarist, producer and arranger, which advanced rapidly during the later stages of his life, suggest that this part of his career would also have developed.

Acting was another career Cochran would have seriously contemplated, and with his personality and good looks, he had the ability to succeed in that field as well. Rumours have sprung up over the years that Eddie was offered a role in the movie *Rally Around The Flag, Boys* and it has also been reported that shortly before his death he was contacted to appear in the John Wayne epic, *The Alamo*.

One thing is for certain: Eddie would have remained a central figure within the Los Angeles music scene and his outstanding talent would have taken him wherever he wanted to go.

Eddie Cochran is certainly not forgotten, and as long as the world wants to listen to a musician with exceptional abilities, he never can be.

Technical Comments on Early Stereo Recording *by Bob Jones*

Most popular music these days is recorded onto wide multi-track tape on 24- or 32-track machines. This practice permits great flexibility for producers and engineers to record any combination of instrumentation at any time. It also allows re-recording of individual tracks or additional effects to be done at a later date for the required mixing to stereo. In the late 1950s, before the advent of stereo, all the musicians had to be in the studio at the same time as the vocalist and the mixing had to be done by the engineer on the mixing desk at the time of recording. This was recorded onto a full-track (mono) tape machine – or in earlier days onto a disc recording machine.

Eddie Cochran's career coincided with a technological development of enormous significance, namely the advent of two-track Ampex tape machine and two-track output desks, thus enabling the industry to experiment with stereophonic sound. Before the arrival of this equipment at Goldstar, Eddie, creative musician that he was, had already been using multi-dubbing techniques in order to record classics such as *C'mon Everybody* and *Summertime Blues* on which he played all the instruments and did the trick vocals himself. This technique involved recording the basic track onto a mono tape machine which, when played back, could be mixed with a new 'live' instrument or vocal from the studio. The resulting mix of the two would be recorded onto a second tape machine, this process being repeated several times if necessary, thus permitting the flexibility of so-called 'overdubbing'. The main disadvantages with this process were the noticeable loss of quality with every successive overdub and the fact that it was time consuming.

The advent of stereo recording, followed quickly by the introduction of three-track machines, facilitated this process enormously without apparent quality loss. Stereo releases of Cochran's music were unknown during his lifetime and none was available until twenty years after his death. It must be remembered that the new stereo gear was welcomed as a convenient means of producing a mono-only master – certainly as far as rock'n'roll music was concerned. The binaural tapes produced in this way were not meant for stereo release, as they usually feature the vocalist on one channel and the entire backing track on the other with precious little in between! Examples of this are *Ah, Pretty Girl* and *Jeannie, Jeannie, Jeannie*. Binaural recording (or two-track mono) was used extensively in this manner by RCA and others; even Elvis's pre-army sessions from 1957 were recorded thus. These tapes were only made as a precaution in case the first mix was rejected and had to be re-mixed (in mono) and then the original binaural tapes were erased.

Three Steps To Heaven, Cut Across Shorty and *Cherished Memories* were recorded at Eddie's last record session in 'straight stereo' (i.e. 'live') and are fine examples of true early stereo. When researching the Liberty archives in Hollywood, Tony Barrett of Rockstar Records discovered that four titles (*Teresa, Think Of Me, My Way* and *Teenage Heaven*) had also been recorded in stereo, but sadly found that the master cards for these gems were marked 'erased'. (The same fate befell Elvis's first binaural (stereo) session; only a few of the tapes survived the instructions to erase and these were featured on the RCA *Stereo '57* album.)

The first stereos were unearthed when Tony was compiling and researching the first box set in 1980 for United Artists Records, which featured *Three Steps To Heaven, Pretty Girl* and *Weekend*. During further research, he dug out the remaining 2- and 3-tracks that had survived – a total of ten songs; this gave him the idea of issuing an album of all the stereos together and so the *Portrait Of A Legend* LP was born. There were no stereo masters of *Hallelujah, I Waited So Long* and *Little Angel* which existed on three-track originals, so I mixed them to stereo.

Hallelujah I Love Her So was not originally meant to have strings; the basic track was recorded and finished in mono, but when Snuffy Garrett at Liberty received the tape, he decided it would sound better with strings and overdubbed them in stereo at Liberty Recorders studio. This stereo overdub – along with the fact that Eddie's last session was recorded in stereo – was almost certainly due to the current fad for stereo jukebox singles that were flooding the market. Although ultimately to fail, we can be thankful for this trend, as we would other-wise have found very few vintage rock'n'roll tapes in stereo.

Bob Jones is held in high esteem by rock'n'roll aficionados, as well as the music industry itself through his work in remastering original recordings by artists such as Elvis Presley, Eddie Cochran and Duane Eddy. With some of the unissued Cochran material Tony Barrett has discovered over the years, Bob has been responsible for attaining Rockstar's outstanding sound quality, by transforming severely damaged master tapes and acetates that might otherwise have remained unissued.

Recommended Listening

The Eddie Cochran Box Set EMI – ECB1, 1988
A four CD set featuring a fairly comprehensive collection of original masters, alternate versions and out-takes spanning Eddie's career from The Cochran Brothers right up to his performances on the *Boy Meets Girls* shows in 1960.

From Rockstar Records
LA Sessions Rockstar – RSR CD 003, 1992
Mighty Mean Rockstar – RSR CD 008, 1995
Cruisin' The Drive-In Rockstar – RSR CD 009, 1996
One Minute To One Rockstar – RSR CD 010, 1996
Rockin' It Country Style (The Legendary Chuck Foreman Sessions) Rockstar – RSR CD 011, 1997
The Town Hall Party TV Shows (With Gene Vincent) Rockstar – RSR CD 016, 1999

An excellent collection of CDs from Rockstar. Tailored not only for Cochran completists, these well packaged releases, with great photos and informative liner notes, are essential for anyone wanting to hear Cochran at work in the studio, both on his own recordings and the recordings he made with other artists. Special mention must be given to *Rockin' It Country Style* as it contains the earliest known recordings by Eddie with Chuck Foreman and *The Town Hall Party* TV shows that feature both Eddie and Gene playing live in front of a studio audience. Recorded only days after Buddy Holly's death in February 1959, Eddie is backed by Dick D'Agostin and the Swingers although Guybo is on bass. Eddie and the band perform songs such as *School Days, Be Honest With Me, Have I Told You Lately That I Love You, Summertime Blues, Don't Blame It On Me, C'mon Everybody* and *Money Honey* and the CD also includes an eight-minute interview between Eddie and country artist Johnny Bond. Gene Vincent performs *Be Bop A Lula, Rip It Up, Dance To The Bop, She She Little Sheila* and *You Win Again* among others. This is an excellent CD featuring superb quality sound and photos.

Acknowledgements

We would like to thank everyone for their valuable contributions to this book. So many people went out of their way to help. Rock legends past and present gave up their valuable time to talk to us, as did Eddie's surviving family – who all helped enormously – together with Eddie's friends and musical associates who worked with him during his brief career.

For their valuable memories we would like to thank Bill and Betty Cochran, Pat and Hank Hickey, Ed Julson, Sharon Sheeley, Hank Cochran, Connie and Marilyn Smith, Chuck Foreman, Stan Ross, Simon Waronker, Glen Glenn, Gary Lambert, Warren Flock, Bob Denton, Sir Cliff Richard OBE, Brian Setzer, Phil Everly, Joe Brown, Big Jim Sullivan, Brian Bennett, John Rook, Hal Carter, P.J. Proby, Duane Eddy, Mike Deasy, Sonny Curtis and Dave Shiver.

Many world-renowned Cochran historians supplied valuable information for this book, and Tony Barrett, Derek Glenister and Rob Finnis deserve a special mention. Tony founded Rockstar Records in the 1970s for the specific purpose of discovering and releasing rare Cochran material. He has done more than anyone to keep Eddie's memory fresh and alive for future generations. Derek Glenister, who runs the Record Museum in Southend, is a noted historian who has helped corroborate masses of information throughout the years of Eddie's career as a studio musician, and is mainly responsible for most of the session details within this book.

Rob Finnis is a highly respected mine of information on the 1950s musical scene in Los Angeles. He writes the informative liner notes to many releases for Rockstar and Ace and is a regular contributor to the leading rock'n'roll magazine *Now Dig This*. Rob wrote the booklet for *The Eddie Cochran Box Set*, which was released by EMI in the late 1980s as a six LP or four CD retrospective on Cochran's career. Rob very kindly agreed to lend us as much information as we needed from his excellent notes, which proved invaluable.

We kept in contact with Tony, Derek and Rob throughout the writing of this book, as their trusted and valued opinions validated many of our own regarding previously unknown material that was discovered while researching Eddie's life and career. Tony also helped with photographs, personal advice and anything we required in order to complete this book. For further information, contact Rockstar Records, PO Box 22, Woodford Green, Essex IG8 0EH, England.

Alan Clark helped enormously by allowing us to use information from his excellent publications on Eddie, such as *Never To Be Forgotten* and *Eddie Cochran: The Legend Continues*. For further information contact Alan Lungstrum, PO Box 1062, West Covina, California 91793, USA.

Spencer Leigh, a broadcaster and respected authority on 1950s British rock'n'roll, and rock'n'roll in general, allowed us to use information that he worked hard to obtain on Eddie and Gene's 1960 tour. His help is greatly appreciated.

Michael Kelly (aka Doc Rock) was incredibly helpful in allowing us to use information from his excellent and highly comprehensive book *Liberty Records: A History of the Recording Company and Its Stars, 1955–71* (McFarland & Company Inc).

Will Beard, founder of *The Cochran Connection*, a highly informative newsletter on Eddie Cochran, provided us with the relevant police and hospital documents on Eddie's death, for which we are extremely grateful. Will can be contacted via The Cochran Connection, 15 St Clements Court, Mardyke Park, Purfleet, Essex RM19 1GL, England.

Trevor Cajiao is the founder and editor of *Now Dig This*, perhaps the best 1950s orientated rock'n'roll magazine on the planet. For many years, this monthly magazine has been a valuable source of information on every leading rocker from that era up to the present day. As well as its highly informative articles, it features all the latest rock'n'roll/rockabilly record and CD releases, and is essential reading for anyone remotely interested in the music, not just Eddie.

Trevor helped enormously by allowing us to use many articles on Eddie that have been printed in his magazine over the years. Thanks, Trevor – you're a diamond! *Now Dig This*, 19 South Hill Road, Bensham, Gateshead, Tyne & Wear, NE8 2XZ, England.

Other valuable suppliers of information that we are extremely grateful for include Kevin Coffey for his liner notes to *The Big D Jamboree Live, Vol. 1 & 2* – Dragon Street Records (Dallas, Texas, USA), 2000; Candace Rich, for the information on *Dick Clark's American Bandstand* (www.fiftiesweb.com); Mike Callahan and David

Edwards at Both Sides Now Publications for their research on the history of Liberty Records (www.bsnpubs.com) and Paul Vidal for the information on Ray Stanley (http://perso.wanadoo.fr/rockin.paul/).

Thank you to the many fans who shared their memories of Eddie's UK tour in 1960: Pauline Amey, Victor Azzopardi, Diane Beckett, Keith Bent, Sheila Bishop, Liz Burnett, Peter Burrows, James Clark, Norma Crowther, Chris Fergus, Michael Hine, Annie Harris, Mrs M. Harrison, Mrs B. Hunter, Mrs J. James, Margaret Jones, Rasina E.M. Le Bas, Peter Lidbury, Edna Lightfoot, Michael Lynch, Bill MacGregor, John Marston, George Milne, Mr G. Page, Marion Parker, Sheila Read, Barry Robinson, Wendy Rose, Gillian Seaman, Jackie Smith, Gloria Snellgrove, Mary Southway, Mrs E. Stone, Stanley Surr, Ken Sykes, Terry Taylor, Brian Urch, David Venn, Pat Wallis, Danny Walmsley and Leighton Wardell.

Thank you to the following people for their help, organisation, inspiration and encouragement: Bill Campbell, Peter Williams, Spencer James, Graham Walker, Sir Jimmy Saville OBE, Gill Snow, Bob Jones, Martha Moore, Geoff Barker, Bill Hyde, Rod Pyke and Bob Timmers (Rockabilly Hall Of Fame www.rockabillyhall.com), David Dennard, Roger Nunn, Tim Whitnall, Neil Foster, Nalle Westman, Seannie Foy and Tony Freer.

Finally, we would like to thank all the local and national newpapers, radio stations, rock'n'roll publications and promoters who have supported this book, and continue to support Eddie Cochran.

We felt that it was about time a book was written about this great artist. It seems totally unjust that he has been overlooked for so long. Eddie Cochran was a pioneer, an innovator, a rock'n'roll genius and, according to those who knew him, a very nice, kind-hearted guy with a great sense of humour. Eddie Cochran's life and musical career deserve to be written about, documented and celebrated. We sincerely hope you have enjoyed this book as much as we enjoyed writing it for you . . . and Eddie!

Julie Mundy and Darrel Higham

Visit the Eddie Cochran website at:
www.eddiecochran.co.uk

Index